Business Design Thinking and Doing

Angèle M. Beausoleil

Business Design Thinking and Doing

Frameworks, Strategies and Techniques for Sustainable Innovation

Angèle M. Beausoleil
University of Toronto
Toronto, ON, Canada

ISBN 978-3-030-86488-0   ISBN 978-3-030-86489-7 (eBook)
https://doi.org/10.1007/978-3-030-86489-7

© The Editor(s) (if applicable) and The Author(s), under exclusive license to Springer Nature Switzerland AG 2022
This work is subject to copyright. All rights are solely and exclusively licensed by the Publisher, whether the whole or part of the material is concerned, specifically the rights of translation, reprinting, reuse of illustrations, recitation, broadcasting, reproduction on microfilms or in any other physical way, and transmission or information storage and retrieval, electronic adaptation, computer software, or by similar or dissimilar methodology now known or hereafter developed.
The use of general descriptive names, registered names, trademarks, service marks, etc. in this publication does not imply, even in the absence of a specific statement, that such names are exempt from the relevant protective laws and regulations and therefore free for general use.
The publisher, the authors and the editors are safe to assume that the advice and information in this book are believed to be true and accurate at the date of publication. Neither the publisher nor the authors or the editors give a warranty, expressed or implied, with respect to the material contained herein or for any errors or omissions that may have been made. The publisher remains neutral with regard to jurisdictional claims in published maps and institutional affiliations.

This Palgrave Macmillan imprint is published by the registered company Springer Nature Switzerland AG
The registered company address is: Gewerbestrasse 11, 6330 Cham, Switzerland

To the curious and inquisitive ones, keep questioning the status quo.

Preface

Good design is good for everyone. It serves a purpose and communicates that purpose effectively. Through form, function and simplicity, design expresses beauty and efficiency.

Good design also builds trust, value and profits. Organizations deserve good design. Business leaders are now demanding it.

In today's uncertain economic climate, business schools are increasingly expected to prepare future leaders to navigate unforeseen crises, embrace new knowledge systems and manage teams and their firms towards prosperity. At the same time, many organizations continue to struggle with their innovation mandates, hobbled by a mix of pragmatism, fear and arrogance. With significant investments in current systems and structures, they resist change. Why invest in new ways of working and profiting? The curse of that past success is that they lack the courage to retool their human and technological systems to adapt to uncertain socio-economic conditions. And crucially, they both lack the curiosity to learn how their customer needs are changing, and from the best practices of those in adjacent sectors.

Innovation processes inherently require continuous reinvention. This dilemma can be solved by:
1. first understanding how innovation actually happens
2. observing and identifying key issues relating to market needs and
3. strategically designing an improved, integrated and multidisciplinary approach that can be sustained over time.

This textbook introduces Business Design as an emergent and important pedagogy and practice to enable a mindset and skillset that integrates business thinking with design doing.It's a recipe that draws on courage to deliver what customers actually need, and what stakeholders and shareholders want.

Authored and crafted by a design practitioner turned innovation scholar and pedagogue, this book is a guide of sorts that integrates over 25 years of business design and innovation leadership practice with over 10 years of innovation literacy research and teaching. It aims to instruct and inspire the next generation of innovation designers, managers and leaders.

Building upon personal and proven design industry practices and innovation development processes,[1] this book introduces, explains and provides visual models, frameworks, strategies and case examples of Business Design—an agile approach to design-driven innovation. Business Design is a way of thinking and working that applies human-centred design to improving or transforming business activities. It draws upon social science, design, marketing and strategy to

---

1 Rogers et al. (2014). *Diffusion of innovations* (pp. 432–448). Routledge.

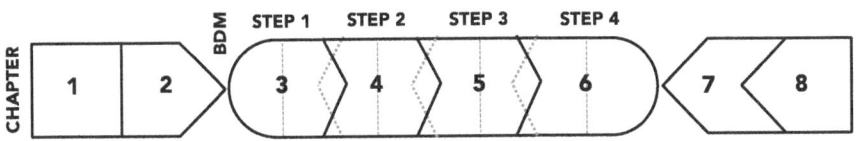

Fig. 1 Diagram of textbook chapters and Business Design Method steps as modules

create business value, from innovative new products, services and processes, to creative strategies and business models.

The Business Design method (BDM) simplifies the innovation development process into four steps or actions: start, find, frame and solve. The BDM is primarily a competency-building framework for design-driven innovation. The BDM's steps, techniques and exercises nudge one's orientation towards more responsible and responsive innovation. The four-step Business Design method is unpacked, verified through a complement of mini-case examples, and packaged into critical learning blocks leading to insightful decision-making and sustained value creation.

Designed for both instructors and students, this 'actionable book' offers key learning objectives for each chapter, warm up and associated exercises, case examples and worksheets. It offers a suite of prompts and templates for active learning, discussion and practice. Its modular design is flexible and adaptable for both linear and topic-based teaching and facilitating. Each chapter is a self-contained module that offers key topics that can be introduced as single subjects, or can be combined with other chapters, to suit your unique instructional needs. For example, if you are focused on new product development, you might begin with ▶ Chapter 5 or BDM step 3 (i.e. integration) and explore how best to integrate your new product concept into existing systems using design-driven business frameworks, and then skip back to the ▶ Chapter 3 or BDM step 1 (i.e. initiation) to craft an updated product design brief. Choose your own adventure (and direction) (Fig. 1).

This book embodies the principles of project-based learning. Similar to workplace initiatives, project-based learning (PBL) aids students (as active project participants) to develop deep content knowledge as well as critical thinking, collaboration, creativity and communication skills. Project-based courses are designed to guide students to learn by doing. A challenge brief is offered as the 'project' which serves as a real-world problem that requires further articulation and ultimately, solving. Similar to a capstone or practicum course, students demonstrate their knowledge and skills by creating a prototype or proposed solution to a real audience (company and/or customer). The project (or course unit) is team based, however individuals are expected to contribute equally to its completion. Note: for industry trainers, the project is replaced by a real and urgent business problem.

For instructors or trainers, this book reflects the double-loop learning educational concept,[2] which involves teaching learners of all types, to think more

---

2 Argyris. (1977). Double loop learning in organizations. *Harvard Business Review*, 55(5), 115–125.

deeply about their own assumptions and beliefs prior to engaging in the design or redesign of organizational products, structures, strategies and policies. If you're applying this book as a curricular course unit, the chapters offer a sequential breakdown of the process of innovation to move from initiation to implementation guided by a proposed 'project'. If you're training in-house managers or teams, the four stage and four-step sequence provides facilitators a structured pathway for innovation development, professional collaboration and workplace application to a real business challenge. Throughout the book, students and participants are encouraged to build awareness of their personal thinking and decision-making style and how to adapt it to participate effectively in the exciting, albeit challenging, innovation process. It's the place where business and design meet. If referencing this book for short, modular-based training programmes, each chapter offers specific topics for discussions along with techniques for practice, and it's designed as self-contained modules.

As a comprehensive guidebook, notebook, workbook and reference book, the use of doodles, markings and sketches is strongly encouraged. Make it your personal navigation guide through the challenging and complex innovation development journey.

Each chapter (as module) invites reflection. It's designed to grant the reader permission to pause, reflect and appreciate how an innovation project gets initiated, what and who is investigated, why, what and how the process involves end-users and internal stakeholders, and when the new offer (product or service) is brought to market. At the end of each chapter the reader is prompted to reflect on the section topics, as well as their own and/or companies' innovation journey and processes. By the end of this book, readers will have gained an innovation and design literacy required to better navigate the volatile, uncertain, complex and ambiguous (aka VUCA) world in which we currently work and live. Below is a brief outline of each chapter.

▶ *Chapter* 1 introduces the building blocks of innovation: how it's defined, what it means and how it works. Influential ideologies, conditions and factors are outlined. A simple four-stage design-driven innovation development model acts as the critical framework for understanding how it happens, how some organizations have failed and why others have succeeded. This chapter outlines and explains each stage: (1) initiation, (2) investigation, (3) integration and (4) implementation. Short business cases are provided throughout.

▶ *Chapter* 2 introduces the origin, practice and discipline of Business Design, and the four-step Business Design Method (BDM). The BDM is an agile, integrative and rigorous approach to navigating the four stages of innovation. This method guides learners to design, participate in and/or manage a design-driven innovation development process or project. This chapter introduces the most common business-oriented design practices, and unpacks each of the four BDM steps: (1) Start, (2) Find, (3) Frame and (4) Solve. Each step is presented in an optimized sequence through ▶ Chapters 3, 4, 5 and 6.

▶ *Chapter* 3 launches the first stage of the innovation process (Initiation) and the first step of the Business Design Method (Step 1: Start). This chapter is divided into two parts that can be delivered as two sequential classes or two distinct and separate modules. Part I introduces key mindsets and competencies associated with each innovation stage and business design step. Part II kick-starts the project-based learning experience, through a challenge brief and innovation design brief. Because innovation, unlike invention, is a team sport, team mapping and forming techniques are provided along with case examples. A proposed challenge brief is offered as an outline for a course or workplace training programme.

▶ *Chapter* 4 outlines the second stage of the innovation process (Investigation) and the second step of the Business Design Method (Step 2: Find). This chapter is divided into two parts which can be delivered as two sequential classes or as two distinct and separate modules. Part I introduces need finding, design research principles and data collection methods. Part II introduces thick data sorting and analysis techniques to arrive at key insights. Both sections build upon the Innovation Design Brief. Observational or field research and empathy interviews are explained with the focus on human, culture and context understanding and narrative data (thick data) collection.

▶ *Chapter* 5 introduces the third stage of the innovation process (Integration) and the third step of the Business Design Method (Step 3: Frame). This chapter is divided into two parts that can be delivered as two sequential classes or as two distinct and separate modules. Part I introduces problem framing and reframing. Part II offers ways of translating insightful problems into novel and relevant ideas and rough prototypes.

▶ *Chapter* 6 outlines the fourth and final stage of the innovation process (Implementation) and the fourth step of the Business Design Method (Step 4: Solve). This chapter is also divided into two parts that can be delivered as two sequential classes or as two distinct and separate modules. Part I outlines final prototyping and evaluation strategies. Part II introduces storytelling, pilot implementation plan development and performance measures design. Story-based frameworks are introduced throughout the chapter and serve as the most effective approach to stakeholder-buy in of new strategies, products, services, plans and measures. Of note, the outputs (as artifacts) generated from each step (from ▶ Chapters 3 to 6) serve as important building blocks and communicate elements for the implementation plan.

▶ *Chapter* 7 makes an explicit case for reflective practice and introspection. Although each chapter ends with a series of question prompts for instructors to ask, and/or for students to reflect upon, this chapter outlines why reflection is important for innovation participants, managers and leaders.It offers a suite of reflection techniques for individuals and teams to pause and reconsider each stage and step of their learning journey, before proceeding to the next, or returning to the previous one.

▶ *Chapter* 8 offers a comprehensive set of templates and worksheets referenced from each chapter. The Appendix section offers examples of completed worksheets as reference for both instructors and students (or participants).

This work was crafted by a designer, manager, strategist, educator and innovator. It embodies multidisciplinary theories, practices, methods, techniques and voices. It offers an alternative perspective from other business and innovation management books as it exposes the failures of over-investing in technologies and profit-first myopia. It offers evidence and strategies that demonstrate the why and how of investing in our human and social systems as a means of delivering impactful success and sustained prosperity.

As a professor at an elite business school, it's my responsibility to educate and inspire students and future leaders to develop an evolved world view. I strive to act as an example of how you can thrive by earning the permission to question stale management frameworks that focus on trade-offs instead of tensions. I'm also here to provide guidance on gaining new perspective or view into how decisions are made, and insights into human needs.

In response to an unprecedented era of global pandemics and disruptive supply chains, management education must redesign its offerings to include both traditional frameworks and more innovative, empathic and enabling methods of leadership. If implemented, business design, as a type of design leadership, may enable large and small firms to redesign their value systems and support their transition to new economies. In uncertain contexts, climates and conditions, innovation participants and managers can all benefit from thinking and acting more like business designers.

This textbook is designed for educators—university professors and corporate facilitators. It is a starting point to your journey of thinking and doing, learning and teaching others, the ways of business design. I hope it proves to be informative, instructional and transformative. I encourage you to use it as reference book or source for case examples and techniques for innovation management and strategy courses.

"Business Design is like therapy for your business"—Starbucks executive

Angèle M. Beausoleil
Toronto, Canada

Acknowledgements

It takes a team to design anything of consequence, and make good design available to everyone.

I've been fortunate to have the opportunity to teach and learn from a lot of people over the past 25 years. This section is to acknowledge their influence, inspiration and contribution to my work.

A big thanks goes to my husband who read my early drafts, offered important edits and reduced my use of jargon. You continue to be my biggest champion.

Un merci pour mon fils Olivier, mon cadeau le plus précieux; mes parents et ma famille pour vos enseignements et conseils.

Thank you Anjana Dattani, Andrew Seepersad and Fifile Nguyễn, my team at the Rotman Business Design Initiative.

Thank you Michelle Hopgood and Elizabeth Phillips, my creative collaborators and co-communication designers.

Thank you to my mentors, Moura Quayle, Sara Beckman, Stefan Miesek, Daved Barry, Nathan Shedroff, Darren Dahl, David Vogt, Brian Fisher and Thomas Kemple.

Thank you to my advisors and colleagues, David Soberman, Delaine Hampton, Chris Ferguson, Emma Aiken-Klar, Richard Blundell, Alex Ryan, Susan Gorbet, Jennifer Nachshen, Judy Mellet, Ken Corts, Stephanie Hodnett, Joanne Goveas, Julie Minielly, and Kate Applin from the Rotman School of Management.

Thank you to Jonas Kronlund, David Schmidt and Alan Faljic and the members of the global Business Designers community of practice group.

Thank you to my friends and early collaborators: Marcelo Bravo, Mary Connolly, Kari Marken, Federico Goroztieta, Karin Watson, Prem Gill and Sang Mah.

Thank you to my students from the Rotman School of Management at the University of Toronto, the Sauder School of Business at the University of British Columbia, and the Haas School of Business at the University of California, Berkeley.

Thank you to my creative muses Joel Gregorio, Alexander Manu, Michael Seven, Bruce Mau, John Couch, Tim Galles and Greg Judelman.

Thanks also to Palgrave MacMillan and Springer for publishing this book and for the Bauhaus design-inspired cover.

A special thank you to the founders, educators, students and practitioners of Bauhaus design. As a designer, the importance of the art form of communicating anything is paramount. I strive for a minimalist design that is understandable, yet provokes. In a complex and complicated world, we need more simplicity. Simplicity that is smart, not dumb. Simplicity that strips away excess, over-engineering and technological abundance, to arrive at the basics. The basic forms and shapes are used in new ways to help you navigate the fundamentals of innovation. The reflective prompts demand that you immerse yourself in the full range of materials and tech-

niques available, and learn by doing. The flexible structure is intentionally adaptive to a linear, circular or bi-directional experience. The strategies and frameworks aim to advocate new ways of approaching multi-faceted problems. These are Bauhaus design principles.

Contents

1	**Introduction to Design-Driven Innovation**	1
1.1	Introduction	2
1.1.1	Warm Up Exercise: Word Association	2
1.2	Defining and Demystifying Innovation	3
1.2.1	Discussion Exercise: Objects and Actions—Innovation as You See It	4
1.3	Key Influences and Orientations	4
1.4	Critical Factors and Skills	5
1.5	Innovation Development: Past and Present	6
1.5.1	Case Map Example: Blockbuster and Netflix	8
1.6	Organizations: To Design or Not to Design	10
1.6.1	Former Innovators: RIP	11
1.6.2	Resilient Innovators: Survivors	11
1.7	Summary and Reflection	12
2	**Introduction to Business Design**	15
2.1	Introduction	16
2.1.1	Warm Up Exercise: Design an Object	16
2.2	What Is Business Design?	17
2.2.1	Discussion Exercise: Designed Innovation	19
2.3	Designing Change and Managing Innovation	21
2.4	Business Design Method: Four Steps to Design-Driven Innovation	23
2.5	Chapter 2: Summary and Reflection	26
	References	27
3	**Business Design Method Step 1: Start**	29
3.1	Introduction	30
3.1.1	Warm Up Exercise: Story of Me	30
3.1.2	Part I: Initiating Innovation by Design	31
3.1.2.1	Human-Centred Design Mindsets	32
3.1.3	Innovation Teams and Participant Types	34
3.1.4	Chapter 3: Part I—Summary and Reflection	38
3.2	Part II: Initiating a Business Design Challenge	39
3.2.1	Warm Up Exercise: Pass the Message	39
3.2.2	Innovations Team Forming	42
3.2.2.1	Exercise: Personal SWOT	43
3.2.2.2	Exercise: Team SWOT	43
3.2.3	Team Forming and Innovation Design Brief Crafting	44
3.2.4	Chapter 3: Part II—Summary and Reflection	47
4	**Business Design Method Step 2: Find**	49
4.1	Introduction	50
4.1.1	Warm Up Exercise: Trading Card	50

4.1.2	Part I: Need Finding as Qualitative Research Method	51
4.1.2.1	Generating Insights from Need Finding	55
4.1.2.2	Case Examples: How Have Organizations Used Need Finding?	56
4.1.3	Key Design Research Methods: Observational Research and Empathy Interviews	58
4.1.4	Creating a Lean Field Research Plan	59
4.1.4.1	Preparing for Field-Based Research	60
4.1.4.2	Empathy Interviews	62
4.1.5	Part I: Summary and Reflection	64
4.2	**Part II: Thick Data Collection and Analysis**	**64**
4.2.1	Warm Up Exercise: Items Sorting	65
4.2.2	Thick Data Analysis	65
4.2.3	Data Sorting: Sift, Sort and Label	66
4.2.4	From Analysis to Synthesis	68
4.2.4.1	Exercise: Insight Statements	68
4.2.4.2	Exercise: Problem Statement (with Insight)	69
4.2.5	Design Critique Session = Feedback Loop	70
4.2.6	Part II: Summary and Reflection	71
5	**Business Design Method Step 3: Frame**	**73**
5.1	**Introduction**	**74**
5.1.1	Warm Up Exercise: Alternative Uses	74
5.1.2	Part I: Framing the Right Problem to Solve	75
5.1.3	Framing Personas from Insights and Problem Statements	76
5.1.3.1	Exercise: Empathy Map	77
5.1.3.2	Exercise: Personas	77
5.1.4	Framing Problems and Questions for Ideation	78
5.1.4.1	Exercise: How Might We Question	78
5.1.5	Design Critique Session = Feedback Loop	79
5.1.6	Part I: Summary and Reflection	80
5.2	**Part II: Framing Ideas, Analogies and Prototypes**	**80**
5.2.1	Warm Up Exercise: Analogy Maker	81
5.2.2	Creative Framing and Ideation	81
5.2.2.1	Generating Ideas Using Metaphors and Analogies	83
5.2.2.2	Exercise: Rapid Ideation	83
5.2.3	Framing Prototypes from Ideas	85
5.2.3.1	Exercise: Rapid Prototyping	86
5.2.3.2	Exercise: Journey Map	86
5.2.4	Design Critique Session = Feedback Loop	87
5.2.5	Part II: Summary and Reflection	88
6	**Business Design Method Step 4: Solve**	**89**
6.1	**Introduction**	**90**
6.1.1	Warm Up Exercise: Paper Airplanes	90
6.1.2	Solving the Right Problem Through Prototyping	91
6.1.3	Evaluating Problems Through Prototypes	94

6.1.4	Evaluation Strategies for Prototypal Solutions	95
6.1.5	Part I: Summary and Reflection	100
6.2	**Part II: Solving Through Implementation**	**100**
6.2.1	Warm Up Exercise: Story Madlib	100
6.2.2	Storytelling	101
6.2.2.1	Exercise: Three-Act Story	104
6.2.3	Designing a Pilot Implementation Plan	104
6.2.3.1	Wayfinding: Designing Better Plans and Pathways	106
6.2.4	Designing Performance Measures	108
6.2.5	Part II: Review and Reflection	115
7	**Reflective Practice and Design**	**117**
7.1	**Introduction**	**118**
7.1.1	Warm Up Exercise: Success Paths	118
7.2	**Reflection Is the Most Impactful Strategy**	**119**
7.2.1	Teaching, Learning and Assessing Reflective Practice	124
7.2.1.1	Exercise: Reflection Paper	126
7.2.1.2	Exercise: Journaling	127
7.2.1.3	Exercise: One-Minute Paper	127
7.2.1.4	Exercise: Free Writing	127
7.2.1.5	Exercise: Free Drawing	127
7.2.2	Reflecting on Business Management Tools	128
7.2.3	Reflecting on the Business Design Learning Journey	131
7.2.3.1	Exercise: 360 Reflection and Evaluation	131
7.2.3.2	Exercise: Personal Learning Journey Map	132
8	**Templates and Worksheets**	**135**
8.1	**Introduction**	**136**
8.2	**Chapter 1: Templates and Worksheets**	**137**
8.3	**Chapter 2: Templates and Worksheets**	**140**
8.4	**Chapter 3: BDM Step 1: START Templates and Worksheets**	**142**
8.5	**Chapter 4: BDM Step 2: FIND Templates and Worksheets**	**154**
8.6	**Chapter 5: BDM Step 3: FRAME Templates**	**168**
8.7	**Chapter 6: BDM Step 4: SOLVE Templates**	**179**
8.8	**Chapter 7: Reflection Templates**	**191**

Supplementary Information

Appendix	198
Glossary	209
Index	219

Abbreviations

BD	Business Design	KPIs	Key Performance Indicators
BDM	Business Design Method	PBL	Project-based Learning
CPMs	Contemporary Performance Measures	PDP	Pre, During, Post
		POEMS	People, Objects, Environments, Messages, Services
HMW	How Might We		
IPMs	Innovation Performance Measures	POV	Point of View

List of Figures

Fig. 1.1	Traditional two-stage innovation development process.	6
Fig. 1.2	Design-driven innovation development process across four stages.	7
Fig. 1.3	The design-driven innovation development process with prompting questions.	8
Fig. 1.4	Comparative case mapping model illustrating traditional vs design-driven innovation	9
Fig. 1.5	Case mapping framework to analyze innovation-focused business cases	10
Fig. 2.1	The Business Design Method steps alignment with design-driven innovation stages	24
Fig. 2.2	Visual model of BDM steps with list of key outputs	25
Fig. 3.1	BDM steps and associated participant types.	36
Fig. 3.2	Divergent and convergent thinking modes and strategies	37
Fig. 3.3	Visual model of the BDM, highlighting how the outputs of divergent thinking are analyzed through convergent thinking to produce key outputs along the innovation journey	38
Fig. 6.1	Visual model of the three interrelated traits of designed innovations.	97
Fig. 6.2	Sample three-act story structure	103
Fig. 6.3	Sample BMPN chart of a pilot implementation plan	107
Fig. 6.4	List of key outputs and artefacts from each BDM step	108
Fig. 8.1	Word association template/worksheet	138
Fig. 8.2	Case mapping template/worksheet.	139
Fig. 8.3	Design and object template/worksheet.	140
Fig. 8.4	Personal thinking map template/worksheet	141
Fig. 8.5	Story of me template/worksheet.	143
Fig. 8.6	Pass the message template/worksheet.	144
Fig. 8.7	Challenge brief template/worksheet (page 1 of 2).	145
Fig. 8.8	Challenge brief template/worksheet (page 2 of 2).	146
Fig. 8.9	Personal SWOT template/worksheet	147
Fig. 8.10	Team SWOT template/worksheet.	148
Fig. 8.11	Innovation design brief template/worksheet (page 1 of 2)	149
Fig. 8.12	Innovation design brief template/worksheet (page 2 of 2)	150
Fig. 8.13	Stakeholder map (internal) template/worksheet	151
Fig. 8.14	Stakeholder map (external) template/worksheet	152
Fig. 8.15	Five whys analysis template/worksheet	153
Fig. 8.16	Trading card template/worksheet.	155
Fig. 8.17	Lean field research plan template/worksheet (page 1 of 2)	156
Fig. 8.18	Lean research plan template/worksheet (page 2 of 2)	157
Fig. 8.19	PDP framework template/worksheet	158
Fig. 8.20	POEMS framework template/worksheet	159
Fig. 8.21	Empathy interview script template/worksheet	160
Fig. 8.22	Items sorting template/worksheet	161

Fig. 8.23	Sift.Sort.Label template/worksheet (page 1 of 3)	162
Fig. 8.24	Sift.Sort.Label template/worksheet (page 2 of 3)	163
Fig. 8.25	Sift.Sort.Label template/worksheet (page 3 of 3)	164
Fig. 8.26	Insight statements template/worksheet	165
Fig. 8.27	Problem statement template/worksheet	166
Fig. 8.28	Problem statement feedback sheet template/worksheet	167
Fig. 8.29	Alternative uses template/worksheet	169
Fig. 8.30	Empathy map template/worksheet	170
Fig. 8.31	Persona template/worksheet	171
Fig. 8.32	How Might We template/worksheet	172
Fig. 8.33	How Might We feedback sheet template/worksheet	173
Fig. 8.34	Analogy maker template/worksheet	174
Fig. 8.35	Rapid ideation template/worksheet	175
Fig. 8.36	Rapid prototyping template/worksheet	176
Fig. 8.37	Journey map template/worksheet	177
Fig. 8.38	Rapid prototypes feedback sheet template/worksheet	178
Fig. 8.39	Paper aeroplanes template/worksheet	180
Fig. 8.40	Storyboarding template/worksheet (page 1 of 3)	181
Fig. 8.41	Storyboarding template/worksheet (page 2 of 3)	182
Fig. 8.42	Storyboarding template/worksheet (page 3 of 3)	183
Fig. 8.43	Service blueprint template/worksheet	184
Fig. 8.44	Three traits framework template/worksheet	185
Fig. 8.45	Five factors analysis template/worksheet	186
Fig. 8.46	Story Madlib template/worksheet	187
Fig. 8.47	Three-act template/worksheet	188
Fig. 8.48	Pilot implementation plan template/worksheet	189
Fig. 8.49	Three-factors measurement framework template/worksheet	190
Fig. 8.50	Success paths template/worksheet	192
Fig. 8.51	Reflection paper template/worksheet (page 1 of 2)	193
Fig. 8.52	Reflection paper template/worksheet (page 2 of 2)	194
Fig. 8.53	Personal learning journey map template/worksheet	195
Fig. A.1	Challenge Brief example for curricular use (page 1 of 2)	199
Fig. A.2	Challenge Brief example for curricular use (page 2 of 2)	200
Fig. A.3	Innovation Design Brief example for curricular use (page 1 of 2)	201
Fig. A.4	Innovation Design Brief example for curricular use (page 2 of 2)	202
Fig. A.5	Stakeholder Map (Internal) example for curricular use (page 1 of 2)	203
Fig. A.6	Stakeholder Map (External) example for curricular use (page 2 of 2)	204
Fig. A.7	Lean Research Plan example for curricular use (page 1 of 2)	205
Fig. A.8	Lean Research Plan example for curricular use (page 2 of 2)	206
Fig. A.9	Persona (Customer) example for curricular use	207

List of Tables

Table 1.1	Deceased companies	11
Table 1.2	Resilient and surviving innovative companies (as of 2021)	12
Table 3.1	Mindsets for design-driven innovation	33
Table 3.2	Key competency measures for learning assessment	35
Table 4.1	Quantitative and qualitative research—comparative summary	52
Table 4.2	Comparative summary: big data versus thick data	54
Table 4.3	Traditional needs analysis vs. need finding	55
Table 4.4	Comparing needs and problems	66
Table 4.5	Problem hypothesis and problem statement examples	69
Table 5.1	Idea generation examples: problems, metaphors and analogies	83
Table 6.1	Prototype categories	93
Table 6.2	Problem-based Alpha prototype development techniques	96
Table 6.3	Three traits framework for discussion	98
Table 6.4	Three traits decision-making framework $(Y = 1/N = 0)$	98
Table 6.5	Prototypal solution adoption evaluation: five factors analysis	99
Table 6.6	KPIs vs CPMs: sample performance metrics and measures	109
Table 6.7	Innovation performance measures and the three-factors framework	110
Table 7.1	Reflective practice frameworks (adapted for this textbook)	121
Table 7.2	Bain's 5Rs of reflection framework	125
Table 7.3	Reflective practice rubric example (applying Bain's 5Rs model)	128
Table 8.1	Chapter-based templates/worksheets list	136

Introduction to Design-Driven Innovation

Supplementary Information The online version contains supplementary material available at (▶ https://doi.org/10.1007/978-3-030-86489-7_1).

© The Author(s), under exclusive license to Springer Nature Switzerland AG 2022
A. Beausoleil, *Business Design Thinking and Doing*,
https://doi.org/10.1007/978-3-030-86489-7_1

> **Learning Objectives**
> At the end of this chapter, readers will be able to:
> - Identify the key influences and orientations for innovation.
> - Identify the critical factors and skills for sustainable growth.
> - Identify the four stages of innovation.

1.1 Introduction

This chapter introduces the building blocks of innovation: what it is, what it means and how it works. Influential ideologies, conditions and factors are outlined. A simple four-stage design-driven innovation development model acts as the critical framework for understanding how innovation happens, why some organizations have failed and why others succeeded. This chapter outlines and explains each stage: (1) initiation, (2) investigation, (3) integration and (4) implementation. Mini-business cases are provided to prompt further discussion and reflection.

1.1.1 Warm Up Exercise: Word Association

> *Warm ups* prepare students to engage in the exploration of new topics or techniques. Similar to fitness or sport-based warm ups, individuals engage in a quick and gentle introduction to a topic and become more comfortable and confident with its relevance and broader application.
> **Word Association** is an associative thinking technique to generate words or phrases that are perceived to be related. A central word is presented to participants, who quickly generate words that come to their mind.
> **How to**: Show a mind-mapping template with the central word being 'innovation' (a template is provided in ▶ Chapter 8).
> - Use a notebook or have paper and pencil or tablet and stylus available.
> - Generate a set of words or images that you associate with this word.
> - Ask participants to generate at least three words.
>
> **Duration**: 1 minute.
> **Discussion**: Ask participants to detect and unpack the patterns with words or images generated from the cohort (classroom or boardroom). Categorize the words into shared meanings. Discuss how one word can present many different and diverse perspectives and meanings.

1.2 Defining and Demystifying Innovation

To navigate, manage and ultimately lead an innovation team, project or innovative organization, you need to understand how others define and interpret 'innovation'.

Innovation is most often associated with successfully bringing a new and improved product or services to market, resulting in consumer adoption and with it, profits. However, people confuse the what (as in new or improved product, service or application) with the how (as in the process of ideating and bringing the new product to market). Many also confuse invention with innovation. Invention is the precursor to innovation. Invention is the process of exploring a hypothesis or prototyping a new idea, while innovation translates an invention into a solution that is adopted at scale.

Innovation is both a noun and a verb. As a noun, it is an idea or object perceived as new; a new idea or object adopted by many; or the output of the process of innovating. Simply stated, innovation often describes the thing perceived as new by the proclaiming party. As a verb, innovation is a structured process of generating, developing and commercializing an idea into a new or improved solution or offer.

Why bother with the semantics (or meaning) of innovation? To start with, it's important you appreciate that without a process, there is no output. The verb trumps the noun. And without an effective innovation process, there is no innovation or new and improved product or service, no market adoption, no revenue or impact. It's also important to understand that at any given time in your teams and organizations, many will be thinking that innovation is a new 'thing', while others will be thinking it's a 'process'. Unfortunately, most won't care because it's not in their job titles or listed in their job descriptions.

This lack of understanding of what innovation is, how it occurs and the role that many have in its success needs serious attention. It is costing companies millions of dollars in operations costs, loss of jobs, low return on investment (ROI) or gross domestic product (GDP). Unsuccessful innovations also result in unexpected consumer waste that impacts our environment, circular supply chain and health. It is exactly this confusion and lack of innovation literacy this module and this book ultimately addresses.

To build your innovation literacy, consider describing innovation as something perceived as new, deemed valuable and has been adopted by a market segment. It is the result of a complex process. Innovation's complex process is due to the fact that it is inherently a communication process that involves all of the activities, decisions and outputs from investigating and defining a problem, through to solving a problem, developing a solution and proposing it to the intended market. It involves on ongoing dialogue with customers and stakeholders, integrates the process of invention, the final output of experiments and prototypes, and the packaging and delivery of new ideas to the market. This process is rife with uncertainty and risk and requires curiosity, courage and insight.

1.2.1 Discussion Exercise: Objects and Actions—Innovation as You See It

> As a cohort or in table teams, take a moment to think of innovations as objects (or things) as well as innovation as actions (or processes). Use a notebook to generate a list or doodle some quick sketches.
> – Generate examples of real-world innovations as objects, or things.
> – Generate examples of real-world innovations as actions or processes.
> **Discuss**: As a large group or at small table groups
> Did you list notable innovation-objects such as the telephone, fax machine, television, internet, smartphone, iTunes platform, etc?
> Did you list or sketch notable innovation processes such as Stage-Gate, Agile Development or design thinking?
> Explain the value of surfacing the dependency of innovative outputs with effective innovation development processes and methods.

1.3 Key Influences and Orientations

To effectively participate in an innovation process, we must first acknowledge our personal orientation and relationship with innovation.

What is your innovation POV? Our individual relationship with innovation likely stems from two influential ideologies from the early twentieth century: techno-economics and socio-economic innovation.

The most pervasive is the economic orientation, an ideology examined by economist Joseph Schumpeter, who described innovation as 'creative destruction'. He was referring to how waves of disruptive technologies and tech-driven innovation were motivated by human ego and progress. He stated that 'while an invention is merely theoretical, an innovation is an invention that has been put into practice'.[1] He would influence scholars and business leaders to study and think that invention is when you take a lot of money and get an idea, while innovation is when you take an idea and make a lot of money with it.[2]

A societal orientation of innovation, on the other hand, is nicely explained through Gabriel Tarde's sociological ideology, often cited from his seminal 'Laws of Imitation' work. He stated that 'all new machines are made up of old tools and old procedures, differently arranged'.[3] Tarde observed that humans love to imitate others and that we continuously evolve and improve our situations into preferred ones, reflecting a more iterative or incremental innovation approach.

---

1   Schumpeter (1942). Creative destruction. *Capitalism, Socialism and Democracy*, 825, 82–85.
2   Davila et al. (2012). *Making innovation work: How to manage it, measure it, and profit from it*. FT Press.
3   Tarde, G. (1903). *The laws of imitation*. H. Holt.

Both Tarde and Schumpeter's ideologies have shaped our personal philosophies, our mindsets and associated behaviours quite profoundly. Gaining an awareness of our influences will aid in developing a literacy and readiness for sustained innovative activities, including developing a hybrid socio-economic innovation orientation should result in a more resilient and prosperous future for all.

Design-driven innovation combines both economic and societal perspectives—[USE EMS] with the aim to imagine better or improved products, services, organizations and societies.

Reflection Prompt: Take a moment to reflect on your personal orientation. Ask yourself if you relate innovation more to economics, society or a hybrid of the two.

1.4 Critical Factors and Skills

To effectively participate in an innovation process, we must also appreciate the critical factors that influence our way of thinking as we introduce a new product or service, strategy or process. These factors have the potential to transform our organizations. Consider the following:
- *Political factors* involve trade policy uncertainty and geopolitical tensions that impact supply chains, manufacturing and trade.
- *Economic factors* include the what and how of production, and for whom, and navigating the circular economy tensions.
- *Technological factors* include the increasing relevance of privacy issues (such as hacking) and the race to set up Big Data and AI teams and databases.
- *Social factors* revolve around the likes of growing social unrest (such as riots in Hong Kong, South America and the USA) and global world health issues (which of course includes pandemics).
- *Environmental factors* include weather-related disasters, ranging from Caribbean hurricanes, to fires in Australia and California, to floods and drought in Africa.

These factors have a huge impact on business innovation. And they can impact you regardless of whether you're in a startup, a small medium enterprise, a corporation or public service organization. They also require new and evolved leadership skills, particularly in the areas of problem diagnostics, problem solving, communications and innovation-readiness. Let's unpack each skillset:
- *Problem diagnosis skills*: To effectively solve problems, you must first learn how to diagnose, define and frame the right problems. This requires critical, reflective and empathic thinking. These skills are radically different from those used by today's analytical thinkers and by those who tend to over-engineer approaches to human needs.

- *Navigating complexity skills*: Today's and tomorrow's leaders need to develop the ability to deal with complexity and ambiguity and learn to adapt to changing needs of customers, contexts and climates.
- *Communication skills*: Those who have the willingness and courage to communicate their thoughts and ask more questions and solicit ideas from their team will prevail. Future-proofing your communication skills starts now, as you will be required to learn how to listen, observe and then translate customer needs into desirable products, services, marketing campaigns and ultimately, innovations.
- *Innovation-readiness*: Those who are open to new experiences, accept failure as pre-condition for success, quickly adopt new ideas and who have the ability and willingness to adapt to changing situations.

> **Reflection Prompt**: Take a moment, and ask yourself:
> a. What is your innovation orientation?
> b. How well prepared are you to engage in an innovation initiative?
> c. How well have you prepared your team, and your company to navigate these factors and forces?
>
> **Discuss**: As a large group or at small table groups.

1.5 Innovation Development: Past and Present

Traditionally, the most researched and practiced organizational innovation development process involves two critical stages: initiation and implementation.

The *first stage* of initiation involves initiating the project based on a problem to be solved; investigating the problem and then deciding to invest in development of a solution to that problem. It is focused on defining the problem to solve.

The *second stage* of implementation involves developing a new idea into a solution; producing, manufacturing, packaging, marketing and distributing the new solution; and evaluating if the solution solved the intended problem. It is focused on developing and delivering the solution to the assumed problem.

Why is this model (◘ Fig. 1.1) still employed by most companies? It favours one key decision-making event (tight control from the C-suite), who logically use existing operational infrastructures, systems and resources. This approach generally results in incremental innovation or improvements to existing products and services, thus offering executives low risk or seemingly predictable returns.

◘ Fig. 1.1   Traditional two-stage innovation development process

1.5 · Innovation Development: Past and Present

Unfortunately, as this visual model shows, the traditional innovation process spends little time and effort defining the problem. Instead, most of the effort, time and resources are spent on generating a solution to that problem. It gravely assumes that the problem identified is the right problem to solve. It reflects an under-investment in research and investigating the right problem to be solved, and over-investment in development and engineering a solution to solve the assumed problem.

Close examination of the traditional model, in part by mapping evidence-based research and industry practice models, unearths inefficiencies in such practices. Out of this, a more sustainable innovation process emerged: a design-driven innovation development model. Design-driven innovation is the design, development, delivery and effective management of an innovation that meets the needs of the target-end user or customer. It invests strategically in defining the right problem to solve, and results in a designed solution that offers value and meaning for consumers. As a customer-centred design model, it involves four-stages initiation, investigation, integration and implementation.

- The *first stage* of initiation involves initiating a project based on problem hypothesis, creating a project (design) brief and research plan to investigate the assumed problem.
- The *second stage* of investigation involves investigating and validating needs associated with the problem hypothesis; researching, collecting and analyzing data; ultimately finding needs and the right problem to solve.
- The *third stage* of integration integrates insights and ideas into prototypes, frame and reframe the problem to solve, test prototypes with external and internal stakeholders.
- The *fourth stage* is implementation involves designing, testing and implementing final prototypes, and then designing and delivering a solution to the problem; followed by evaluating the solution to determine if the problem is solved or not.

This four-stage model's first two stages focus on defining the right problem to solve. The last two stages focus on designing the right solution. This model (◘ Fig. 1.2) shows a better balance with investing in defining the right and solvable problem and generating solution prototypes, before investing significant resources in the final design and delivery of the solution. Each stage demands reflection prior to decision-making, granting permission to both management and innovation teams to determine if they should move forward or backward. This process separates research from the traditional R&D, investigating the intended customer's needs prior to defining the problem—which positively impacts the design of a solution that is solving

◘ Fig. 1.2 Design-driven innovation development process across four stages

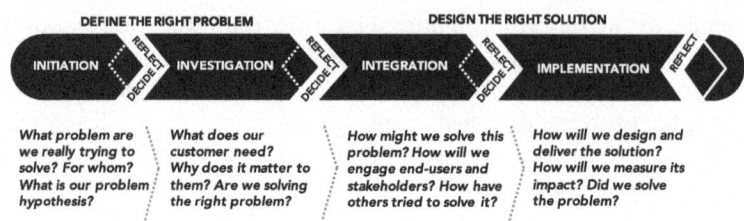

☐ **Fig. 1.3** The design-driven innovation development process with prompting questions

the right problem for the target end-user. The four stages highlight a design-driven innovation process as a best practice.

Designing a process for success involves moving from intention (initiation) to inquiry and insight-based problem framing (investigation), to integrating insights into ideation, prototyping and existing production systems (integration); to packaging and delivering the solution to a demanding market (implementation).

Design-driven innovation aims to facilitate ongoing dialogue with stakeholders (internal and external), resulting in insightful and informed decision-making between each stage. The innovation manager or participant is guided with a series of questions to spark discussion and reflection before moving forward or towards action (☐ Fig. 1.3).

For example, the initiation stage prompts the team to ask: What problem are we really trying to solve? For whom, the company or the customer? The investigation stage asks: Who does our customer need? Why does it matter to them and the company? The integration stage asks: How might we solve their problem? And, the implementation stage poses: How will we design and deliver a solution that solves their problem? The questions serve as prompts to surface assumptions, biases and beliefs that may affect the effectiveness of the innovation process. For the manager or project owner, the benefits for a design-driven approach include:

- Collaborative approach to decision-making.
- Customer or user-informed insights.
- Multiple decision points for stakeholder engagement and buy-in.
- Strategic integration of person-led, low-tech techniques with existing processes.
- A combined fluid and adaptive approach with a structured system.
- Stage-based costs projections for effective budget management.

1.5.1 Case Map Example: Blockbuster and Netflix

A case map is a diagram that visually illustrates the relationships between key concepts, inputs and outputs of a case study. Case mapping is a technique to visually reconstruct and analyze relevant information from a case study. It guides individu-

1.5 · Innovation Development: Past and Present

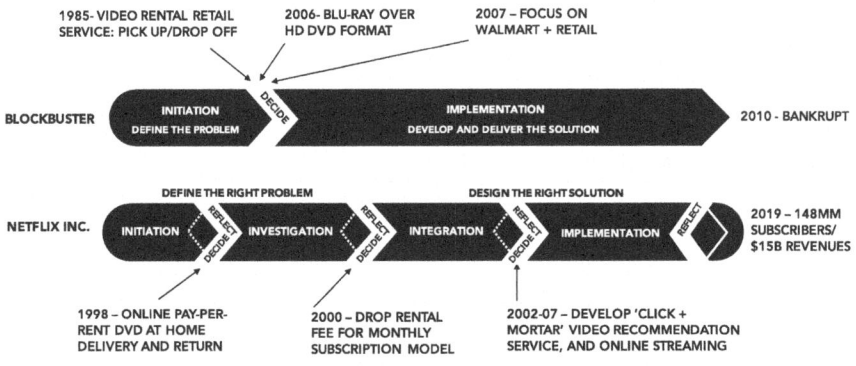

Fig. 1.4 Comparative case mapping model illustrating traditional vs design-driven innovation

als and teams to think analytically and visually, aiding in the exploration and surfacing of key problems, issues, decisions and actions within a case. The case map below (Fig. 1.4) highlights the key innovation-related decisions made by Blockbuster and Netflix over their corporate lifecycles.

This case mapping has been created to highlight the different strategies and decisions involving innovation activities between two companies operating in similar territory. It examines and summarizes how Blockbuster and Netflix each offered different services to the same customers, enabling the customers to decide the victor. Blockbuster, founded in 1985 in Texas, was a brick-and-mortar retail chain who once led the North American and global video rental industry, then filed for bankruptcy in 2010. Blockbuster grew into a successful company by initially offering VHS video rental customers a choice of movies, albeit limited to physical retail locations for selection, pick-up and drop-off. Their business model combined revenues from rentals and from late fees—charging the same customer for withholding future sales of the video or DVD. Throughout the nineties, Blockbuster would make shareholder-focused corporate decisions over customer preferences by offering only Blu-Ray over HD-DVD titles, restricting rentals to physical retail locations only (including a limited partnership with Walmart), and ultimately declining an alternative strategy for rentals-by-mail and web-based services from a couple of guys who had just founded Netflix. Blockbuster filed for bankruptcy in 2010.

Netflix launched in 1997 from California, with a simple rent-by-mail service for customers to order and return the new CD-ROM video formats (Blu-Ray and HD-DVD) from the comfort of their home, and without late fees. Their online subscription service pilot proved successful, aiding them to secure a $30 million investment to scale their services across the US. Netflix pivoted their business model from post-delivered DVDs to a complete online subscription service. The company then dropped their monthly fee and introduced an annual flat fee for limitless access to internet-based streamed movies. With thousands of subscribers, they built an algorithm to identity film genre, consumer preference and choice, and introduced a 'smart' recommendation feature. From 2002 to 2013, Netflix grew to serve over $36 million subscribers across the USA and internationally. In 2019, Netflix[4] operated in over 190 countries, offering the largest subscription-based online streaming service—a library of long and short-form films and television series—while emerging as a producer and distributor of in-house, original content.

Blockbuster originally succeeded with a business model focused on delivering entertainment to people's homes. Blockbuster maintained its original business model and delayed responding to changing customer needs and disruptive technologies. Netflix continued to pivot and redesign their business model, offering what customers desired and profits to shareholders. Netflix is one example of design-driven innovation—a strategic approach to generate sustainable and desirable products or services.

Reflection Prompt: Are you able to discern and diagnose the different stages of innovation in this mini-case?

Discussion: What are your interpretation of the decisions made by both Blockbuster and Netflix?

To analyze additional innovation development focused business cases (or workplace case studies), consider using or referencing the case mapping framework. It provides a set of guiding questions for each stage (◘ Fig. 1.5). A templated worksheet is provided in ▶ Chapter 8.

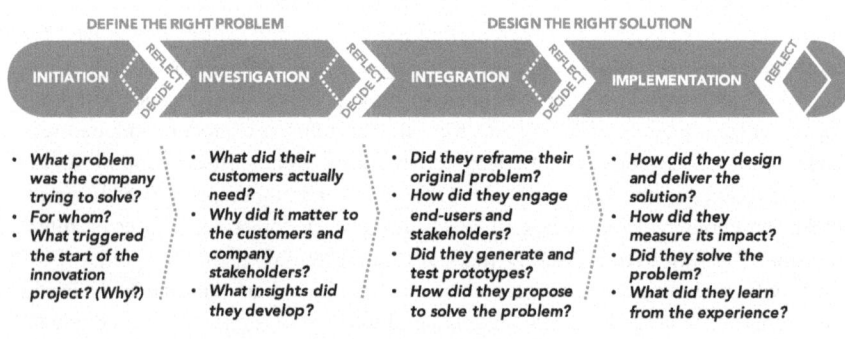

◘ **Fig. 1.5** Case mapping framework to analyze innovation-focused business cases

1.6 Organizations: To Design or Not to Design

We now have a better understanding of what innovation means, along with the influences on its practice, and factors and skills critical to successful participation. Let's examine a few examples of companies that failed to innovate sustainably, and compare their experiences to those of companies that are currently thriving.

---

4 Randolph (2019). *That will never work: The birth of Netflix and the amazing life of an idea*. Little, Brown.

1.6 · Organizations: To Design or Not to Design

Table 1.1 Deceased companies

Company (operating years)	Simplified description of demise
Pan Am (1927–1991)	• Overinvested in business model, mismanagement
British Home Stores (BHS) (1928–2016)	• Traditional book store that stagnated into unprofitable community tea shop
Polaroid (1937–2001)	• Unable to anticipate impact from digital cameras
Toys R Us (1948–2017)	• Signed 10-yr deal with Amazon, no in-house e-commerce
Tower Records (1960–2004)	• Disrupted by music piracy, iTunes and streaming
Parmalat (1961–2003)	• Dairy food manufacturer to fraudulent financial model
Borders (1971–2011)	• Too late to offer online books, too much debt
Compaq (1982–2002)	• Lost pricing war with PC makers
Blockbuster (1985–2010)	• Unable to transition towards a digital model
Pets.com (1998–2000)	• Lacked integrated e-commerce and warehouse management systems

1.6.1 Former Innovators: RIP

This table outlines a sample of organizations no longer operating (Table 1.1), and offers simplified reasons for their demise, to illustrate their innovation challenges.

What can we learn from these once, now fallen innovators? These companies fell into the 'success trap' by exploiting their (historically successful) business activities. They neglected to explore evolving customer needs to enhance their long-term viability.

1.6.2 Resilient Innovators: Survivors

Table 1.2 outlines a sample of existing companies (2021) that are positioned to survive and thrive through the global pandemic and beyond:

Why have they succeeded? What is their secret formula? The innovation development patterns from these companies suggest they share some common practices in their paths to success:

– They have all managed to evolve their original business models to meet evolving customer needs.
– They combine design with engineering.
– They created a culture of experimentation.

◘ Table 1.2 Resilient and surviving innovative companies (as of 2021)

Company (founding year)	Evolution (from > to)
Nintendo (1889–	> from local playing cards to global at-home entertainment products
Nokia (1865–	> from paper mill to manufacturer to telecom services
Microsoft (1975–	> from software to cloud and team-based tools as service
Alibaba Group (1999–	> from B2B online marketplace to C2C platform
Tesla (2003–	> from R&D to clean energy product manufacturer
Shopify (2004–	> from platform to powering global online pop-ups
Big Hit Entertainment (2005–	> from music management to music fan generator
Beyond Meat (2009–	> from single retail provider to global plant-based meat manufacturer
Snap/Snapchat (2011–	> from social messaging to content publisher
White Claw (2016–	> from Mike's Hard Lemonade to crafted low calorie seltzers

These companies are examples of sustainable innovation in practice. Designing and redesigning your business in response to what your market needs is crucial for survival and sustained competitive advantage. 'Sustainable innovation' in this book is defined as an approach to innovation development that is designed to be maintained, sustained and supported over many cycles or years.

1.7 Summary and Reflection

Innovation is both a process and an output. It is important to have the right process that generates desirable goods or services that are deemed innovative and are adopted widely. The traditional innovation development model puts most of the time, effort and money in developing the solution, and less on understanding and framing the right problem to solve. In response to this rigid, solution-focused approach, a design-driven innovation model is proposed. The contemporary four-stage design-driven innovation model has emerged as a sustainable approach that balances time, effort and resources to find the right problem for your organization to solve, focused on a target customer or end-user.

Students: Reflect on topics presented and answer the following:
– How do you define innovation?
– What are the key influences and orientations for innovation?
– What are the critical factors and skills for sustainable business growth?
– What are the four stages of design-driven innovation?

Reflect on your own process and/or your companies' innovation process. Take a few minutes to quickly sketch out how a project gets initiated, what and who is investigated and why, what and how the process involves end-users and internal stakeholders. Also reflect on the how and when the new offer (product or service) being brought to market. From that quick 'memory check', compare your process to the four stages: are they similar or different? Identify gaps, ask how you might retool.

Introduction to Business Design

Supplementary Information The online version contains supplementary material available at (▶ https://doi.org/10.1007/978-3-030-86489-7_2).

© The Author(s), under exclusive license to Springer Nature Switzerland AG 2022
A. Beausoleil, *Business Design Thinking and Doing*,
https://doi.org/10.1007/978-3-030-86489-7_2

> **Learning Objectives**
> At the end of this chapter, readers will be able to:
> - Describe the value of design for business
> - Identify the principles and practices of human-centred design
> - Identify the four steps of the Business Design Method

2.1 Introduction

This chapter introduces the origin, practice and discipline of Business Design, and the four-step Business Design Method (BDM) as an agile, integrative and rigorous approach to navigating the four stages of innovation. This method guides learners to design, participate in, and collaboratively manage a design-driven innovation development process or project. The most common design practices in business innovation are explained, and the four BDM steps are unpacked: (1) Start; (2) Find; (3) Frame) and (4) Solve. Each step is presented in an optimized sequence from Chapters 3, 4, 5 to 6.

2.1.1 Warm Up Exercise: Design an Object

> *Warm ups* prepare students to engage in the exploration of new topics or techniques. Similar to fitness or sport-based warm ups, individuals engage in a quick and gentle introduction to a topic and become more comfortable and confident with its relevance and broader application.
> **Design an Object** is a design thinking exercise practiced at IBM which involves two prompts that elicit two different yet meaningful outcomes. One focuses on the functional needs associated with an object, the other focuses on the emotional needs of the object's end-user.
> **How to:** Take a sheet of paper/pen or tablet/stylus and draw a line in the centre to create two panels or sections.
> - The first panel states 'Design a vase (as object)' as a prompt
> - Ask participants to generate words and sketches that come to mind.
> - The second panel states 'Design a better way for people to enjoy flowers (object of vase)' as a prompt
> - Ask participants to generate new or unexpected responses that come to mind.
>
> **Duration:** 3 minutes (1.5 min per panel).
> **Discussion:** Explore the power of reframing a question to develop empathy for the people using the object and/or seeking a desirable and designed experience. Discuss functional and emotional needs.

2.2 What Is Business Design?

Design has become increasingly the crucial ingredient for businesses competing for a share of today's global, fast-paced and uncertain marketplace. Better designed products and services attract customers. Well-designed organizations attract and retain top talent. Design-driven leaders craft their companies and cultures based on the logic of design's appeal and a designer's approach. Welcome to Business Design.

Business design is a modern construct, making its first appearance in academic and industry literature in the early 1990s. It was first described by systems engineer J.L. Dietz in 1993 as the modeling, design, engineering and re-engineering of a firm.[1] Dietz's research focused on informational and technological mechanisms that facilitated organizational structures. Management consultant Adrian Slywotzky, in his 1996 book 'Value Migration', offered a straightforward definition of *business design* as encompassing all activities involving the design of a profitable business. As a respected author, he guided business leaders to consider critical questions to inform their business design, such as asking about the customer, their firm's unique value proposition, profit model and strategic control, and how all of these elements work together. He stated the **discipline of business design is to take exactly the same approach to designing the business as one takes to designing a great product—bringing new value to the customer from concept to product, and then to market, profitably.** He also offered Google as an example of a firm practicing business design and redesign, obsessed with constant improvement based on the customer's need to find and rank information. Google's approach has resulted in the invention of AdSense and AdWords services, and a new business design (for internet browsers) with a sustainable competitive advantage.[2]

As a phrase, business design implies the integration of business (as organization) with design (as to make or mark), or **the act of designing or redesigning an organization**. From a multidisciplinary research literature review, business design is described as organizing and actively engaging in new value creation, using design-related principles and practices, resulting in sustained competitive advantage. Hence, business design is the practice of design-driven innovation.

In practice, **Business Design (BD) is generally understood as a way of thinking and working that applies human-centred design to improving or transforming business activities**. Its combinatory approach draws upon management and social science, design, strategy and marketing to create business value—from innovative new products, services and processes, to sustainable business models.

As a discipline, we define **Business Design as an approach that integrates management frameworks, anthropological methods and design principles to solve organizational challenges.** It offers a structured methodology to orient organiza-

---

1 Dietz (1993). *Business modelling for business redesign.* Faculty of Economics, Limburg University.
2 Slywotzky (1997). Value migration: How to think several moves ahead of the competition. *Long Range Planning*, 2(30), 314.

tions to recognize that the marketplace and customers are evolving, and to evolve their business processes and models accordingly. Its purpose is to align leaders and their teams to reframe business problems, prototype solutions and deliver what customers need, and stakeholders want—resulting in sustainable business operations. A senior executive with a global corporation described Business Design as 'it's like therapy for your business'.

Human-centred design (HCD) involves a dynamic and reflective process of observing humans to understand their needs, wants and motivations, and proposing a desired state or outcome. Human-centred design is defined as an approach to designing platforms, products and services, that model end-user behaviour, and are intuitive, desirable and commercially viable. The aim of HCD is to develop empathy for others in order to make insightful decisions and take impactful action. The key principles of HCD include:

- Focus on understanding people
- Focus on solving problems for people
- Understand that human systems are interconnected (platforms and planet)
- Be iterative and generative
- Always be seeking feedback
- Test prototypes
- Learn, do, refine and repeat

Business Design (BD) employs HCD methods that involve customer understanding delivered through ethnographic methods when spreadsheets and big data analytical tools are insufficient. More accurately, yet less commonly stated is how **BD applies a holistic form of HCD or stakeholder-centred design approach to business innovation**. Stakeholder-centred design (SCD) is an approach to designing platforms, products and services, that model both end-user and ecosystem member behaviours, and are desirable, and commercially feasible and viable.

As an emergent discipline, BD is introduced (or trained) and practiced horizontally and vertically across organizations. It involves cross-functional teams that span marketing, strategy, HR, product design and development, finance and operations. It involves both internal and external stakeholders (i.e. customers or end-users) and is focused on the effective management of the design, development and delivery of an innovative solution. Examples of its diverse practices include: strategic design, business model design, employee experience design, service design and customer experience design. The following integrate the needs of both internal & external stakeholders:

- **Strategic Design** applies design principles and practices to guide strategy development and implementation towards innovative outcomes that benefit both people and organizations. Strategic design involves systems thinking and considers user needs and business goals when designing a strategy.
- **Business Model Design** involves the designing or redesigning of an organization's or division's business model to create value and prosper. Business Model Design involves business planning frameworks and business model maps to articulate the source of future value and a proposed distinctive value proposition to remain competitive.

- **Employee Experience Design (EXD)** applies design methods to designing programmes and experiences that employees desire. EXD involves employee-centred activities (as internal customers) to research, map, prototype and develop new or improved interactions between employee and employer.
- **Service Design** applies design principles and methods to service planning, development and implementation that benefit both users and organizations. Service design involves both internal and external (customer facing) activities to map, prototype and propose an improved or new external service and/or internal process.
- **Customer Experience Design (CXD)** applies marketing principles and design methods to designing product/service experiences that customers desire and firms profit from. CXD involves customer-centred activities to research, map, prototype and market new or improved interactions between end-users (as customers) and your organization.

As an overarching approach to navigate and manage design-driven innovation, *business design* orients organizations to recognize that the market place, consumer segments and customers are evolving, and that business models and strategies must evolve accordingly. As users (or customers) continue to leave for competitor offerings, organizations need to rediscover who their customers are. For organizations to survive, let alone thrive, they will need to effectively embrace a business design approach to connect with customers, understand their unmet needs and find effective yet profitable ways to make their lives and jobs better. **If the organization doesn't adapt, they will continue the slow and inevitable decline towards bankruptcy or irrelevance.**

2.2.1 Discussion Exercise: Designed Innovation

> Take a moment and think of examples of designed innovations that span strategic design, business model design, employee experience design, service design and customer experience design. Use a notebook to generate a list.
> - Generate examples of real-world strategic innovations
> - Generate examples of real-world business model innovations
> - Generate examples of real-world EXD innovations
> - Generate examples of real-world service design innovations
> - Generate examples of real-world CXD innovations
>
> **Discuss:** As a large group (cohort) or at small table groups ask:
> - What are the similarities between the designed innovations?
> - What are the differences between the design innovations
> - What role does human-centred design (HCD) play?
>
> Explain the value of integrating HCD principles into innovation development processes, for different types of business designs or outputs.

Business Design and Design Thinking: A Literature Review Synopsis

As an emergent discipline, Business Design scholars and practitioners suggest it involves the re-engineering or redesigning of the organization in response to market changes and customer needs (Dietz 1993; Talwar 1993; Kilov and Simmonds 1996; Slywotzky 1997; Sia 2000). Some propose that Business Design is a framework comprising a firm's structures, cultures and sources of capital (Denning 1996; Baroudi and Lucas 1994; Osterwalder, Pigneur and Tucci 2005; etc.) or even its DNA (Turner 2000). As a modern management practice, Business Design is inherent in business model design, combining a firm's logic and processes in creating and commercializing value (Osterwalder et al. 2005; etc.) or a strategic competitive advantage (Slywotzky 1997; Martin 2009; Fraser 2012). At business schools, it is associated with design thinking (Martin 2005; Dunne and Martin 2006; Martin 2009; Brown 2009; Liedtka and Ogilvie 2011; Kelley and Kelley 2013; Dunne 2018; Fraser 2012) and described as a human-centred approach to innovation (Beausoleil 2018). As a design management practice, Business Design is associated with systems thinking (Van Ackere et al. 1993; Kumar et al. 2009; Caisse and Montreuil 2014; Gharajedaghi 2011), strategic design (Manzini 1999; Manzini and Vezzoli 2003; Stevens and Moultrie 2011; Liedtka et al. 2007; Quayle 2017), service design (Faber et al. 2003; Mager 2008; Reason et al. 2015; de Rouw and Johnson 2017) and customer experience design (Berry et al. 2002; Lockwood 2010; Oswald 2016). Practicing business designers offer business design as an activity that uses design methodologies, a design mindset and business tools to solve business challenges (Faljic 2019).

From the management discourse on business design, most authors discuss the need for organizations to welcome new 'designs' to adapt, survive and prosper. It appears the combinatory power of business with design has driven an exponential rise in business design-related discourse, particularly with the concept of design thinking. Design thinking commonly refers to a creative problem-solving approach that draws from the designer's toolkit to integrate the needs of users with the requirements for business success (Kelley 2006; Brown 2009).

Originating from Stanford University's engineering school and associated with professors Robert McKim, Rolf Faste and David Kelley in the 1980s and 1990s, design thinking was introduced as a way of incorporating end-users (known as human-centered design) into traditional engineering processes (Oxman 2017). Published research articles focused on design thinking are extensive and span engineering, science, design, education, sociology and management journals.

Most management scholars encourage firms to adopt design thinking approaches to increase customer understanding and therefore a competitive advantage (Owen 2005; Beckman and Barry 2007; Dunne and Martin 2006; Martin 2009; Ungaretti et al. 2009; Esslinger 2009; Liedtka and Ogilvie 2011; Lockwood 2010; Matthews et al. 2011; Martin and Euchner 2012). A few argue it lacks a clear definition, rigorous theoretical frameworks and effective practice (Kimbell 2011; Panda 2016; Iskander 2018; Ersoy 2018).

This book introduces business design as a distinct construct and practice from design thinking, noting three key differences:

- first, its origin is with organizational redesign;
- second, it integrates both customer and stakeholder needs (rather than customers or end-users only) and,
- third, its focus is on both the management of innovation work, and engineering or product/service design.

The steady increase of published articles and scholarship in the domain of design-oriented and design-driven innovation studies suggests it is an emerging discipline in management education and more precisely in innovation management.

Reflection Prompt: Take a moment and reflect on the value of design to customers and companies. Do you consider these trade-offs or tensions?

Discussion: Ask students (or participants) to consider your professional experience in designing a service or experience, and your personal experience of being a customer or end-user. What are their similarities and differences with the experiences?

2.3 Designing Change and Managing Innovation

Any action involving the design or redesign of a process, product or business model requires innovation management. Therefore, *business design* is aligned with organizational change, product improvement and the 'management of innovation' perspective inside firms.[3] Innovation scholars have subtly introduced the need for *business design* when highlighting the four main problems that innovation creates for managers: human, process, structural and strategic problems. They suggest the role of senior management teams is to effectively manage innovation inside a firm with the intent to improve business performance and firm competitiveness. They provide compelling evidence for the need to equip senior managers and future leaders (e.g. MBAs) with innovation management methods, frameworks and mindsets that integrate *business design*.[4]

Business Design triggers a new typology of key design actions and owners that intersect with core business functions and involve design-as-process activities

---

[3] Cunningham and Walsh (2019), Disciplinary perspectives on innovation: Management, Foundations and Trends® in Entrepreneurship: Vol. 15, No. 3–4, pp. 391–430.
[4] Damanpour (1991). Organizational innovation: A meta-analysis of effects of determinants and moderators. *Academy of Management Journal, 34*(3), 555–590. Shoham and Fiegenbaum (2002). Competitive determinants of organizational risk-taking attitude: The role of strategy reference points. *Management Decision, 40*(2), 127–141. Van de Ven (2017). The innovation journey: You can't control it, but you can learn to maneuver it. *Innovation, 19*(1), 39–42.

(methods) across an organization, in contrast to design-as-artifact (things). Examples of design-as-process activities and their common associated roles comprise:

- What are we designing? (R&D, Sales, Marketing, HR, Management and Finance)
- Who are we designing for? (Marketing and HR = customer facing)
- Why are we designing? (Strategy and CEO)
- How will we design it? (Production/Operations and Finance)
- How will we know if we succeeded? (Management and Finance)

These core roles all engage in innovation-related activities. They drive, manage and participate in the improvement, reinvention and transformation of processes, structures, products and systems (aka organizational change).

Innovation is synonymous with change. Introducing a new idea or technology is one thing (it actually is invention). Introducing a new idea or technology that is adopted by many, is change (aka innovation). Design-driven innovation involves thoughtful planning and execution of an idea, proposal or technology with the intent to design change. Business Design denotes an intended or designerly approach to craft and embed change in an organization. There are four basic types of designed business innovations relating to what the firm's leaders believe requires changing and improvement:

- **Product/Service**: changing what you do or offer (e.g. mobile phone)
- **Position/Market**: changing who consumes it (e.g. new user)
- **Process**: changing how you do it (e.g. Lean, Six Sigma, etc.)
- **Paradigm**: changing why it matters and what value it creates (e.g. platform (iTunes) and organizational culture (flat or decentralized)

Business examples for each type of design-driven innovation include:

Product Design Example: OXO, founded in 1990 in NYC by Sam Farber, is a manufacturer of kitchen utensils and housewares. Farber, an industrial designer and entrepreneur, observed his wife struggling to hold her potato peeler due to her arthritis, and questioned why ordinary kitchen tools hurt, instead of help, the home cook. Sam prototyped, tested and launched a Good Grip series of inclusive-design cooking tools that could benefit all people (with or without arthritis). OXO has grown to offer over 1,000 Good Grips products designed to delight end-users.[5]

Position/Market Design Example: Umpqua Bank is a commercial bank based in Oregon. Umpqua was founded in 1953 by a group of timber industry workers seeking a way for their employees to cash their payroll checks. Over the years, the bank has redesigned their product, service and retail strategies to meet the needs of both the citizens and businesses located near their branches. They shifted their

---

5   OXO Corporation (2021) Behind the scenes. Retrieved May 2021 from ▶ https://www.oxo.com/blog/behind-the-scenes/behind-design-oxos-iconic-good-grips-handles.

focus from convenience and speed, to connecting with the locals (people) who value community prosperity as much as their own. They offer a café and community resource centre and exemplify the concept of 'slow banking'. Their business design approach has resulted in sustained growth for them and their clients, from their early start of $120M to $8B in 2019.[6]

Process Design Example: Slack Technologies, founded in 2009 in Canada, started as a gaming company that had developed an internal process, application and platform for collaborative and remote-based teams. Although the game failed, their internal communication process, called Slack (acronym for "Searchable Log of All Conversation and Knowledge) proved to be an improved design over most competing project management and communication tools. Users from around the globe adapted the platform leading to a successful acquisition by Salesforce in 2020.[7]

Paradigm Design Example: IBM, a multinational computer and information technology corporation, is a leading example of a company that has redesigned their business model, products and services, systems and markets over their 100 years in operation. With a 350,000-plus workforce, IBM has infused a design orientation with their proprietary 'Enterprise Design Thinking' formula, a simple approach to transformation and reinvention. They have evolved from mainframe experts, to designing and prototyping driverless cars and launching cyber security and AI services with an empathic understanding for both end-users and stakeholders. Their transformative DNA reflects a human-centred design orientation that can be measured in patents, retaining Nobel Prize winning employees and annual sales of over $77 billion (2019).[8]

2.4 Business Design Method: Four Steps to Design-Driven Innovation

Business Design (BD) is a way of thinking and working that applies human-centred (as stakeholder-centred) design to improving or transforming business activities. Human-centred design involves understanding and ultimately solving a problem or resolving a need for the end-user or consumer, while stakeholder-centred design involves both the end-user of the process (internal stakeholder) and the end-user of the product. Designing change requires stakeholder-centred design, as it impacts the whole organization and associated ecosystem. Examples of innovation-led change includes product design (changing your offering), strategic and customer experience design (changing your target market and their experience), process and service design (changing how you offer it) and business model design (changing how you operate, your mission or culture).

---

6   Umpqua Bank (2021) Retrieved May 2021 from ▸ https://www.umpquabank.com/.
7   Slack Software (2021) Retrieved May 2021 from ▸ https://en.wikipedia.org/wiki/Slack_(software).
8   IBM Corporation (2021) Retrieved May 2021 from ▸ https://www.ibm.com/about.

To navigate the complexity of innovation and business design (and redesign), a structured methodology and process map is required. Maps represent the real world on a much smaller scale. They help us travel from one location to another. They help with organizing information and figuring out where we are, and where we aim to go. Without maps, we process blind. Mapping is a technique extensive practiced across all design domains. They invite one to participate in the collection, capture and analysis of a pathway—a new or evolving process, situation or scenario (aka innovation or change).

The Business Design Method (BDM) is quite simply a map and navigation system. BDM is an end-to-end and step-by-step approach to sustained innovation, enabling organizations to (re)design their processes, systems and offers to focus on customers (internal or external). Developed from extensive research on innovation development and management frameworks and design processes, the BDM involves four action-oriented steps mapped to the four stages of design-driven innovation: (1) start; (2) find; (3) frame and (4) solve. It is important to note that this methodology is explorative and reflective in its design, enabling bi-directional activity and movement.

The BDM is ultimately an agile framework that simplifies the complexity of an innovation development process. It's designed to aid the structure of your thoughts, questions and actions along the uncertain and ambiguous innovation journey. Think of the steps as prompts and guides for business design thinking and doing, leading to resilient and sustainable innovation. The four steps align directly with the four design-driven innovation stages:

1. *Start (Initiation):* Trigger or initiate the innovation project; form team
2. *Find (Investigation):* Find human needs, problems and insights
3. *Frame (Integration):* Frame the right problem to solve, generate ideas and prototypes and test; reframe if warranted.
4. *Solve (Implementation):* Solve problems and resolve the need, measure the innovation as solution's impact.

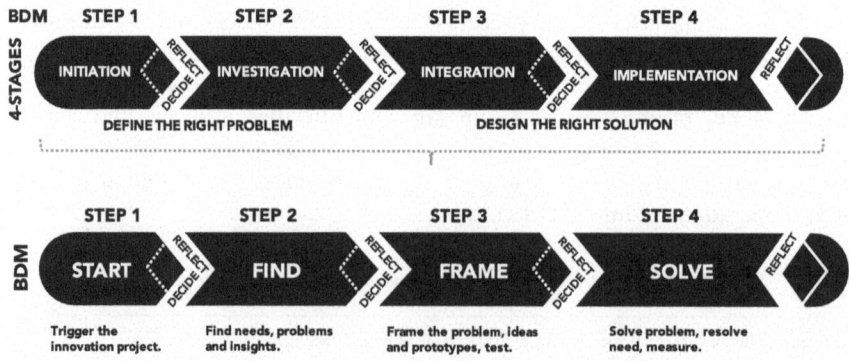

◘ **Fig. 2.1** The Business Design Method steps alignment with design-driven innovation stages

2.4 · Business Design Method: Four Steps to Design-Driven Innovation

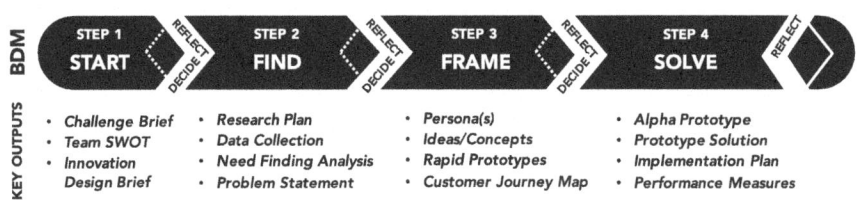

◘ **Fig. 2.2** Visual model of BDM steps with list of key outputs

The four steps are sequential as a best practice. However, you can 'start' (◘ Fig. 2.1) at different steps, depending on which stage you begin your innovation initiative. For example, you might begin at step 3 (frame) to discover you are solving the wrong problem, and therefore must return to step 1(start) to articulate a better brief, or move back to step 2 (find) to lead more field research on the right and solvable problem to focus your efforts upon. *Note: Presenting the BDM as a process helps you and your team untangle the complex innovation development process and visualize it with ease. With repeated referencing, the BDM serves as a process map, guiding and preparing you and your organization to better respond to uncertainty, and enabling strategic and resilient decision-making.*

Each step of the BDM (◘ Fig. 2.1) has a set of outputs that align innovation managers and teams to reflect on project status. Each step prompts further inquiry into defining the right problem and designing the right solution. The key outputs should be valued as knowledge elements, leading to actionable insights and decisions and include (◘ Fig. 2.2):

1. **Start**: challenge brief; team profile and innovation design brief
2. **Find**: data collection; data analysis; needs analysis and problem statement
3. **Frame**: persona(s); ideas/concepts; rapid prototypes and customer journey map
4. **Solve**: alpha prototype, prototype solution; implementation plan and performance measures

As a process map and framework, the Business Design Method reduces the complexity of innovation development and the fear associated with uncertainty, and increases your confidence with how best to navigate it. By following the map, efforts focus on uncovering the needs that lay below the surfaced problem. For many organizations, this can effectively minimize the pressure of being a fast-follower who constantly struggles to innovate. BDM allows companies to outline a sustainable roadmap. Practitioners of this method have emphasized the value of being liberated from being boxed into specific solutions, so that they can access a wider array of possible solutions. When practiced as a 'recipe', BDM opens the door to going beyond business stakeholder assumptions about their customers and gaining a deeper understanding of their needs and motivations. It minimizes biases and increases insight, resulting in more impactful solutions. The next four chapters launch you into understanding and practicing each step in its optimized sequence.

> **Exercise: Personal Thinking Map**
>
> A personal thinking map is a visual thinking technique to reflect and then express your thinking process in simple steps or stages, making your decision-making process visible.
>
> **Think and Do:**
> - Reflect on the Business Design Method steps
> - Identify a past situation involving adopting a new idea, object or technology (i.e. a simple everyday example)
> - Use the template (or paper/tablet) to sketch out the steps involved in your thinking and actions
> - Annotate your mapping with key decisions or actions
> - Reflect on how it compares with the BDM steps
> - Prepare to share with table group or larger cohort
>
> **Discuss**: As a large group or at small table groups:
> - How does your thinking process compare with the BDM?
> - What does your thinking process compare with peers?
> - What issues and opportunities does the map surface?

2.5 Chapter 2: Summary and Reflection

> The Business Design Method (BDM) is an agile innovation development framework designed to aid the launch, management and effectiveness of your business improvement or transformation initiatives. Aligned with the stages of design-driven innovation, BDM's four steps (start, find, frame and solve) serve as prompts and guides for business design thinking and doing, leading to sustainable innovation. Students: Reflect on topics presented and answer the following:
>
> - What is the value of design for business?
> - What are the key principles and practices of human-centred design?
> - What are four steps of the Business Design Method?
>
> Reflect on your own experiences with design, as a customer, manager or business designer. Take a few minutes to list the features—both functional and emotional—of designed products, experiences, strategies and business models.

'The framework and Business Design method is the most valuable learning I had. This framework will go a long way in solving day-to-day business problems, and also for new initiatives I am contemplating'.—GEMBA student.

References

Baroudi and Lucas Jr. (1994). The role of information technology in organization design. *Journal of Management Information Systems, 10*(4), 9–23.
Beausoleil (2018). Revisiting Rogers: The diffusion of his innovation development process as a normative framework for innovation managers, students and scholars. *Journal of Innovation Management, 6*(4), 73–97.
Beckman and Barry (2007). Innovation as a learning process: Embedding design thinking. *California Management Review, 50*(1), 25–56.
Berry et al. (2002). Managing the total customer experience. *MIT Sloan Management Review, 43*(3), 85–89.
Brown (2009). Change by Design.
Caisse and Montreuil (2014). Polar business design. *SAGE Open, 4*(1), 2158244014522632.
de Rouw and Johnson (2017). *Collaborative Business Design: Improving and innovating the design of IT-driven business services.* IT Governance Ltd.
Denning (1996). Business designs for the new university. *Educom Review, 31*(6), 20–30.
Dietz (1993). *Business modelling for business redesign.* Faculty of Economics, Limburg University.
Dunne and Martin (2006). Design thinking and how it will change management education: An interview and discussion. *Academy of Management Learning & Education, 5*(4), 512–523.
Dunne (2018). *Design thinking at work: how innovative organizations are embracing design.* University of Toronto Press.
Ersoy (2018). Why design thinking is failing and what we should be doing differently. *UX Design, 19*.
Esslinger (2009). *A fine line: How design strategies are shaping the future of business.* Wiley.
Fraser (2012). *Design works: How to tackle your toughest innovation challenges through business design.* University of Toronto Press.
Faber et al. (2003, June). Designing business models for mobile ICT services. In *Workshop on concepts, metrics & visualization, at the 16th Bled electronic commerce conference etransformation, Bled, Slovenia.*
Faljic (2019). The Ultimate Business Design Guide. ▶ www.d.mba.
Gharajedaghi (2011). *Systems thinking: Managing chaos and complexity: A platform for designing business architecture.* Elsevier.
Kelley (2006). Design thinking. Accessed November 26, 2014.
Kelley and Kelley (2013). *Creative confidence: Unleashing the creative potential within us all.* Currency.
Kilov and Simmonds. (1996). Business patterns: reusable abstract constructs for business specification. In *Implementing systems for supporting management decisions* (pp. 225–248). Springer, Boston, MA.
Kimbell (2011). Rethinking design thinking: Part I. *Design and Culture, 3*(3), 285–306.
Kumar et al. (2009). Embedding innovation: design thinking for small enterprises. *Journal of Business Strategy.*
Iskander (2018). Design thinking is fundamentally conservative and preserves the Status Quo. *Harvard Business Review, 5.*
Liedtka et al. (2007). The practice of breakthrough strategies by design. *Journal of business strategy.*
Liedtka and Ogilvie (2011). *Designing for growth: A design thinking tool kit for managers.* Columbia University Press.
Lockwood (2010). Design Thinking: Integrating Innovation, Customer Experience, and Brand Value. Design Management Institute.
Mager (2008). Service design. In *Wörterbuch design* (pp. 361–364). Birkhäuser Basel.

Manzini, E. (1999). Strategic design for sustainability: Towards a new mix of products and services. In *Proceedings first international symposium on environmentally conscious design and inverse manufacturing* (pp. 434–437). IEEE.

Manzini, E., & Vezzoli, C. (2003). A strategic design approach to develop sustainable product service systems: Examples taken from the 'environmentally friendly innovation' Italian prize. *Journal of Cleaner Production, 11*(8), 851–857.

Martin (2005). Embedding design into business. *Rotman Management*, 5–7.

Martin (2009). *The design of business: Why design thinking is the next competitive advantage*. Harvard Business Press.

Martin, R., & Euchner, J. (2012). Design thinking. *Research-Technology Management, 55*(3), 10–14.

Matthews, J. H., Bucolo, S., & Wrigley, C. (2011). Multiple perspectives of design thinking in business education. *Design Management Towards a New Era of Innovation*, 302–311.

Osterwalder, A., Pigneur, Y., & Tucci, C. L. (2005). Clarifying business models: Origins, present, and future of the concept. *Communications of the Association for Information Systems, 16*(1), 1.

Oswald, J. (2016). *What is business design-and why is it the most important design job of the future*. Retrieved November, 28, 2017.

Owen, C. L. (2005). Design thinking. What it is. Why it is different. Where it has new value. In *A speech given at the international conference on design research and education for future*.

Oxman, R. (2017). Thinking difference: Theories and models of parametric design thinking. *Design studies, 52,* 4–39.

Panda, N. (2016). *10 reasons why your design thinking program is failing*. Medium.

Quayle, M. (2017). *Designed leadership*. Columbia University Press.

Reason, B., Løvlie, L., & Flu, M. B. (2015). *Service design for business: A practical guide to optimizing the customer experience*. John Wiley & Sons.

Stevens, J., & Moultrie, J. (2011). Aligning strategy and design perspectives: A framework of design's strategic contributions. *The Design Journal, 14*(4), 475–500.

Talwar, R. (1993). Business re-engineering—A strategy-driven approach. *Long Range Planning, 26*(6), 22–40.

Turner, R. (2000). Design and business who calls the shots? *Design Management Journal (Former Series), 11*(4), 42–47.

Ungaretti, T., Chomowicz, P., Canniffe, B. J., Johnson, B., Weiss, E., Dunn, K., & Cropper, C. (2009). Business+ design: Exploring a competitive edge for business thinking. *SAM Advanced Management Journal, 74*(3), 4.

Van Ackere, A., Larsen, E. R., & Morecroft, J. D. (1993). Systems thinking and business process redesign: An application to the beer game. *European Management Journal, 11*(4), 412–423.

Business Design Method Step 1: Start

Supplementary Information The online version contains supplementary material available at (► https://doi.org/10.1007/978-3-030-86489-7_3).

© The Author(s), under exclusive license to Springer Nature Switzerland AG 2022
A. Beausoleil, *Business Design Thinking and Doing*,
https://doi.org/10.1007/978-3-030-86489-7_3

Learning Objectives

At the end of Part I of this chapter, readers will be able to:
- Describe the mindsets associated with design-driven innovation.
- Identify key competencies for navigating innovation.
- Identify the stage-based innovation participant types.

At the end of Part II of this chapter, readers will be able to:
- Initiate a design-driven innovation project.
- Form an innovation project team.
- Craft an innovation design brief.

Key Outputs:

- Challenge Brief.
- Personal and Team SWOT.
- Innovation Design Brief.

3.1 Introduction

This chapter launches the first stage of the innovation process (Initiation) and the first step of the Business Design Method (*Step 1: Start*). The first stage provides the critical context for starting a project or initiative, involving team forming and innovation project framing. This chapter is divided into two parts that can be delivered as two sequential classes or two distinct and separate modules. Part I introduces the key mindsets, competencies and participant types associated with the innovation stages and BDM steps. Part II launches the project-based learning unit through a challenge brief, people-based SWOT analysis and an innovation design brief.

3.1.1 Warm Up Exercise: Story of Me

Warm ups prepare students to engage in the exploration of new topics or techniques. Similar to fitness or sport-based warm ups, individuals engage in a quick and gentle introduction to a topic and become more comfortable and confident with its relevance and broader application.

Story of Me is a visual and associative thinking technique on a topic you're familiar with (yourself). It also engages participants in reflective practice—where you are now, how you got here and where you might be going. It encourages futures thinking and is used as a team forming exercise.

> **How to**: Take a sheet of paper/pen OR tablet/stylus and divide the sheet into three equal sections (draw lines): label 'Past' on the left; 'Now' in the centre and 'Future'. Write your name at the top and then:
> – Describe/sketch your NOW (you are here).
> – Describe/sketch your PAST.
> – Describe/sketch your FUTURE.
> – Use few words or images (keep it simple).
> **Duration**: 2 minutes.
> **Discuss**: Ask students to share their personal map with cohort or table team. Ask what they discovered from this exercise about themselves and others. (i.e. values, wants, motivations, etc.)

3.1.2 Part I: Initiating Innovation by Design

The first step in the Business Design Method is appropriately called 'start'. As an initiation stage, it involves all the activities included in the start or launch of an innovation project or initiative. In industry, the majority of trigger events that launch organizational events are negatively correlated with low revenues, dropping market share, poor Net Promoter Scores or losing a pricing war with competitors. Other trigger events involve business opportunities, such as scaling or growth, new product development or new market exploration.

Launching an innovation project is both exciting and overwhelming. It involves a series of activities to first understand, then solve a problem specific to a particular context, which is validated by the adoption or consumption of that solution. If you strip away the perceived complexities and barriers from over-engineered internal systems and fear of failure, innovation is fundamentally a communication process.

It concerns most people and their social systems intersecting with technological infrastructures and economic forces, to make decisions on the design and development and adoption of new ideas. **Design-driven innovation is a persistent company-wide research and development function that involves all members of an organization in various capacities. As such, all members of the organization have a role to play**.

Innovation is all about people, the mindsets they bring, the knowledge they offer and discover and the roles they play. Innovation is not invention. Invention is all about creating or discovering something new. Innovation is about generating and transforming inventions into ideas that get used, consumed or adopted. Innovation is the lifeblood of an organization, yet its path is often unpaved, unfamiliar or completely new. As discussed in ► Chapter 2, organizations need to learn how to navigate its winding and risk-infused path in order to design strategies, systems and environments that engage employees and teams in positive change, leading to a culture rich in adaptability, creativity and renewal. Companies eager to succeed at innovation need new methods and diverse mindsets that bring in new insights, fresh viewpoints and question the status quo.

The most common innovation development methods are actually tools, techniques and systems engineered to produce and replicate incrementally innovative solutions (i.e. Stage-gate; Six Sigma, Lean Manufacturing, etc.). Their value is in their systematic design and deployment, as they offer a seemingly predictable and less risky process. Unfortunately, many business leaders mistakenly apply these process improvement tools as innovative thinking and working methods, unaware of the mindset and competence required to operate and optimize them. This is evident by a focus of capital and resources on new tools, and less on the human dimension, which is about hiring the diverse mindsets and developing the skillsets needed to navigate and manage innovation.

3.1.2.1 Human-Centred Design Mindsets

Innovation is inherently a human-centred learning process. The Business Design Method (BDM) is designed to enable the development of this mindset and skillset as it embeds social learning and modeling theories with active learning.[1] For instructors and facilitators, the BDM acknowledges that individuals can learn and change their behaviour from observing others, while not necessarily experiencing the direct exchange (verbal or visual) themselves. Directly seeing or sensing another's experience builds empathy which is a powerful influencer to behavioural change. The BDM integrates double-loop learning[2] as a way to first explore the problem space prior to jumping into problem solving. It grants permission for individuals and teams to reflect and question underlying assumptions behind goals, beliefs, values and plans, prior to investment and implementation.

Design-driven innovation demands an exploratory and combinatory mindset, one that blends critical thinking with strategic thinking, and curiosity and empathy with analysis and creative synthesis. A mindset is a set of assumptions, methods and beliefs held by one or more people, or groups of people. It's is a mental map that arises from one's world view or philosophy, and is expressed through attitudes and actions. Your mindset plays a critical role in how you cope with life's challenges. The learning mindset, growth mindset, creative mindset and design mindset are most often associated with innovative work (◘ Table 3.1).

For example, in school, a learning mindset can contribute to greater personal fulfillment, achievement and increased effort. When facing an employee conflict in the workplace, a growth mindset shows greater resilience and perseverance to resolve it. At home, a creative mindset is expressed through the plating of your favourite meal, the way you write letters to friends, or how you tell stories to your children. While commuting by train, a design mindset might lead you to observe how people behave and respond to the environment. The design mindset generates the seeing of unarticulated needs and patterns, and that triggers ideas and models for improvement that may be sketched or developed.

---

1   Beausoleil (2016). *The case for design-mediated innovation pedagogy* (Doctoral dissertation, University of British Columbia).
2   Argyris (1977). Double loop learning in organizations. *Harvard Business Review, 55*(5), 115–125.

3.1 · Introduction

Table 3.1 Mindsets for design-driven innovation

Mindset	Description	Verifying Questions
Learning mindset	Knowing that failure has something to teach you, and everything you learn helps you grow. Every great success requires some kind of struggle	*Are you curious?* *Are you courageous?* *Do you love learning?*
Growth mindset	Having the desire to work hard and discover new things. To tackle challenges and grow as a person	*Do you seek out new experiences?* *Do you possess grit?* *Do you view problems as opportunities?*
Creative mindset	Living with an attitude that allows you to think, feel and express yourself creatively, confidently and consistently	*Are you imaginative?* *Do you express yourself?* *Do you make your thoughts visible?*
Design mindset	Seeing and sensing a need or problem, and being driven to solve it. Combines learning and creative mindsets to propose new futures	*Do you see things others don't?* *Do you empathize with others?* *Do you experiment with ideas?*

A design mindset fluidly moves between problem finding, framing and solving, and in appreciating that these are intrinsically linked. Those possessing a design mindset display the trait of innovativeness. Innovativeness has been studied as one's early adoption of a new idea, innovative capacity and aptitude associated with innovators. A new idea can be an unarticulated need or problem, a new process or technology, or a new concept, prototype or proposed solution. Innovativeness is the willingness to experiment with new approaches of inquiry, the commitment to master new knowledge and the ability to exhibit innovative behaviour over time.[3] Innovativeness is achieved through the ability and willingness to adopt new ideas, think creatively and critically, act with curiosity and tolerate uncertainty through an innovation process.

Simply put, innovativeness is the capacity and willingness to actively participate in the learning activities of the innovation process. It's like a journey. It involves thinking (head), doing (hands/body) and reflecting (soul). Innovativeness as a learned trait is an important indicator of one's level of innovation-readiness and innovative capacity. It is mindset-dependent, but transcends roles, functions and job titles.

Mindsets are informed by traits and driven by the development of competencies. Competencies are individual capabilities, aptitudes and skills that are learned. They draw and build upon what you know, how you think and what you

---

3 Beausoleil (2016). *The case for design-mediated innovation pedagogy* (Doctoral dissertation, University of British Columbia).

can do. Key competencies are specific qualities in an individual that an organization deems desirable for an employee to possess, with the idea that it creates a competitive advantage. For students and continuous learners, competencies are critical building blocks of the knowledge, skills and attitudes required to navigate innovation and personal learning journeys for both life and work. The key competencies or qualities associated with a design mindset and innovativeness include:

- **Communication skills**: Ability to first listen and observe, and then to speak, write and interact effectively with others.
- **Perspective taking skills**: Ability to take on someone else's point of view when thinking and acting. They are directly associated with empathy.
- **Analytical and critical thinking**: Integrative ability to analyze (processing data and facts into information), evaluate (questioning bias and interpretation) and conclude (converging on a decision or statement).
- **Strategic thinking**: Ability to analyze critical factors and macro variables, and to synthesize information into an intent or vision for a course of action.
- **Creative problem-solving**: Ability to think creatively about a problem, generate ideas and develop solutions to solve it.

Although it may be difficult to develop all these competencies, it's not impossible, nor expected. These competencies are often bundled within individual mindsets and each contribute to the whole, such as a team, department or organization. What is important is to have an awareness of the different qualities that individuals possess, and how these qualities can assist in designing more effective and resilient innovation development teams.

How does one develop a design mindset and innovative capacity? Measuring competencies is important in understanding if the knowledge and skills have been learned (or adopted) through thinking and doing practice. Competencies serve as benchmarks to help focus individual behaviour (in students, employees and managers) and align teams on what matters most to them and the organization, helping drive sustained success. For companies, competency measures provide a common framework and benefits for hiring, developing and retaining talent. The following table (◘ Table 3.2) outlines a sample set of measures for each competency.

3.1.3 Innovation Teams and Participant Types

Most design-methods curricula (i.e. design thinking, product development, service design, user experience design, etc.) focus on technical tools training. By contrast, this textbook outlines an approach to develop key competencies relating to innovation management and leadership, that can be applied to a suite of techniques and tools. Competencies serve as critical learning assessment measures for the classroom or the workplace. The Business Design Method (BDM) is a series of steps involving stage-based activities designed to enable competencies-development from within and across the design-driven innovation process.

3.1 · Introduction

Table 3.2 Key competency measures for learning assessment

Competency	Description	Measures (sample only)
Communication skills	Ability to first listen and observe, and then to speak, write and interact effectively with others	*Did you listen/observe before speaking?* *Did you solicit opinions and feedback?* *Did you craft impactful messages?*
Perspective taking skills	Ability to take on someone else's point of view when thinking and acting; associated with empathy	*Did you lead desk field research?* *Did you sense another's POV?* *Did you check your biases?*
Analytical and critical thinking	Ability to analyze (processing data and facts into information), to evaluate (questioning bias and interpretation) and to conclude (converging on a decision or statement)	*Did you collect facts?* *Did you translate data into interpretations?* *Do you translate data and interpretations into insights?*
Strategic thinking	Ability to analyze critical factors and macro variables, and to synthesize information into an intent or vision for a course of action	*Did you consider all stakeholders, factors and conditions?* *Did you integrate insights from all contexts?* *Did you generate many scenarios?*
Creative problem-solving	Ability to think creatively about a problem and to generate ideas and develop solutions to solve it	*Did you reframe the problem?* *Did you generate ideas and prototypes?* *Did you propose a solution and evaluative measure?*

The BDM characterizes participant profile-types based on motivation and behaviour relating to key activities. The participant types include initiators, investigators, integrators, implementers and connectors. As innovation process participants, they are not limited by job title, role or function, and are encouraged to engage in multiple steps and activities concurrently. The BDM steps, key outputs and participant types include (see ◘ Fig. 3.1):

Step 1: START: Trigger the innovation project.
– **Key activities**: Initiate project; form team; propose problem hypothesis; create an innovation design brief.
– **Participant type**: *Initiators* have the drive to start something; the curiosity to explore; and, focus on strategic problem solving.

Step 2: FIND: Find needs, problems and insights.
– **Key activities**: Investigate and validate needs; collect and analyze data; discover patterns and insight(s).

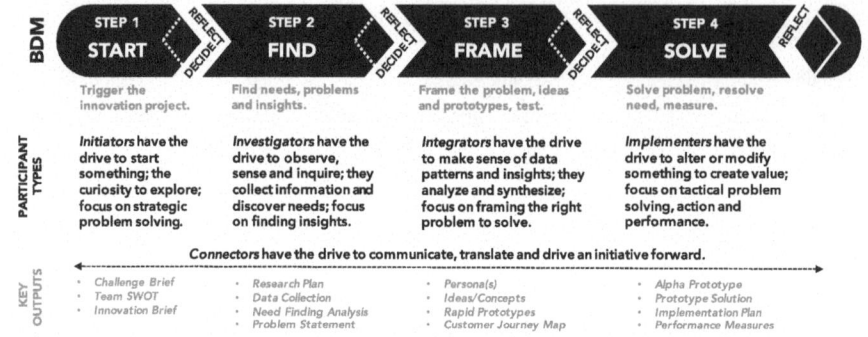

☐ Fig. 3.1 BDM steps and associated participant types

– **Participant type**: *Investigators* have the drive to observe, sense and inquire; they collect information and discover needs; and, focus on finding insights.

Step 3: FRAME: Frame problems, ideas and prototypes; and, test.
– **Key activities**: Define and frame the real problem; generate ideas; design prototypes and test with end-users and stakeholders.
– **Participant type**: *Integrators* have the drive to make sense of data patterns and insights; they analyze and synthesize and they focus on framing the right problem to solve.

Step 4: SOLVE: Solve the problem, resolve the need; and, measure.
– **Key activities**: Produce and package 'solution'; diffuse and evaluate solution and measure if problem is (or is not) solved.
– **Participant type**: *Implementers* have the drive to alter or modify something to create value; focus on tactical problem solving, action and performance.

Across all BDM steps, and bridging between stages…
– **Activity:** Manage the process.
– **Rely on** the *Connectors* participant type, as they have the drive to communicate, translate and drive an initiative forward.

Each BDM step prompts participants to engage in a set of activities that generate outputs that are the building blocks of knowledge for reflection and decision-making (☐ Fig. 3.1). How one acquires knowledge, forms opinions, solves problems, makes decisions is called a thinking style. While no one thinking style is better than another, a balance of the various types results in better decision-making.

Human-centred designed efforts require that all participants engage explicitly in divergent and convergent thinking practice. Divergent thinking involves generating or creating many ideas or choices. Convergent thinking involves narrowing or choosing a single idea or choice. Divergent thinking spans creative, generative and imaginative thinking modes, while convergent thinking spans analytical,

3.1 · Introduction

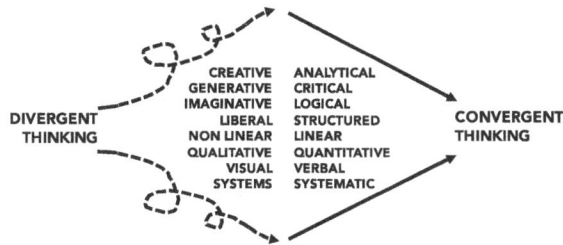

◘ **Fig. 3.2** Divergent and convergent thinking modes and strategies

critical and logical thinking modes (◘ Fig. 3.2). When combined, these thinking modes help flex your mental muscles and push individual and team-based boundaries towards design-driven mindsets and innovative capacity building. Their value is in facilitating open-ended and divergent dialogue, discussion and discovery. This can avoid the potential negative consequences of making early—or quick converging—decisions based on one idea or choice.

The visual model (◘ Fig. 3.2) represents a flattened and simplified framework of the BDM in terms of stages, goals, steps, activities, thinking modes and outputs. As a teaching and learning device, this model serves to highlight and explain the key elements of a complex process without overwhelming the reader.

The diamonds are visual metaphors for divergent and convergent thinking, proposing a size and width as a guide to where to best invest effort and resources over time. The diamond shape represents the act of opening (or exploring) with divergent thinking and the act of narrowing (or applying rigour) with convergent thinking. Adapted from Banathy's original model,[4] in 2005 the British Council introduced and has since popularized their 'Double Diamond design process'. The double diamond highlights a design-centred dialogue between problem and solution spaces, ways and modes of thinking to better discover and define the problem, and ways to design and deliver a solution.[5]

This model (◘ Fig. 3.3) is figurative and intended to visually and simplistically display the complex architecture of a design-driven innovation process. Consider the elements as modular, flexible and adaptable depending on the specific context, initiative, project and organization.

The Business Design method (BDM) is foremost a competency-building framework for design-driven innovation. It advocates for design-driven innovation to be practiced as an explicit learning process engaging the whole organization—both human and technological systems. It also offers simple and low-tech techniques to make decisions, document the process and engage a larger partici-

---

4   Banathy (1996). *Designing social systems in a changing world*. New York: Plenum Press.
5   UK Design Council (2015). The design process: What is the double diamond [online]. The Design Council. Available at: ► https://www.designcouncil.org.uk/news-opinion/design-process-what-double-diamond (Accessed 21.11. 2018).

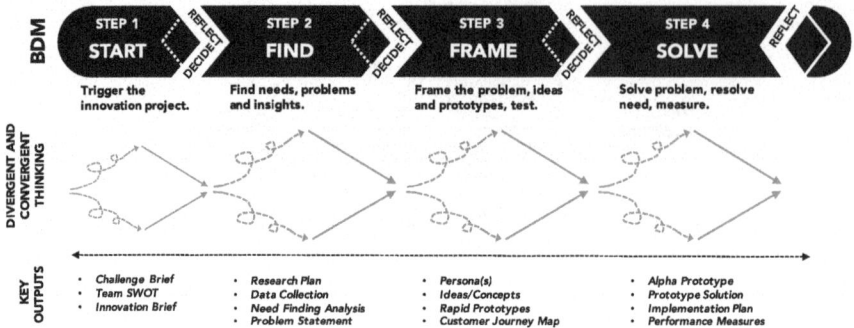

■ **Fig. 3.3** Visual model of the BDM, highlighting how the outputs of divergent thinking are analyzed through convergent thinking to produce key outputs along the innovation journey

pation from across the organization. *The BDM is ultimately a framework designed to structure your thoughts, questions and actions. It's a recipe that enables curiosity and openness to experience through the ambiguous yet rewarding innovation journey.*

3.1.4 Chapter 3: Part I—Summary and Reflection

Summary of topics discussed in Part I: Although one inventor could create a new technology, one innovator can't create an innovation. Invention is about creating or discovering something new. Innovation is about generating and transforming inventions into ideas that get used, consumed or adopted. An innovation is only as successful as the process that created it, and requires various humans with diverse mindsets, including the technical skills to research user needs, the ability to invent new ways to resolve those needs and the business savvy to package it and bring it to market in a sustainable and profitable way.

Innovation takes a team of diverse players with mindsets and competencies. Remember that working as part of a team does not make you a team player. To effectively participate in a design-driven innovation initiative, individuals require a level of self-awareness and self-management. They must begin with a learning mindset, and over time and with practice, they will develop a design mindset.

Students: Reflect on topics presented in Part I and answer the following:

— What are the key mindsets associated with innovation?
— What are the key competencies associated with Business Design?
— What are the four participant types for innovation projects?

Reflect on your own mindset and prior experience as a participant in the innovation process. Take a few minutes to think about your thinking modes and approach to facing failure and navigating uncertainty.

> *The Business Design course has been designed in a way that it breaks down the way you are thinking and shows you of the holes you leave – once you are aware of these holes you are able to refine your approach and come up with a more suitable idea or thought'.—EMBA student*

3.2 Part II: Initiating a Business Design Challenge

Part I introduced key mindsets, competencies and participant types associated with each innovation stage and business design step. Part II introduces the role of challenge and innovation design briefs to kick-start the project and align teams. A challenge brief is introduced to frame the project-based learning unit experience and is offered as an outline for a course or workplace training programme. An innovation design brief is then proposed as a way to align teams and trigger discussion on assumptions and hypothetical problem spaces to be investigated. Templates and worksheets for this chapter's exercises are provided in ▶ Chapter 8.

3.2.1 Warm Up Exercise: Pass the Message

Warm ups prepare students to engage in the exploration of new topics or techniques. Similar to fitness or sport-based warm ups, individuals engage in a quick and gentle introduction to a topic and become more comfortable and confident with its relevance and broader application.

Pass the Message can be used as an icebreaker activity and as a group communications exercise. It engages participants to translate information using words and illustrations. It encourages analytical and creative thinking and is used as a team forming exercise.

How to: Divide the cohort into groups of four or five people. Give each group one sheet of paper and a pencil.

- The first person in each group writes a sentence/message at the top of the paper and folds the paper to cover the sentence (Any sentence at all).
- This person passes the paper to their colleague on the left, who unfolds the paper, reads the sentence, folds it back, and in the next section illustrates their interpretation of it.
- Keeping the original statement hidden under the fold, the paper is then passed to the next person, who looks at the drawing, folds it back and writes the sentence of what they think it is.
- The paper continues to be passed along and this until each person has had a turn.
- Return the folded paper to the first person who unfolds it and shares with group.

Duration: 5 minutes

Discuss: This fun exercise illustrates how quickly a message can be altered even when passed from person to person in a relatively short period of time. It high-

> lights that people interpret information differently and that the intent of the original message can be completely lost. Ask: How does this relate to team projects? (i.e. clear communication, multiple perspectives, alignment, etc.)
> Reference the template provided in ▶ Chapter 8.

Successful projects result from effective communication, enabled by a well-articulated project brief. A brief is a document that outlines key information, a plan and a process relating to a project. A clear brief aligns team members and stakeholders, reduces conflicting objectives and enables strategic decision-making. Project briefs span roles and purpose: account managers write business briefs, marketers generate communication and creative briefs, strategists create planning briefs, and designers use design briefs. Innovation instructors and trainers create challenge briefs. To facilitate an effective project-based learning experience, a business challenge brief is used. The challenge brief outlines an open-ended driving question or business challenge that invites investigation and resolution.

> **About Project-Based Learning (PBL).** Project-based courses are designed to guide students to learn by doing. Students work on a project over an extended period of time to solve a real-world problem or answer a complex question. Project-based learning[6] (PBL) aids students in developing deep content knowledge as well as critical thinking, collaboration, creativity and communication skills. Design-driven project-based instruction requires more facilitation and coaching skills, guiding students to learn by doing, collaborating and reflecting. PBL courses are designed for project teams, but individuals are expected to contribute equally to their completion.

This textbook proposes a challenge brief that is suitable for a course unit outline, case competition or workplace design challenge. The brief contains the following elements: aim, learning objectives, teaching method, business challenge, assessment and schedule and is shared with the students (or participants). An example of a challenge brief is provided in the text box. For instructors, a challenge brief for Business Design course is outlined below. For industry trainers, the unit is replaced by a real business problem. Templates are provided in ▶ Chapter 8.

> **Challenge Brief (Project-Based Learning Unit Outline)**
> This outline offers key elements that can be adapted to meet the instructor's needs and context in terms of learning experience (i.e. unit course, capstone, design challenge or case competition). Supplementary templates for all BDM steps are in ▶ Chapter 8, and serve as exercise worksheets for students.

---

6 Krajcik and Blumenfeld (2006). *Project-based learning* (pp. 317–334).

Aim: Design-Driven Innovation Experience

The unit aims to provide students with real-world experience that requires the understanding and application of the Business Design Method and related techniques.

Learning Objectives

For this project-based unit, students will be expected to:
- Actively practice the 4-step Business Design Method, using the recommended frameworks, strategies and techniques.
- Collaboratively select and define the context and target population for in-depth investigation identified in the innovation design brief.
- Independently conduct in-field and desk research, guided by the brief.
- Collectively analyze and synthesize narrative data.
- Undertake professional innovation project management through the use of project and research planning and team management tools.
- Collaboratively frame and reframe problems and generate problem-solving ideas.
- Generate and present insightful prototypes and proposals that reflect end-user and stakeholder needs.
- Develop and present a proposed design solution that demonstrates understanding of, and engagement with, critical needs, problems and opportunities presented.
- Articulate the effectiveness and experience with the innovation project process through reflective reporting, peer review and evaluation.

Learning and Teaching Method

The project-based learning approach integrates activities and resources designed to support an active learning and learning-by-doing experience. Students are expected to work independently to gather materials and in groups to fulfill the requirements of the innovation design brief. Instructors are expected to provide guidance to both teams and individuals, supporting their project management, stakeholder engagement and self-directed learning skills development. As an experiential course or unit, it aims to enable the development of skills associated with problem framing and solving, critical and creative thinking, improved communications skills and knowledge management. The unit is designed to challenge students to work in consulting-like teams and to navigate uncertainty, ambiguity and complexity—critical skills for all managers and leaders.

Business Challenge Options

Project-based units are intentionally real-world and feature professionally practiced activities. They are introduced as business challenges and may originate from industry classroom sponsors, competitions or research questions. Although each challenge offers a distinctive context (i.e. industry sector or problem area), the students apply core and foundational knowledge and methods that include:
- Applying multidisciplinary knowledge to a real-world context.

- Developing and responding to innovation design briefs.
- Team dynamics, management tools and frameworks.
- Communications issues and stakeholder expectations.
- Qualitative research methods.
- Documenting project developments, artifacts and evolutions.
- Presentation skills.
- Critical and reflective practices.

Assessment

Assessment provides evidence of the understanding and application of the design-driven innovation process and the business design method, as described by the learning objectives. Students are expected to deliver the assessable items (assignments) based on the class or unit schedule. Deliverables and deadlines should be published prior to the start of the class or unit.

Assessment Schedule
Item/Weighting/Due.
Innovation Design Brief/10%/Week 3.
Data Analysis/10%/Week 5.
Insight and Problem Statements/10%/Week 7.
Prototype Presentation/10%/Week 10.
Design Solution Presentation and Report/30%/Week 12.
Team 360 Evaluation/10%/Week 12.
Reflection Paper/20%/Week 13.

The assessment is staged and reflects both formative and summative assessment mechanisms. Instructors should add supplementary contextual and relevant references. Students will be expected to locate additional resources independently, reflecting the project-based unit.

The challenge brief is the official start of the applied or practical learning section of a PBL course unit or training programme. With the foundational knowledge of how innovation happens and why design-driven innovation is the best competitive strategy (topics from Chapters 1 and 2), the students are now ready to begin their project-based and active learning journey.

3.2.2 Innovations Team Forming

Humans are driven to innovate, be it by fear and necessity, or by ego and opportunity. People are motivated, to varying degrees, to solve problems, try new things or compete in the spirit of innovation or self-preservation. We engage in innovation initiatives through project-based learning classes or by job-related functions in the workplace. Prior to starting your design-driven innovation journey, it's important to understand who you are, what you bring and who's part of the team. Start by engaging in personal and team SWOT exercises. Using a familiar framework (such as SWOT) individuals can self-reflect and also learn about others, as they begin to connect and form their innovation project team.

3.2.2.1 Exercise: Personal SWOT

The SWOT analysis framework has been used for over 60 years as a strategic planning tool to identify an organization's strengths, weaknesses, opportunities and threats. It's a simple tool that prompts a high-level analysis of internal capabilities (strengths and weaknesses) and external factors (opportunities and threats). It aids in the understanding of the general context of where and how a firm is operating and positioned. As an analytical tool, it can also be applied to humans, as individuals and teams.

The **personal SWOT** is a version of the original framework applied to individuals. It facilitates a series of 'asking' questions and capturing observations and insights from answering the questions. Use the template provided in ▶ Chapter 8 or in your notebook, take a sheet of paper and create four quadrants:
Title the top left quadrant 'Strengths' and top right as 'Weaknesses'
Title the lower left quadrant 'Opportunities' and lower right 'Threats'.
- Ask yourself: What are my strengths? Fill in the top left quadrant
- What do I do well?
- What unique resources can I draw on?
- What do others see as my strengths?
- Ask: What are my weaknesses? Fill in the top right quadrant
- What could I improve?
- Where do I have fewer resources than others?
- What are others likely to see as weaknesses?
- Ask: What opportunities can I chase? Fill in the lower left quadrant
- What opportunities are open to me?
- What trends could I take advantage of?
- How can I turn my strengths into opportunities?
- Ask: What threats do I face? Fill in the lower right quadrant
- What threats could harm me?
- What is my competition doing?
- What threats to my weaknesses expose me to?

Complete each quadrant and reflect on your answers. Prepare to share the highlights of your personal SWOT with your project team.

3.2.2.2 Exercise: Team SWOT

The **team SWOT** is a version of the original framework applied to project teams or groups. It facilitates a dialogue between team members and enables curiosity and empathy by engaging each member to share their personal SWOT and map it onto an aggregated team SWOT profile. On a large sheet of paper or whiteboard, create four quadrants: Title the top left quadrant 'Strengths' and top right as 'Weaknesses'; Title the lower left quadrant 'Opportunities' and lower right 'Threats'. In teams, take turns describing your individual strengths, then weaknesses. Capture these on sticky notes or with a marker or type it on a digital whiteboard.

- Ask team members: What are our strengths? Fill in the top left quadrant
  - What do we do well?
  - What unique resources can we draw on?
  - What do others see as our strengths?
- Ask: What are our weaknesses? Fill in the top right quadrant
  - What could we improve?
  - Where do we have fewer resources than others?
  - What do others see as our weaknesses?
- Ask: What opportunities can we chase? Fill in the lower left quadrant
  - What opportunities are open to us?
  - What trends could we take advantage of?
  - How can we turn our strengths into opportunities?
- Ask: What threats do we face? Fill in the lower right quadrant
  - What threats could harm us?
  - What is our competition doing?
  - What threats to our weaknesses expose us to?

Complete each quadrant and reflect on your answers.

Team Forming: To complete the team forming exercise, as a group:
- Share your innovation participant type and mindset.
- Identify words and images that describe your team's opportunities (goals), then threats (challenges).
- Discuss which attributes from the SWOT best describes your team.
- Propose a name or symbol/logo that reflects your team.
- Share your name/symbol and logo with the class.

Innovation, unlike invention, is a team sport. Following the team forming exercise (Team SWOT), prepare to collaborate on the crafting of your innovation design brief and 'lean' research plan.

3.2.3 Team Forming and Innovation Design Brief Crafting

As mentioned in ▶ Chapter 1, innovation is triggered by specific events, issues, problems or opportunities. For example, a local coffee shop observes the need to offer mobile order and delivery services to attract new customers; a national grocer seeks to reduce fresh produce waste and disposal costs; or, a bank reviews their Net Promoter Score that shows below-average customer recommendation results.

In a project-based learning classroom, a simulated business challenge is provided, representing a typical business problem, (such as one of the earlier examples) for students to solve. In a workplace, a real and timely business challenge is presented that is relevant to the organization and its clients/customers. The observed and pressing issue is framed (simulated or real) into a challenge question and packaged into a challenge brief. The challenge brief serves as the prompt to trigger the formation of an innovation project team, and is the source from which they will craft their innovation design brief.

Unlike a project requirements document, an innovation design brief proposes a hypothesis of what the problem is assumed to be and informs a lean research action plan. The research plan seeks to investigate, verify or validate the assumed problem and discover what the right and solvable problem actually is. It's purposefully developed with a project's starting point, listing a set of assumptions of the problem space (as problem hypothesis) and company and customer motivations. It's crafted with facts and interpretations, and acts as an innovation intent document. The innovation design brief combined elements of a design brief with a business brief.

All successfully designed, consumed and adopted products, services, brands and customer experiences started with a design brief. If the intent is to design a new and improved process, strategy, business model or policy, a design brief is required.

Borrowing from a designer's toolkit, a design brief triggers the start of a project, guiding the team with a clearly written document that outlines the goals, objectives, timelines, target audience information and budget. It acts as a reference point for both company and the 'innovation design' team throughout the process, and directly informs a lean research plan.

A business brief is a communication device that informs a decision-maker (senior stakeholder) on an important issue or situation. Business briefs serve to summarize all the relevant facts and considerations to inform a decision or course of action.

An innovation design brief integrates a business brief with a design brief. It provides a situational analysis and an invitation for further investigation. The innovation design brief is a critical document that launches a design project, aligns teams and serves as the initial statement of intent between a company's senior stakeholders and the innovation project team/manager (internal or external stakeholders if the team is positioned or acting as a consultancy). The brief's key objective is to fuel the curiosity and creativity of the innovation team who will use it to design and deliver an innovative proposition to the market.

The innovation brief borrows elements from the Innovation Intent framework,[7] and is comprised of four critical questions for you to answer:

1. *What problem are we trying to solve? (For the company and for the customer or end-user)*

---

7   Paradis and McGaw (2007). *Naked innovation*. Chicago, IL: IIT Institute of Design.

2. *For whom? (Who is the company and the end-user or customer?)*
3. *Why does it matter? (For the end-user/customer and for the company)*
4. *Where and how will we observe and better understand them? (To gain insight)*

The innovation design brief is prompted by an overarching business challenge or problem hypothesis and is designed to question assumptions and direct the research and discovery of needs-based insights, relating to a specific company and its customers (external or internal). The key elements include:

— **Problem hypothesis**: the articulation of an assumed problem(s) relating to your organization (as problem-owner) and the assumed needs of your target end-users or customers (as need-owners). As a hypothesis, it summarizes a situational or contextual analysis of the proposed problem and target end-user population, and grants the team an opportunity to investigate the problem space, verifying it or discovering an alternative. Guiding questions include: *What problem(s) are you trying to solve? (as problem hypothesis); What customer problems (s) are you trying to address? (as needs)*
— **Stakeholder map**: a summary of key individuals or groups that have a stake in, directly influence or are impacted by the assumed problem. Guiding questions include: *Who is most interested in solving this problem? Who is most influential in solving this problem?*
— **Stakeholder motivations**: the goal-oriented drivers behind human decision-making and action. Guiding questions include: *Why does this problem matter? What is the internal stakeholder motivation to start the project and solve the problem? What is the external stakeholder motivation to resolve the need?*
— **Target end-user population**: a group that shares similar characteristics and is an intended audience for product, service or process design research. Guiding questions include: *Who is our intended customer/end-user for this problem/challenge? Why do they buy? Where are they located?* Etc.
— **Project team schedule**: an outline of the team's initial schedule as to who will lead which task on which day, over what timeframe. Guiding questions include: *Who will participate in the innovation project? What is the timeline? Provide details of team members and associated tasks, activities (be feasible and realistic).*
— **References and sources**: a section that captures all your references, citations, links associated with your desk research. Note: This brief, like most, combines assumptions, biases and facts.

Reference the Innovation Design Brief, Stakeholder Map and Five Whys Analysis templates and worksheets provided in ▶ Chapter 8.

Briefs are powerful initiation tools as they combine a provocation with limitations (or time and resource-based constraints). In design-driven innovation teams, you challenge the assumptions imposed in the initial challenge brief. You will question and collect facts, generate interpretations and craft insights to better define a needs-based problem. As creative problem solvers, you will aim to view and define problems free from solution biases, bounds and prejudices. The value and benefits of an innovation design brief includes:

- enabling continuous questioning and reflection on the proposed business challenge
- facilitating team alignment on a problem hypothesis
- informing your observational and empathic research efforts
- demanding that you iterate to solve the right problem for the target user and associated system (e.g. a grocery store or chain)
- enabling a rich discussion on assumptions on prior knowledge
- ultimately, guiding the team to design an effective customer-centred solution, leading to a successful business results.

All designers, creative directors and innovation consultancies begin their projects with briefs. Why don't more companies do the same? Think about how differently you would approach a project if, instead of referring to a list of 'requirements questions', you renamed it as an innovation brief with a set of questions that ignited discussion about your customers, and not your costs.

Once the innovation teams are formed, their journey continues over the next three chapters, experiencing the four universal stages of design-driven innovation through the four-step Business Design Method.

3.2.4 Chapter 3: Part II—Summary and Reflection

Innovation is a communication process. It involves people, processes and systems aligned to solve problems that matter. Innovation projects require a multidisciplinary and cross-functional team. Most innovation projects begin with business challenge, issue or opportunity. A challenge brief is the prompt that triggers the need for a team and for that team to frame their intent with a design brief. The innovation design brief is a critical document that serves as the starting point of a collaborative project. It frames a problem hypothesis, the key stakeholders and their motivations, the intended target user/customer, and directs a lean research plan. This brief focuses on the target end-user/customer POV and serves as a living document, ever-evolving with more research, more data and more insight.

Students: Reflect on topics presented and answer the following:
- What did you discover about yourself and your team members?
- What is the difference between a project brief and an innovation design brief?
- What is the value of starting projects with a design brief?

Reflect on your experience with your personal and team SWOT. Connect with your team and create your innovation design brief, which is required to move to the next stage and step.

Business Design Method Step 2: Find

Supplementary Information The online version contains supplementary material available at (▶ https://doi.org/10.1007/978-3-030-86489-7_4).

© The Author(s), under exclusive license to Springer Nature Switzerland AG 2022
A. Beausoleil, *Business Design Thinking and Doing*,
https://doi.org/10.1007/978-3-030-86489-7_4

> **Learning Objectives**
> At the end of Part I of this chapter, readers will be able to:
> – Describe research methods in the context of need finding.
> – Create a lean research plan to understand people and context.
> – Practice observation skills and interviews in the classroom.
> – Develop an empathy interview guide.
>
> At the end of Part II of this chapter, readers will be able to:
> – Practice need finding, field research and data collection.
> – Practice empathy interviews in the field.
> – Practice narrative data analysis and synthesis.
> – Detect patterns, generate key themes and insights.

> **Key Outputs:**
>
> – Lean Research Plan
> – Data Collection
> – Need Finding Analysis
> – Problem Statement

4.1 Introduction

This chapter outlines the second stage of the innovation process (Investigation) and the second step of the Business Design Method (Step 2: Find). The chapter is divided into two parts that can be delivered as two sequential classes or two distinct and separate modules. Part I introduces need finding and associated qualitative research and data collection methods. Part II introduces narrative data analysis techniques to arrive at key insights. Both sections build upon the Innovation Design Brief. A lean research plan is proposed as the guide to the team's field research activities. Observational research and empathy interviews are explained with the focus on human, cultural and contextual understanding, and narrative data (thick data) collection. Templates for all the exercises are provided in ▶ Chapter 8.

4.1.1 Warm Up Exercise: Trading Card

> *Warm ups* prepare students to engage in the exploration of new topics or techniques. Similar to fitness or sport-based warm ups, individuals engage in a quick and gentle introduction to a topic and become more comfortable and confident with its relevance and broader application.

> **Trading Card** can be used as an icebreaker activity for a class, meeting or workshop, and as an interviewing and visual thinking technique. It provides a quick and structured way to ask basic questions of an interviewee and record one's observations. Designed for teams of two, it aims to build rapport between individuals, and facilitates active listening and visual thinking skills.
> **How to**: Take a sheet of plain paper or use a new page in your tablet. With a pen or stylus, divide the sheet into two sections. In one section draw a large box and label it 'image'. In the other section write down the following words and add a line:
> Name_____
> From _____
> Current Position (Job Title) _____
> Superpower_____
> After the sheet or page is complete (as your template), turn to a colleague or peer and ask the following questions. Fill in the lines:
> - What is your name?
> - Where are you from?
> - What is your current position or job title?
> - What is your special talent (aka superpower)?
> - From this information, quickly sketch an image of your peer in the box (Stick figures are great).
> - Ask your peer to interview you. Note: one person asks the questions, listens, writes the answers in the lines and creates a quick sketch of the person. Take turns being the interviewer and interviewee.
>
> **Duration**: 3 minutes. Introduce your colleague by sharing the trading card you created for them, to the cohort.
> **Discuss**: Ask students to share their personal map with cohort or table team. Ask what they discovered from this exercise about themselves and others (i.e. values, wants, motivations, etc.).

4.1.2 Part I: Need Finding as Qualitative Research Method

The second step in the Business Design Method (BDM) is titled 'find'. As the investigation stage, it involves activities focused on finding knowledge about and deeply understanding a population (your customers or end-users) within the context of a business challenge. This step is guided by the innovation design brief which directly informs the other stages of the design-driven innovation process. The first BDM step or 'start' involved initiating a project or innovation process and generating an innovation design brief. The design brief acts as the starting framework for end-user or customer-centred research efforts focused on finding the unarticulated needs relating to the proposed problem space (problem hypothesis).

The investigation stage and second BDM step involves questioning the assumed problem or problem hypothesis, developing a lean research plan, and then

Table 4.1 Quantitative and qualitative research—comparative summary

Quantitative research	Qualitative research
• Aim: to generate confirmatory insight from structured datasets	• Aim: to generate exploratory insight from unstructured datasets
• Deductive methods: survey, questionnaire, poll and lab experiment	• Abductive methods: interview, focus group and observational or field research
• Inquiry: seeks to answer tangible 'what is' or 'what was' queries: e.g. 'how much', 'how many', 'where' and 'when'	• Inquiry: seeks to answer narrative 'what, how and why' or 'what if' queries below 'where' and 'when'
• Value: numbers-driven decision-making	• Value: needs-driven decision-making
• Output: transactional data patterns, statistics and broad segment-level trends	• Output: narrative data patterns, latent needs and niche population-based insights

leading field research with the aim of discovering end-user desires and drivers, resulting in need finding.

Need finding is a scientific approach to understanding humans and borrows from anthropology and marketing. Anthropology is the study of human behaviour, and the origin and development of social cultures. Marketing is the study of an end-user or intended customer segment behaviour, with the intent to communicate the value of a product, service or experience.

Need finding is a qualitative research approach that collects data, as observed facts and interpretations, sourced from field research and interview-based interactions with people. The goal of need finding is to collect and analyze data to draw insight, which informs the design of a desirable new or improved product, service or experience (design-driven innovation). Need finding is a stream of qualitative research that seeks to uncover unarticulated needs leading to key insights, as opposed to broader trend-based insights provided by quantitative research. See Table 4.1 for a simple comparative summary of quantitative vs. qualitative research.

> Qualitative research data is often referred to as unstructured, narrative or 'thick description' data. It is collected from primary, secondary and tertiary research sources:
>
> – **Primary research** involves direct engagement with the intended end-user, customer or research subject population. Methods include observation, interviews, focus groups, online chat rooms, questionnaires and surveys.
> – **Secondary research** involves reviewing and analyzing information from primary research activities. Also known as 'desk research', its methods include document analysis of print or digital media reports, whitepapers, and industry reports from libraries and other professional/rigorous sources.

4.1 · Introduction

> — **Tertiary research** involves referencing or citing summaries of completed analyses sourced from third-party primary and secondary research. Sources include industry reports, mass media published articles, Wikipedia, etc.

Need finding is focused on primary research methods. Referred to as design research or customer insight research, need finding is a systematic process of discovering end-user or customer needs involving observational research and empathy interview methods. Need finding aims to surface deep motivations, drivers and needs of the intended end-user or customer. Its two most practiced primary research methods are field-based observational research and empathy interviews in the users' (aka subjects) own environment.

Need finding activities typically involve interdisciplinary teams who observe, research and analyze the data collected. From the data, the 'need finding researchers' apply their insights to the design of new products, services and experiences, as well as strategies, processes and business models. These methods are considered relatively agile, low cost and low risk in identifying and testing critical user/customer needs. This type of research position inside organizations may be titled as a market researcher or analyst, customer insights manager, design researcher, design ethnographer or brand anthropologist.

Need finding centres on collecting narrative data, also known as thick description or thick data. Thick data describes the rich stories shared by the subject under study, and the researcher's interpretation of the observed context. This type of qualitative research involves small sample sizes to deeply understand the needs, motivations and drivers of a specific population under study.

Unlike focus groups, need finding research is led by the customer or end-users' natural habitat. Unlike surveys, interactions with end-users are open-ended questions focused on understanding their experience with a product or service. Thick data complements the more popular 'big data' (collected from large data samples) and when combined, they offer a complete view of the problem space in terms of what it is, how it occurs and why it exists. A comparison of big data and thick data is provided in ◘ Table 4.2.

For organizations, big data offers quantifiable evidence from a broad sample size for informed decision-making. Alternatively, thick data offers qualitative evidence from a very small sample size, shifting the dataset from scale (macro trend) to uniqueness of experience (micro meaning) based on human motivations and choices.

Since around 2010, organizations have increasingly integrated thick data analysis with big data focused projects. Data analysts now include anthropologists, sociologists and economists providing cultural insights into effective and adoptable solutions.

The value of need finding and its associated practice of design research is to create models of:

— **Behaviour**: human and social, technical, environmental, political and economic systems; leading to empathy and clues about practices and patterns;
— **Relationships**: how and why we connect with others, our things, our routines, our view of the world and our beliefs;

◘ Table 4.2 Comparative summary: big data versus thick data

Big data	Thick data
• Big data is a combination of structured and semi-structured data collected by organizations, that can be mined for information, machine learning and predictive modeling	• Thick data is unstructured data in the form of thick description or narratives, that is mined for insights on human behaviour
• Big data draws broad patterns from massive amounts of data from large end-user or customer samples	• Thick data draws deep human-centred patterns from small end-user or customer samples
• Big data is used for informed decision-making to improve operations, customer service, marketing campaigns, and generate revenue models, and profit-oriented strategies	• Thick data is used for insightful decision-making to better understand people, their contexts, motivations and behaviour, and to design desirable products, services and impactful strategies
• Big data aims to answer the 'what' happened or happens based on transactional events	• Thick data aims to answer the 'why' behind what consumers do or think

– **Contexts**: how, where, when and why a customer and a business intersect is an important part of defining context, strategies and tactics;
– **Concepts, Ideas and Prototypes**: what characteristics a product/service/process should have, plus testing to see if it's working as intended.

Models are useful tools in learning science that can be used to improve explanations, generate discussion, make predictions, provide visual representations of abstract concepts and generate mental models. Behavioural and prototype-based models help explain complex concepts in visible and meaningful ways.

In summary, need finding is a qualitative research approach that is most valuable in the early stages of innovation. Gaining deep understanding of an intended end-user is vital prior to investing resources and capital in new product or service development. Need finding draws on collecting data from primary research methods that lean on direct observation and engagement with the end-user in their natural environments (vs. focus group rooms or labs), with the intention of reducing or avoiding any possible personal or organizational biases. This qualitative research method is focused on small, targeted populations.

The Vital Few as Small Research Sample = Pareto Principle

The universal rule known as 80-20 was first observed by Italian economist Vilfredo Pareto in the early 1900s. Pareto studied different societies and noted a pattern: a very small population typically controlled and influenced the larger population. He described the small population as the 'vital few', representing approximately 20% and described the larger population, or approximately 80% of the population, as the 'trivial many'. His research theorized how small things (actions or population percentages) could influence or cause great things to happen, hence the 80-20 rule. In the mid-1900s, management scholar J.M. Juran applied this rule to assessing business production and discovered the 'vital few' or 20% of operational deficiencies were consistently causing 80% of the problems.

As a useful management concept, the 80-20 rule is often reflected in terms of sales (80% of sales are often generated from 20% of clients), productivity (80% of output relies heavily on a few or 20% of employees) and marketing (80% of website traffic is generated from 20% of the marketing content produced). When applying this principle to qualitative research, managers and need finding researchers should be able to identify the key sources of the problems (i.e. unarticulated needs) by focusing on the issues or needs of a small or 'vital few' population. Note: While the 80-20 rule is not fixed, it provides researchers with the ability to generate observable qualitative data—particularly when understanding that 80% of the output or consequences tend to be produced by 20% of the input or causes.

4.1.2.1 Generating Insights from Need Finding

Need finding methods give innovation designers and innovative companies the tools necessary to observe unarticulated needs, develop insight and integrate them for effective innovation development. Uncovering needs requires an organized and structured approach with methods that are adaptable and suitable for different research contexts.

Need finding differs from the more common practice of business needs analysis. Traditional needs analysis is a structured and systematic process to identify needs, employing scripted tools such as surveys and questionnaires to direct the re-

◘ Table 4.3   Traditional needs analysis vs. need finding

Needs analysis	Need finding
• Aim: to generate information from quantifying patterns; to affirm expected behaviour and validate problem hypothesis (prescriptive)	• Aim: to generate meaning from stories, collect data (natural language), discover patterns of meaning and behaviour and develop insights (iterative)
• Methods: survey; questionnaire; focus group; interviews (scripted, closed)	• Methods: observational research and empathy interviews (guided, open-ended)
• Output: seeks to answer the 'what' from a research question	• Output: seeks to answer the 'what, how and why' of a research question
• Value: data-driven decision-making	• Value: insight-driven decision-making
• Example: Net Promoter Score (customer recommendation)	• Example: Latent Need Discovery (customer pain points)

search subject to provide answers to pre-articulated problems and issues. Further comparison between needs analysis and need finding is provided in ◘ Table 4.3. Need finding research (and analysis) aims to generate the following:

- **Observations**: Both 'facts' and 'interpretations'. Facts describe a situation or object as explicitly seen or heard. Interpretations describe a situation that is judged based on tacit knowledge of a similar context.
- **Findings**: 'Summarized facts' that propose common meanings or themes reflecting the facts, based on patterns and/or bias.
- **Insights**: Synthesized interpretations of the facts, findings and patterns reflecting a deeper understanding of the people and situation or context.

An observation as fact is information that is observed to be true. Facts are verifiable data that we all see and which can be quantified. For example, we can verify that a smartphone is rectangular-shaped, broccoli is a source of iron, or that 600,000 people attended an event. An observation can also be an interpretation, a source of narrative data based on personal beliefs or prior experience. For example, we believe that broccoli is a healthy food choice, or that we attended the biggest event of the year.

Findings are summarized facts that have been sorted and categorized based on patterns of meaning. Findings interpret observed facts as a qualitative dataset to provide important cultural and contextual meaning. Qualitative data can be verified through quantifiable measures, such as noting repeating patterns of similar behaviour within a context. For example, many people choose to add broccoli to their meal for its taste as well as for its added nutrients. And you may conclude the concert you're at is well attended based on scanning the venue, by the long lineups to the bathroom, and the merchandise was sold out. Although findings may reflect personal biases, these can be mitigated by measuring the repeating patterns and converting them into 'factual interpretations'.

While findings are sorted and categorized facts based on patterns of meaning, insights are synthesized findings that offer a deeper understanding of the human needs and behaviour under investigation. It's only by first understanding needs (the why behind the what), that innovation design teams (and organizations) can gain deep insight into the problem hypothesis proposed from the innovation design brief.

4.1.2.2 Case Examples: How Have Organizations Used Need Finding?

> Apple and Kodak: Researchers D. Patnaik and R. Becker offer a compelling argument for need finding for organizations. They outline 'needfinding' as a systematic process to uncovering the deep human needs hidden below surface problems. Their article highlights an example of Apple's mistake in the late 1990s with their digital assistant device called the Newton. While Steve Jobs and his team focused on a host of features, Palm Computing introduced the Pilot. The Pilot was prototyped,

4.1 · Introduction

tested and redesigned as an innovative product that would fit into a pocket, be simple to use, and offer the much-needed address book and day planner. Palm focused on the human need for organizing one's calendar of activities and personal contacts, over Apple's view of shrinking an entire set of desktop computer tools onto a small device. They suggest that needs, not problems, offer a roadmap to innovation development, when one pauses and chooses to observe and understand them. They reflect on Kodak's early days with moving from chemical-based processing to digital photo imaging software, based on observing and questioning amateur photographers seeking digital images for their own use.[1]

NIKE: Over thirty years ago, clothing brand NIKE learned directly from their target users (professional athletes) how to design and develop shoes and clothing. From their extensive observations and interviews, they identified a common need in regular people to celebrate the potential of athletic greatness in all of us. Nike even integrated their customers' language directly into their products, processes and marketing campaigns, and introduced Nike+ and Nike Run Club to help customers collect data on their running sessions.

Capital One: As a financial institution, Capital One was keen to understand young adults and their motivation to save. Their insights team interviewed a series of teenagers and developed a guide for them to save and plan for their first car, by making their savings journey relate to the independence of a road trip.

These examples highlight the importance of discovering and finding needs ahead of solutions.

Why are companies challenged to resolve needs and solve the wrong problems?
- They think they already know their customers and end-users.
- They are overwhelmed by trying to determine who exactly their customers are.
- They focus research on product development (functional needs) and not user-centred design (emotional needs).
- They prioritize operational tasks over market understanding and needs-based research in their R&D efforts.
- They lack an understanding of design's value in their business.
- They focus their capital and resources on repeating past success, and not investing in discovering the right problem to solve.

Design-driven innovation team members engage in both observational and interview-based research activities. The following section introduces the two leading design research methods and explains how to practice them for classroom project or as a real business challenge in your workplace.

---

[1] Patnaik and Becker (1999). Needfinding: The why and how of uncovering people's needs. *Design Management Journal (Former Series)*, *10*(2), 37–43.

4.1.3 Key Design Research Methods: Observational Research and Empathy Interviews

Need Finding borrows from the best practices in social sciences, especially from anthropologists and ethnographers, in addition to marketers. The investigation stage requires innovation team members to lead and complete two need-finding exercises: (a) observational research and (b) empathy interviews. The aim is to experience leading field research and collecting data in the form of observations and field notes.

Observational research is a qualitative research technique where researchers observe subjects or a target population's behaviour in a natural environment. Design-oriented observational researchers capture how end-users (or customers) genuinely behave, in addition to what they say about a company, product or experience. Observational data is qualitative and unstructured, yet offers a deeper understanding of a subject or end-user's needs and motivations. Observational or field research involves identifying a context and target population (i.e. end-user or customer), which are directly relevant to the business challenge or innovation design brief.

The **empathy interview** is a qualitative research technique where researchers engage in open dialogue with a subject or target participant, in a natural environment. Design-oriented researchers craft a simple interview script, approach and ask end-users (or customers) to share their experiences with a specific company, product, place or process. This type of interview is open-ended, and enables the 'amateur ethnographer' or innovation researcher to understand the choices people make and why they make them. Unlike formal qualitative interviews, the researcher prepares a few open-ended questions and explores each answer to uncover patterns leading to deep insights about motivations and desires. Similar to observational research, this type of interview is best led in the field or in the subject's natural habitat.

To design effective solutions for people, it is critical to understand human needs and perspectives, which requires empathy. In business, understanding one's perspective involves speaking to and building rapport with end-users or customers. While observational research provides descriptive or thick data, in terms of the context, the place, space and people interacting within it, the empathy interview invites the researcher to zoom in and better understand the end-user or customer's experience and relationship with a specific experience. (e.g. grocery shopping experience as this classroom project).

Working from the innovation design brief, the next step involves crafting an observational or field research plan that is feasible and adaptive within the context of a class project or time-constrained business challenge.

Business Design Method Step 2: Find

4.1.4 Creating a Lean Field Research Plan

Most organizations are familiar with market research or new product research and development (R&D) planning. Over the past ten years, a growing number of companies have hired anthropologists, ethnographers and design researchers to better understand the relationships between humans and organizational cultures, and between customers and brands (or products/services). These researchers engage in the common practice of ethnography. Ethnography is the study and systematic recording of human cultures and has its roots in anthropology. Ethnographic research is essential to the design process, particularly with need finding. It is not enough to ask users what features they want in a product or service. Ethnographic research gives the researcher/designer the ability to use techniques like observation and interviews (for contextual inquiry) to understand in-depth the user context(s). Lean Ethnography[2] is an agile method for design researchers to observe and engage human-subjects in their natural habitats (e.g. work, grocery stores, cafes, etc.) over a shorter period of time (e.g. one day to three months). Lean field research is an extension of lean ethnography and involves crafting a mini-research plan for a project team.

Design inspired by observing real people living their real lives is not new. Designers—of products, fashion, service, space or media—have long relied upon their observation of the world to understand what will resonate with the people they want to attract. The NEW part is that many businesses must gain better understanding of users/consumers within an authentic setting to remain relevant and competitive.

> **Lean Field Research Plan**
>
> A lean field research plan as a brief document that outlines the target study population (end-users or customers), the context and potential locations to lead qualitative data collection. It guides novice researchers to observe, interact and understand people in their natural environment, over a short period of time.
> **Research plan** describes the design research efforts necessary to discover and the needs lurking below the surface problem. Designing a new and improved output requires qualitative inquiry. This critical step guides the team to seek our key findings leading to insights.
> — *Prompt: How will you investigate the problem or user need? Where will you observe and interview your target customer/end-user in your research?*
> **How to**: Use the template provided in ▶ Chapter 8.

---

2 *"Lean Ethnography" is a concept explored in Dr. Angèle Beausoleil's work on Innovation Process Design*. Published at ▶ https://www.strategicdesigntoolkit.com/lean-ethnography.

> **Research Methods, Objectives and Outputs**: outline the desk and qualitative research methods that will be used to investigate the problem space and discover needs. Each method will have an objective and an expressed output.
> — *Prompt: Which methods will be employed, what objectives do you want to achieve and what outputs will be generated?*
> **Project team schedule**: outline the team's initial schedule as to who will lead which task on which day.
> — *Prompt: Who will participate in the innovation project? Provide details of team members and associated research tasks, activities (feasible and realistic).*
> **References and sources**: list all relevant references, citations and links associated with your desk (computer-based) research.
> **Discuss**: The target population, methods and tasks with team members and complete your research plan. Prepare to lead your field research.
> Note: Teams must identify a specific grocer or type of grocery store that all members can easily observe. Alternatively identify grocer proxies that approximate the target grocer (hint: reference your innovation design brief).

For this innovation challenge (e.g. class project), students will be identifying a specific grocer and engaging in observational research. It's critical they observe end-users or customers in their natural environments. To simulate a real design-driven innovation challenge, consider visiting a grocery store near you or your school.

If the team's brief outlined several possible grocers, consider reconnecting with the team members to seek alignment on the types of places to observe, as the research data is only as good as the thoughtfulness put into ensuring the right context and associated customers. Note: if health and safety issues exist (e.g. pandemic), ensure a safe distance and follow jurisdictional protocols.

- **Lean Research plan**: outlines the design research efforts necessary to discover the needs lurking below the surface problem. Designing a new and improved output requires qualitative inquiry. This critical step guides the team to seek out key findings leading to insights.
  - *Prompts: How will you investigate the problem or user need? Where will you observe and interview your target customer/end-user in your research?*
- **Research Methods, Objectives and Outputs**: outlines the desk and qualitative research methods that will be used to investigate the problem space to discover needs. Each method will have an objective and an expressed output. A worksheet is provided in ▶ Chapter 8.
  - *Prompts: Which methods will be employed, what objectives do you want to achieve and what outputs will be generated?*

4.1.4.1 Preparing for Field-Based Research

To prepare for observational or field-based research, bring a notebook, two pens (two different colours), a small camera or smartphone. Dress comfortably for the outdoors. Consider focusing on three general elements of the context:

4.1 · Introduction

- **Place**: Find a comfortable spot that allows for observation from a distance. You will be required to sit and observe over a period of 30 minutes to one hour. With a notebook in hand, write notes on how people arrive and leave. If possible, use a camera or smart phone to capture objects and specific locations, such as signage or transportation choices (e.g. bikes, vehicles, etc.) or grocer items such as shopping carts. If someone approaches and questions your notetaking, kindly explain that you are leading a course-based research project. Note: observational research requires following best practices with human ethics and privacy protocols, including securing informed consent from individuals you directly engage with (see ethics protocol template in ▶ Chapter 8).
- **People**: Observe with fresh eyes. Take notes on what you see (as facts), and what you interpret (as interpretations). If possible, use a camera or smartphone to take images of how people interact with places, objects and others. But be discreet and very careful not to take any images of faces, and follow proper ethics and privacy protocols (see ethics protocol template in ▶ Chapter 8).
- **Patterns**: While observing and taking notes and photos, look for patterns of behaviour shared across different types of people, objects and/or specific locations. Identify and note any significant outliers. Capture notes with one pen and highlight notable observations with the other coloured pen.

Field observation requires seeing a familiar context with a researcher's lens. Consider your research as a journey, observing interactions of the pre, during and post experience. For example:

1. PRE:
   - How do people arrive (mobility/transportation/etc.)?
   - How do people behave as they arrive?
   - How are they dressed? What might it suggest?
2. DURING:
   - How do they move through the store?
   - What is their visible emotional state? Why?
   - What do they do while interacting with _____?
3. POST:
   - How do people behave as they leave?
   - What are they carrying? And how?

Field research can be overwhelming, with too many objects, people or interactions to observe effectively. To assist with further categorizing field-based observations, a POEMS framework is recommended. It's a framework that organizes notetaking and facilitates alignment with team-based generated datasets. It considers identification of the people, objects, environments, messages and services that end-users or customers interact with over the course of an observational study (e.g. a food shopping experience at a grocery store for this class-based project). Here's a breakdown of the POEMS elements:

- **People**—the demographics, roles, behavioural traits, and quantity of people in the selected environment.
- **Objects**—the items people are interacting with, including furniture, devices, machines, appliances, tools, etc.
- **Environments**—the visual observations about the place and space (i.e. architecture), lighting, furniture, temperature, atmosphere, etc.
- **Messages**—the words and language overheard, and the environmental messages or signage.
- **Services**—the organization's offers (as services) which the target population is interacting with, within the selected field study context.

The POEMS framework can be an effective technique for both novice and experienced observational researchers. A template is provided in ▶ Chapter 8.

For students (or participants): Practice leading observational research in a familiar location. For example, select a location inside your home, your neighbourhood or your favourite people-watching spot. Sit down, get comfortable, and observe an area for 20–30 minutes. Use a notebook to take notes and separate observational facts from your interpreted facts (facts with judgement). Collect the notes and prepare to convert these notes into data from this practice 'observational research' exercise with your team for the capstone project. If you're applying this technique to your class project or business initiative, use relevant and specific field sites.

> **Field Research and Ethical Issues: Consent and Confidentiality**
> Consent:
> - Everyone who participates in your study should have freely consented to participation, without being coerced or pressured.
> - They should be informed about the study and reassured that they can opt out at any time.
> - While written consent may in some situations frighten the individuals you're talking to, you should at the very least obtain verbal consent.
>
> Confidentiality:
> - It's essential to protect the identity of the person from whom you gather information.
> - If collected, the identity of the participants must be protected at all times and not be left lying around in notebooks or in unprotected computer files once the study is completed.
> - Protect their identity with a number (code) and a different name.

4.1.4.2 Empathy Interviews

To lead a successful series of empathy interviews with a few targeted subjects (e.g. end-users or customers), an overarching and open-ended research question must be crafted which reflects the problem space (or context). To ensure quality data

4.1 · Introduction

collection, this question must be used consistently and repeatedly with every interviewee. As a team, follow these three basic rules:

1. As a project team, meet to discuss the overarching research question that all members will be asking the interviewees. Individually generate options for the overarching question, then vote and decide on one. This is critical to collecting accurate data.
2. As a project team, individually contribute to the final short script that all members will follow consistently.
3. Individually (or in groups of two) return to the observational or field research sites and practice getting comfortable speaking to strangers. Individually should aim to interview at least 2–3 people. For project teams comprised of five members, your research unit of analysis should be 10–15 subjects ($n = 10$–15).

To write an empathy interview script, follow the basic outline below:

- Build rapport: "Hello, I am _____ (introduce yourself). I'm working on a research project focused on _____ (e.g. grocery shopping experience) and was hoping you had a few minutes to talk about your best and worst experiences.
- If no, approach another grocery shopper.
- If yes, ask "Before we begin, may I have your verbal consent to take notes or capture this interview with a digital recording assistant? Rest assured that your comments will remain anonymous. Please answer only what is comfortable. Thank you."
- Ask: "Can you share what you enjoy most about shopping for food?" (Don't lead the interviewee. Listen, take notes—prompt for further 'stories' by adding why? can you elaborate? when? etc.).
- Follow up by asking "Can you share what you dislike about shopping for food?" (Don't lead the interviewee. Listen, take notes—prompt for further 'stories' by adding why? how so? when? etc.).
- Actively listen, allow them to answer and capture their story using a notebook or digital recording application. Observe facial behaviour for emotional cues such as excitement or frustration. Code key words or phrases that elicit emotional responses.
- Do: "Thank you for taking the time to share their story today".
- Do: Review your notes, code them with key themes and meet with your project team to begin data sorting and analysis.

To prepare for empathy interviews, bring a notebook, two pens (two different colours), a smartphone or recording device and dress comfortably for both outdoor and indoor environments. Reference the empathy interview script guide and worksheet in ▶ Chapter 8.

4.1.5 Part I: Summary and Reflection

Guided by the innovation design brief completed in BDM Step 1 (▶ Chapter 3), the investigation stage (BDM Step 2) entails human-centred design research methods that offer observations and key findings leading to the critical insights required to uncover a need, solve a problem or a puzzle. A lean research plan serves as your team's field research guide.

The investigation stage involves key activities focused on understanding the context and the customer relating to the innovation challenge. It uses the innovation brief as a compass to guide the innovation team in their research efforts. Need finding is core to the second step of the Business Design Method, and is preferred approach to uncover needs associated with business problems.

From this chapter, students (participants) are expected to practice leading and completing observational research and empathy interviews for a classroom project (or real business challenge). They will be collecting observational data—referred to as thick data—as it reflects the narrative information provided by the field research observations and empathy interviews notes. To collect rich and descriptive data, need finding requires clear alignment on the right context to observe, and the relevant end-users or customers to interview. Consider investing the necessary time between data collection and the next section focused on data analysis.

Students: Reflect on topics presented and answer the following:
— Which research methods are used for need finding?
— What are the key outputs from qualitative research?
— What is the value from observational research and empathy interviews?

Reflect on your direct experience with human-centred design research methods focused on finding needs and deep understanding of a population (e.g. customers, end-users and stakeholders).

4.2 Part II: Thick Data Collection and Analysis

In Part I, need finding was introduced and practiced as a way to investigate a problem hypothesis originating from the innovation design brief. Participants led observational research and empathy interviews as individuals and as a team, and collected data—comprised of observations and interpretations—with the aim of finding needs and motivations relevant to the innovation challenge (e.g. capstone project). In Part II, narrative data analysis and associated techniques are introduced with the purpose of translating observations into insights. Both parts build upon the innovation design brief. Templates and worksheets for the exercises are provided in ▶ Chapter 8.

4.2.1 Warm Up Exercise: Items Sorting

> *Warm ups* prepare students to engage in the exploration of new topics or techniques. Similar to fitness or sport-based warm ups, individuals engage in a quick and gentle introduction to a topic and become more comfortable and confident with its relevance and broader application.
>
> **Items Sorting** is an analytical thinking technique that can be applied to all domains, sectors and topics. It engages participants to observe, sift, sort and group items into categories. It encourages divergent and convergent thinking and is used to introduce unstructured data analysis.
>
> **How to**: Provide a copy of the Items Sort exercise template from ▶ Chapter 8 to the students (or participants).
> – Observe the following objects (e.g. grocery items)
> – Sort the objects into common and contextual categories.
> – Categorize objects with common similarities (e.g. shape); label.
> – Categorize objects with contextual similarities (e.g. use); label.
> – Generate 1–3 groups/labels.
>
> **Duration**: 2 minutes. Share your categories with your cohort.
>
> **Discuss**: Items Sorting is a simple example of open data sorting, which involves the ability to see similarities and differences between datum as words or objects. It involves visual thinking and pattern recognition. Participants are required to quickly observe the various objects, interpret similarities and differences and propose categories and groupings that reflect common or contextual themes for shared meaning and insight.

4.2.2 Thick Data Analysis

Unstructured or thick data analysis involves all the activities involved in making sense of the observations and insights generated by the needs investigation. The goal is to frame the right problem for an innovation team to solve. To assist with making sense of the unstructured data collected from observational research and empathy interviews, it's important to describe the differences between needs and problems (see ◘ Table 4.4).

In business, to survive you may *need* to evolve an existing business model to reflect the changing marketplace. A *problem*, on the other hand, may be the desire to increase profits from an existing market to provide shareholder value.

Needs are commonly categorized into two types: functional and emotional. A functional need is a basic need required for survival, such as food. An emotional need is a psychological need that seeks a connection, such as status. Consumers have both functional needs and emotional needs. Functional needs can

Table 4.4 Comparing needs and problems

Needs	Problems
• A need is something that is necessary; a critical tension with a present state	• A problem is an issue; a tension between the present, and a desired future state
• Need owners focus on the *present state*, since it is something that is essential or very important; wanted or required	• Problem owners focus on the *desired state* since it involves resolving issues associated with goals, values and preferences
• A need requires immediate action, since it demands satisfaction or resolution	• A problem may or may not be solved, based on priorities and the type of unsatisfied needs
• Needs can be difficult to detect. Unlike a problem, a need is something that may kill you if you don't address it. For example, protecting your bare feet in the snow to avoid frostbite is a need	• A problem is surfaced as something that costs time, money or energy. The solution must be an improvement over simply living with the problem. For example, a problem is that you want new boots for use in the snow

be satisfied through rational decision-making such as usefulness, convenience and price. For example, the need to have bread as a food source. Emotional needs can be satisfied in many different ways through instinctive decision-making such as safety, security, acceptance, love and status. For example, the need to buy an artisanal loaf of bread for a dinner with friends.

Problems are surfaced from unsatisfied needs. Finding the needs that are causing issues to surface is essential in defining the *right* problem to solve.

Working with the data collected from the need finding research, this section of the chapter involves sorting data to identify functional and emotional needs from target end-users or customers. At the end of this section and chapter, the goal is to craft a **problem statement**, as the evolved problem hypothesis.

4.2.3 Data Sorting: Sift, Sort and Label

Sorting and analyzing narrative data may feel overwhelming. To assist with navigating and making sense of the many observations collected from the field research and empathy interviews, the POEMS framework is recommended as an effective way to collect qualitative data prior to the data sift, sort and label technique.

Working with an individual or team-generated data set, the first step in data analysis is to sift the data. Sift through the observed facts first, then the interpreted facts. The second step involves sorting the combined facts into categories. The third step is labelling each category. Below are the detailed activities associated with each step.

(1) **Sift through observed facts**: Take time individually to sift through your own data and highlight some key observations as facts. Make sure the facts you choose are verifiable—for example, direct quotes from your interviews or digital photos highlighting a real interaction. Identify each key fact as one datum and add to a data sorting board (e.g. physical or digital whiteboard). For

example, one customer was quoted as saying '*I enjoy grocery shopping as an escape from the busy household*'.

Sift through interpreted facts: Sift individually through the interpreted facts, which are also called assumptions. These usually combine one's personal experience or tacit knowledge of what was seen or heard, and are important contributions to the data set. Be aware to note and sift these interpretations separately from the observed facts. For example, you may have interpreted an observation about a person's possibly escaping a busy household, writing a note describing '*customer X sat in their car, looking like they are escaping a busy household, listening to music for 10 minutes before stepping out to grab a cart*'. You don't know exactly what they were listening to or why they stayed in their car, but their behaviour and the music heard suggests it was enjoyable and they were singing, smiling and bopping their heads. Note: be mindful that others may interpret observations differently, as we infuse unconscious bias to our data collection notes. Acknowledging possible bias with a research team will improve the validity of the interpretation, serving as an important contribution to needs or motivations not explicitly seen or heard.

(2) **Sort both observed and interpreted facts**: Sorting involves moving the key data points into thematic groups based on themes and/or patterns that are observed individually and as a team. Making the data points visible enables others to see all contributions. It also facilitates discussion and encourages curious questions such as, what do you think this quote means? Why do you think they said that? Why do you think there are contradictions? etc. For example, one theme that might be proposed is that food shopping offers customers a break from their busy home life (e.g. capstone project). You would create a group under a general theme of 'break from routing' and sort your data to support this theme accordingly.

(3) **Label facts into themes**: Labelling involves questioning each theme or pattern that you have surfaced and sorted, which are supported by both facts and interpretations. Labelling gives the team members permission to further discuss common or shared meaning and value for each group or cluster, and then generate labels for each grouping. Labels are meant to synthesize the patterns you are seeing or sensing. For example, a label your team might propose based on the theme of 'break from routine', is 'personal time or me time'. The theme should spark that question of why do they need a break from routine, etc.

Work either independently, and/or in real time with your team, with the data analysis data templates provided in ► Chapter 8. Have an open mind and defer from judging others for their perspectives. Instead probe with curiosity into their analysis process and ask how they arrived at the themes and possible labels presented.

The best way to develop a proficiency with unstructured data analysis is through active practice, or learning-by-doing. The more practice you get sifting, sorting and labeling data, the better the final analysis. That's the path to an insightful and evolved problem hypothesis (or statement of need).

4.2.4 From Analysis to Synthesis

Data analysis is challenging and is truly where the arts meet science. The amount of human effort required to unpack needs and motivations is not something most organizations are keen to invest in. That's why many companies choose to generate high-level themes from surveys or polls, and hope their solution solves some customer needs.

At this point the students (or participants) have generated a few overarching labels reflecting a summary of the facts, interpretations and patterns. Working from the initial labels and themes generated from the sift, sort and label exercise, insights can now be developed. The following formula enables teams to synthesize their data analysis into a series of insight statements.

4.2.4.1 Exercise: Insight Statements

> An insight statement is the result of a series of prompts that summarize observations and findings from research activities. This technique requires iteration and practice. The statements reflect discovered needs and motivations, and are written in a series of statements, leading to a concise conclusion.
> **Think and Do:**
> Use the following three sentences as prompts to draw out insights from your investigation efforts. The sequence of sentences are based on analytical and abductive thinking logic—moving from broad observations, to key learnings and then summarized as an inference or reasoned conclusion.
> We observed and/or heard (observations/needs) _____.
> We learned (findings/themes) _____.
> We infer (needs-based problem = insight) _____.
>
> The third and concluding statement reflects your data analysis and synthesis of key themes. The third statement is your insight statement that reframes the original problem hypothesis.

The formula may read like a madlib (a word that combines an improvisational actor's ad-lib with perceived humour or madness), but it's intended to draw insight from your investigation efforts. It's comprised of three statements.

- We observed and/or heard (functional and emotional needs) _____.
- We learned (findings/patterns/themes) _____.
- We infer (user need/problem meaning = insight) _____.

Table 4.5 Problem hypothesis and problem statement examples

Problem hypothesis example	Problem statement (with insight) example
• The problem we (Grocer X) are trying to solve is: To increase basket size and retain everyday grocery shoppers	• The problem we (Grocer X) are trying to solve is: To provide busy grocery shoppers with an experience that combines a mini escape with practical meal planning
• The original problem hypothesis is typically positioned from a company's POV, focused on business objectives	• The evolved statement reflects a customer-centred insight for the company to explore—that still meets their original objective of increasing basket size and retaining customers

The third statement should reflect your data analysis while synthesizing your key themes into an insightful problem statement (as converted problem hypothesis). Here's an example:

- We observed *that some customers combine their food shopping with personal 'me time'.*
- We learned *that some customers view the grocery store as an escape from their daily routine, where they can spend time listening to their favourite playlist or podcast, while also getting food for their family.*
- We infer *that remote working grocery shoppers need an escape from their busy lives, and want an experience that combines a mini getaway with practical meal planning.*

This second BDM step (Find) requires the original problem hypothesis to evolve into a proposed problem statement infused with needs-based insight. For example, a problem statement may read as: *The problem we are trying to solve is that busy grocery shoppers need an escape from their remote working lives, and they want an experience that combines a mini getaway with practical meal planning.* Further examples are provided in Table 4.5.

The key themes, as examples, lead to an insight that combines the emotional need or meaning of 'escape' with the practical or functional need for food, reflecting meal planning. From this example, practice generating several problem statements using this formula. Remember to insert your data analysis output to generate several possible problem statements. Use the templates provided in ▶ Chapter 8 to guide you.

4.2.4.2 Exercise: Problem Statement (with Insight)

A problem statement is a communication tool that clearly defines the problem your project ultimately addresses and why it matters. An insightful statement highlights the target end-user (persona), their needs and the context in which the problem exists.

How to: Working from the insight statement, the problem statement is further infused with the target end-user or customer segment. A clearly articulated and framed problem directly inspires a creative and effective solution.

> State what the problem is, who is suffering with it, why it exists and why it matters to both the end-user and company seeking to solve it. The recommended formula is:
>
> *The problem we_____ (company) are trying to solve for _____end-user/customer (who), is their need _____(what), so/because (why it matters) _____.*
>
> Examples:
> - The problem Instagram (company) is trying to solve for smart phone users (who) is to improve the quality and size of their photos and size (what) so they can share them as best moments in real time (why).
> - The problem Grocer X (company) is trying to solve for the busy young family shoppers (who) is to how to balance routine with discovery of new items (what), so they can stay on budget and introduce new meal options to their families (why).
> - The problem Manufacturer X (company) is trying to solve for engineering teams (who) to innovatively problem solve within a rigid process (what), so they can feel more creative and confident (why).

An insight is a discovery of understanding and needs. It explains why something is happening the way it is. It offers the critical element to frame the right problem to solve. An insight drives novel and relevant ideas and solutions, resulting in competitive advantage and sustainable innovation development.

From the insights generated from this step, the innovation teams can reframe the problem hypothesis and begin to generate novel and relevant ideas, prototypes and innovative solutions, resulting in competitive advantage and sustainable innovation development. ▶ Chapter 5 introduces and explains how to frame and translate insights into innovative ideas and concepts.

4.2.5 Design Critique Session = Feedback Loop

Design-driven innovation combines methods and frameworks from management, anthropology and design. The designer's toolkit in the first step of BDM (Start) offered the innovation design brief as the crucial starting and framing document. The second step of the BDM (Find) recommends the practice of a 'design crit' or critique session. For centuries, designers have engaged in critique sessions as safe places and spaces for constructive criticism or feedback. These sessions, originally housed in a design studio, facilitate both instructor and peer-based evaluation of a concept. As 'critics', they offer positive feedback, pose clarifying questions and identify possible changes or different approaches. The 'crit's' purpose is to openly discuss and reflect on work-in-progress, and not to direct or converge on one idea, or to jump to a designed solution.

Increasingly, organizations have introduced the designer's crit and renamed it as project-based feedback sessions or loops. Feedback loops are simple to understand and easy to put into practice in a classroom or workplace setting. The process involves the creation of something, presenting the 'something' to gain information (feedback) on its clarity or value, and the use of that information (feedback) to improve that something. Feedback loops offer a constant cycle of monitoring and measurement of improvement. For example, feedback loops influence the improvement of problem statements, prototype designs and ultimately the packaged and adopted innovation. Additionally, these sessions increase collaboration between innovation team members and project stakeholders, where they systematically embed diverse perspectives from internal and external stakeholders, and provide visibility into the decision-making process.

Setting up the feedback loop for the problem statements. Once the teams have generated a few problem statements, each member should vote on one problem statement that best reflects the needs discovered from the data analysis process. It's recommended that teams employ the technique of *dotmocracy*, where each member of the team has two votes. Each member selects their top two statements. The statement with the most votes is selected and proceeds to a round of peer or stakeholder feedback.

> **How to engage in a feedback loop**:
> - Post your selected problem statement into the module's Feedback Loop section.
> - Prepare to offer valuable feedback to the other team's submission.
> - When providing feedback follow the best practices of:
>   – stating what is done well
>   – seeking clarification on what is presented then proposing recommendations for improvements
>   – Accepting all feedback, then returning to your problem statement and implementing improvements to generate variations of your problem statement.
>
> Use the template provided in ▶ Chapter 8.

4.2.6 Part II: Summary and Reflection

> Referencing your Innovation Design Brief, the investigation stage entails need finding or design research methods that offer observations and key findings leading to the critical insights required to uncover a need, solve a problem or a puzzle.
>
> The investigation stage involves two critical and distinct steps, need finding research and narrative data analysis. These activities involve making sense of the observations and articulating the insights generated by your research efforts, ultimately resulting in framing the right problem for the innovation teams to solve.

Part II focused on sorting and translating data into insights so that the right or solvable problem can be defined. You practiced giving and receiving feedback on your insight and problems statements. With a well-articulated problem statement, you are now ready to generate novel and relevant ideas and concepts, well-positioned as innovative solutions.

Students: Reflect on topics presented and answer the following:

— What are examples of narrative data sorting methods and frameworks?
— Where else can you apply the practice of thick data analysis?
— What was challenging when developing your problem statement?

Reflect on the experience with sorting unstructured and narrative (thick) data and its value in finding needs and insight into the target population (e.g. customers, end-users and/or stakeholders).

'The empathy interviews have impacted my role. As Vice President of Operations, I support all of our partners in the eastern stores, and spend a lot of our time in the stores, connecting with and supporting our partners who wear the green apron and take care of you, our customers. These interviews have absolutely changed what questions I ask, how I ask them, the level of curiosity, that I go into a store with, and how I suspend any bias or judgment. They (empathy interviews and observational research) have deepened my level of connection with the people, the partners in our stores, and enabled me to make better decisions. It's no longer about what I think is happening, it's about engaging partners to share—because they're really at the center of it all. These techniques have been the most significant for me in my work'.—Corporate executive learner.

Business Design Method Step 3: Frame

Supplementary Information The online version contains supplementary material available at (▶ https://doi.org/10.1007/978-3-030-86489-7_5).

© The Author(s), under exclusive license to Springer Nature Switzerland AG 2022
A. Beausoleil, *Business Design Thinking and Doing*,
https://doi.org/10.1007/978-3-030-86489-7_5

> **Learning Objectives**
> At the end of Part I of this chapter, readers will be able to:
> - Frame and reframe an insightful problem statement
> - Frame key target user/customer personas
> - Craft a 'How Might We' question
> - Understand the value of feedback.
>
> At the end of Part II of this chapter, readers will be able to:
> - Transform insights into ideas and concepts
> - Generate metaphors and analogies for ideation
> - Transform ideas into prototypes for testing
> - Understand the value of feedback.

> **Key Outputs:**
>
> - Persona(s)
> - Ideas/Concepts
> - Rapid Prototypes
> - Customer Journey Map.

5.1 Introduction

This chapter outlines the third stage of the innovation process (Integration) and the third step of the Business Design Method (Step 3: Frame). It's divided into two parts that can be delivered as two sequential classes, or as two distinct and separate modules. Part I introduces problem, persona and opportunity framing. Part II introduces framing ideas, concepts and prototypes from the problem statement and personas. Both sections build upon the insights developed from your need-finding research efforts from BDM step 2 (Find). Templates and examples for classroom-based projects (or real business challenges) are provided.

5.1.1 Warm Up Exercise: Alternative Uses

> *Warm ups* prepare students to engage in the exploration of new topics or techniques. Similar to fitness or sport-based warm ups, individuals engage in a quick and gentle introduction to a topic and become more comfortable and confident with its relevance and broader application.
> **Alternative Uses** is a fun icebreaker activity or as a purposeful creative thinking technique. They engage participants to think divergently and generate options for alternative uses of simple objects such as a pencil, hammer or paper clip. In busi-

ness, this technique is used to surface 'functional fixedness' or unconscious bias towards existing processes, systems or products. Repeated practice of this technique helps develop the ability to reframe orthodoxies, explore different perspectives and think more creatively.

How to: Take sheet of paper/pen OR tablet/stylus and prepare to respond to a visual prompt. The prompt is a simple drawing of an object (i.e. pencil):
- Ask participants to consider alternative uses for this object
- Ask participants to generate as many alternative ideas as possible.

Duration: 2 minutes.
Discuss: Ask participants to share their most 'alternative' use ideas.
Use the template provided in ▶ Chapter 8.

5.1.2 Part I: Framing the Right Problem to Solve

The third step in the Business Design Method is entitled 'frame', as it outlines the importance of framing the right, or solvable, problem to focus on. Framing sets in motion a series of activities focused on resolving the need—or root cause of the problem—by developing a well-articulated problem statement.

Framing is the process of defining an issue, problem or context that influences how it's perceived and evaluated. Framing is important in explaining or making sense of an issue, context or problem, and is influenced by personal narratives and conceptual metaphors.

This framing effect is a well-researched cognitive bias in decision-making, and its effectiveness depends heavily on how the issue, problem or question is presented. That's where we need to put in the work. For example, if we ask the question $x+x=2$, the correct answer for $x=1$. However, if we ask or frame the question as $x+y=2$, the answer for x and y will diverge to include whole numbers, fractions, decimals, etc. How we frame the question is critical in solving problems that seek divergent, novel and innovative solutions.

The most effective way to overcome this cognitive bias is to frame the question or problem differently (i.e. $x+y=2$) and seek out individuals with different perspectives. This strategy is all about reframing, a process of identifying and then changing the way an issue, problem or situation is viewed. The reframing effect enables biases and perceptions to be challenged and potentially changed.

Framing a point of view, problem or insight directly influences our behaviour, decisions and actions. For example, this book frames innovation development as a communications process, which may be incongruent to technology driven, science-driven or market-driven narratives of innovation. When breaking the innovation development process into stages and steps, and framing the human-to-human and human-to-systems dialogue as critical events, the benefits of communicating an effective process—that in turn produces an innovative product for a consumer—become obvious.

However, it can be even more helpful to reframe innovation as a series of signals (of pain) that generate positive responses (of relief).

The problem statement generated from BDM Step 2 is the artifact the innovation teams are framing and reframing in this section. Asking the question 'are we solving the right problem?' triggers the activities for BDM Step 3. This reflective question requires curiosity, confidence and creativity to pose and then answer.

Successful business leaders know that the right problem is a solvable problem, and that a solvable problem should be framed or reframed based on insight. For example, the problem statement may be 'the automated checkout is too slow', which leads to framing ideas about making the checkout machine faster. Instead, the problem can be reframed as 'the process is annoying', with ideas refocusing on making the experience feel shorter. Moving the problem from the terminal to the customer experience generates different and varied ideas, such as installing free wifi, pre-sorting tags, etc.

How to reframe your problem statement:
- Does your problem statement skew towards a functional or technical problem, which is a business frame? If so, then you are trying to solve the 'checkout terminal' problem.
- Does your problem statement integrate an insight from a human need or pain point? If so, then you are trying to solve the 'experience' problem, which is the solvable problem.
- Ask the teams to revisit their problem statement and ask if they are framing the *right* problem to solve. Use the template provided in ▶ Chapter 8 as the guide.

5.1.3 Framing Personas from Insights and Problem Statements

A well-crafted problem statement employs personas designed to represent the target end-user or customer. Personas are used extensively by marketers who have evolved the original psychological profiles introduced by Carl Jung[1] and apply them to user-types of services, products and brands.

Software designer Alan Cooper[2] popularized the concept of introducing user personas in interactive design. They capture general demographic and psychographic data, and specific behavioural data, to help guide business leaders to make informed decisions from a customer's point of view. Personas are models of end-users (or customers) that reflect their goals, beliefs, motivations, thoughts, behaviours and preferences. Personas are not fictional profiles (or characters) created to suit a story conceived from the imagination. The most common persona types include buyer, customer, brand and user personas.

For organizations, personas are vital to the success of any marketing and innovation activity. The highest quality personas integrate both qualitative and quantitative research data (e.g. from in-field observation, interviews, surveys,

---

1 Jung (1971). Personality types. *The portable Jung*, 178–272.
2 Alan (1999). The inmates are running the asylum.

etc.). The aim of personas is to visualize a real person (with a real name) for the purpose of:
- building empathy for a target consumer type.
- understanding hidden behavioural drivers, such as needs and goals, and what they want to accomplish, along with their journey to finding your product.
- identifying obstacles to purchasing, such as hesitations and concerns with a specific product or service.
- reflecting a mindset shared with others, such as personality traits, prior experiences, expectations and preconceived notions (i.e. product and brand affiliations).

To develop personas, first apply the sorted observational data (from ▶ Chapter 4) and any additional data collected from desk research, etc. onto an empathy map. An empathy map is a persona prototyping technique that sorts observational data across four quadrants of what the end-user says, does, thinks and feels. It is a useful technique to build empathy for end-users or customers by understanding their needs, desires and motivations.

5.1.3.1 Exercise: Empathy Map

Build empathy for end-users or customers by understanding what they think, feel, say and do leading to insight into their needs and motivations.
How to create an empathy map: The empathy map is typically split into four quadrants (*Says*, *Thinks*, *Does*, and *Feels*), with a circle representing the end-user, customer or persona in the middle. The two quadrants on the left highlight what can be observed as fact (i.e. quotes or actions) and the two quadrants on the right are observations as interpretations (i.e. thoughts and emotions). The map offers a way to sort field research data into the quadrants to gain a holistic perspective from the user's POV, and directly informs the development of personas. Use the template provided in ▶ Chapter 8.

5.1.3.2 Exercise: Personas

How to Create Personas:
- Reference your empathy map prototype
- Identify target end-user customer demographic info
- Describe their traits and buying habits
- Describe their needs and wants
- Describe key influencers and media channels
- Describe any product/service affiliation
- Propose a name and title for your persona(s)
- Recommend that each team member generates one persona.

> As a project team, discuss and select two personas per team (hint: use the *dotmocracy* technique). Dotmocracy is about voting with dots. Participants vote on their preferred options using a limited number of marks with pens (as dots) or dot stickers. The item with the most dots is selected.

5.1.4 Framing Problems and Questions for Ideation

Once the teams have reframed their problem statements and framed the key personas, they're ready to begin generating ideas. A proven technique to launch into ideation from a reframed problem statement is to ask a How Might We question.[3] The question is comprised of three simple words that frame and trigger innovative and creative problem-solving efforts.

A strong and effective How Might We (HMW) question converts a problem statement into an inclusive and collaborative question. The aim is to trigger novel and relevant idea generation or idea storming for all members of the team. Today, the HMW question is used extensively to frame design challenges inside classrooms and business boardrooms.

The best practice of crafting a HMW question is to ensure it is end-user or customer-centered and that it's sufficiently narrow (so that it is manageable and solvable), yet broad enough to encourage exploration of divergent ideas. For example, the following are HMW questions that reflect the embedded insights and personas in their original problem statement and hint at their solution (i.e. business offers):

- **Nike**: How Might We (Nike) inspire the everyday athlete to feel and celebrate greatness in their daily activities?
- **Starbucks**: How Might We (Starbucks) connect coffee drinkers to baristas and personalize their experience?
- **Instagram**: How Might We (Instagram) enable amateur smart phone photographers to share quality images immediately with friends?

Engage the innovation teams to iterate many HMW questions from the reframed problem statement. Remind them to include their personas. Use the How Might We template in ▶ Chapter 8.

5.1.4.1 Exercise: How Might We Question

> The How Might We question is a divergent thinking technique that launches idea generation. The three words are placed at the start of the problem statement, reframing the statement into a question.

---

3 Parnes, S. J. (1967). *Creative behavior guidebook*. Scribner.

How to: Reframe your problem statement into a problem-solving question. The recommended formula is:
How Might We (company) _____ *(active verb)* _____ *(persona)* _____ *and resolve* _____ *(problem statement)?*
Examples:

- How might we (Instagram) enable (verb) smart phone users (persona) to improve the quality and size of their photos, so they can share them as best moments in real time (problem statement)?
- How might we (Grocer X) inspire (verb) busy young family shoppers (persona) to balance routine with discovery of new items, so they can stay on budget and introduce new meal options to their families (problem statement)?
- How might we (Manufacturer X) support (verb) engineering teams (persona) to innovatively problem solve within a rigid process, so they can feel more creative and confident (problem statement)?

5.1.5 Design Critique Session = Feedback Loop

Design-driven innovation combines methods and frameworks from management, anthropology and design. For centuries, designers have engaged in critique sessions as safe places and spaces for constructive criticism or feedback. Originally housed in a design studio, these sessions facilitate both instructor and peer-based evaluation of a concept. As 'critics', they offer positive feedback, pose clarifying questions and identify possible changes or different approaches. The design crit's purpose is to openly discuss and reflect on work-in-progress, and not to direct or converge on one idea, or jump to a final solution.

Setting up the feedback loop for the How Might We question (as opportunity statement). Once the teams have generated several HMW questions, each member should vote on one HMW question that best reflects the problem statement. It's recommended that teams employ the technique of *dotmocracy*, where each member of the team has two votes to select their top two HMW questions. The question with the most votes is selected and proceeds to a round of peer or stakeholder feedback.

How to engage in a feedback loop:
- Prepare to post or share the selected HMW question into a Feedback Loop.
- Prepare to offer valuable feedback to the other team's submission, in return.
- When providing feedback follow the best practice of:
  - stating what is done well
  - seeking clarification on what is presented, then…
  - proposing recommendations for improvements

> — Accept all feedback, return to your HMW question and implement the improvements to generate more iterations of the HMW question. Use the template provided in ▶ Chapter 8.

Accept all feedback, return to your HMW and consider implementing the recommendations. With a well-articulated problem statement, you're now ready to generate novel and relevant ideas and solutions, well positioned as innovations.

5.1.6 Part I: Summary and Reflection

> The third BDM step involves activities focused on understanding, framing and evolving the original problem hypothesis into a problem statement to better reflect the right problem to solve.
> Working from the revised problem statement and data-driven insights, personas are then developed and combine to form the How Might We question. The HMW question is positioned as the important guide for ideation and concept development.
> Design-driven innovation results from a deep understanding and articulation of end-user or customer needs and drivers. Personas offer a way to visualize customer needs and empathize with their pains and desires in a relevant market context. Personas directly influence the design of the offer (product or service), marketing strategies and go-to-market plans for the implementation stage (or BDM Step 4).
> Note: If the team is lacking insight, or is unable to frame an insightful problem statement or set of personas, it's recommended they return to the investigation stage (or BDM Step 2) and continue to lead field research and data analysis.
> Students: Reflect on topics presented and answer the following:
> — Describe the value of problem framing
> — Develop end-user or customer personas
> — Develop How Might We question crafting skills.
>
> Reflect on the experience with problem framing and reframing. As with each chapter or topic-based module, take a few moments to reflect on key learnings and "aha" moments from the exercises. Capture your thoughts and questions in your notebook.

5.2 Part II: Framing Ideas, Analogies and Prototypes

In Part I, you were introduced to frameworks that enable problem framing and reframing based on insights and deep understanding of your target population (as personas). At this stage, the design-driven innovation process moves from defining the right problem to designing the right solution. This next section is focused on idea generation, prototyping and testing guided by insights and persona(s).

5.2.1 Warm Up Exercise: Analogy Maker

Warm ups prepare students to engage in the exploration of new topics or techniques. Similar to fitness or sport-based warm ups, individuals engage in a quick and gentle introduction to a topic and become more comfortable and confident with its relevance and broader application.

Analogy Maker can be used as an icebreaker activity and creative thinking technique. Analogies are word puzzles that are used to compare and connect two seemingly unrelated concepts. The activity introduces one problem statement as prompt. Participants are asked to generate at least two metaphors and analogies in order to practice idea generation.

How to: Take a sheet of paper/pen OR tablet/stylus and generate a few metaphors and analogies that answer the presented statement.
- Prompt: Cooking a meal was once like _____(metaphor); now, cooking is _____(analogy).
- Generate at least two different metaphors and associated analogies.

_____

Don't overthink. Keep it simple
Example: Finding my car keys was once like finding a needle in a haystack (metaphor); Now, finding my car keys is like having a magnet, simple to locate and quick to detect.
Duration: 2 minutes.

5.2.2 Creative Framing and Ideation

Designing solutions for the right problem is hard work that requires diligence. Contrary to popular myths, creativity is not reserved only for artists, doesn't result from a flash of genius, and isn't the product of a single person's imagination. Creativity is a core human condition, is a learnable skill and occurs through collaboration. Creativity is practiced through intention, process and perseverance. The creative solving process involves a structured approach and a suite of techniques that enable many ideas to be generated, experimented with and tested. Generating ideas or ideation requires strategic, visual and creative thinking, along with an experimental and learning mindset.

A quick and effective way to generate a variety of ideas is the use of analogies and metaphors that reflect the problem you aim to solve. An analogy compares two different things to show and explain their similarities, while a metaphor relates one thing in terms of another. In business, metaphors and analogies are valuable tools that communicate and illustrate complex concepts in familiar and simple ways. Pervasive metaphors include time as money (e.g. spending, wasting or investing it), careers as ladders (e.g. climbing up the corporate org chart) and processes as roadmaps (e.g. planned phases, stages, gates and destinations). Analogies are clever creative thinking devices that explain how a problem can be solved in a different context. For example, ineffective teams can be improved by observing and replicating a race car pit crew, or a blueprint can be used to communicate the complexity of building a new website or service.

Metaphorical thinking is used extensively in creative industries to communicate the intended problem to solve, while analogous thinking enables the generation of novel ideas for solutions. The metaphor for this textbook reflects a set of recipes addressing the need to offer simplified and repeatable instructions, techniques and core ingredients for design-driven innovation. As an analogy, recipes allow novice cooks (i.e. students or participants) to learn basic cooking techniques while following a list of steps and gathering the right ingredients. Each stage and step (or chapter) is comprised of a set of basic ingredients, techniques and outputs. With practice, each recipe can be varied depending on the cooks (i.e. team members) and by swapping ingredients (i.e. contexts and target populations), resulting in tasty alternatives to the original recipe (i.e. innovations).

Industry examples of how problems were framed into innovative solutions through analogous thinking include:

— **Scaling production and industrial butchery.** In 1913, a Ford employee saw a model of industrial butchering efficiency as an analogy to building a car. The systematic butchering or dismantling of an animal into parts could be reversed into building a car engine from individual parts. This powerful analogy of systematic butchering of pigs and cows inspired the moving assembly line that increased Ford's productivity and reduced labour costs. The phrase 'a model Ford is a dead cow' summarized the visceral impact of integrating this analogy into an innovative manufacturing process.
— **Interface design and physical office desks.** Apple Corp., in the early 1980s introduced the analogy of the common physical office desktop to their computer interface by employing visual icons and labels to reflect paper documents, files and folders. This innovative and 'intuitive' interface successfully secured the early 'desktop' computer adopters and continues to be used by most software companies.
— **Retail experience and mazes.** The Swedish retailer, IKEA combined the maze and museum visit analogies when creating their retail shopping experience, now replicated by retailers worldwide. The maze offered multiple pathways to experience and discover products not on one's shopping list, while the museum visit design guided customers to see and experience curated pieces and staged sets showcasing how products could be used or placed in a room.
— **Emergency room teams and race car pit crews.** The University Hospital of Wales modelled its infant delivery rooms on Formula 1 pit crew stops, redesigning their work areas with floor mappings and essential tools-only trolleys.

The F1 pit analogy offered a way to significantly improve the hospital's procedures for resuscitating newborn babies.[4]
- **Dust removal and industrial cyclones.** British engineering designer James Dyson was inspired by a local sawmill's industrial powered cyclones to remove sawdust. He used it to solve the problem of suction and dust removal with his household vacuum. Dyson prototyped thousands of cyclone designs before developing the innovative bagless vacuum cleaner.[5]

Table 5.1 Idea generation examples: problems, metaphors and analogies

Problem	Metaphor	Analogies
Lack a strong workforce	Frail human body	Build stronger muscles (increase protein intake; increase exercise; etc.)
Loss of market share	Leaky bucket	Seal or replace bucket (fix specific leak; change bucket type or size; etc.)
High production costs	Excess weight	Lose weight (curb appetite; drink more water; join a gym; etc.)
Poor customer service	Hot potato	One stop shop (full service; concierge service; soup to nuts service; etc.)

5.2.2.1 Generating Ideas Using Metaphors and Analogies

Great ideas result from generating many ideas. One way to generate multiple ideas quickly is to use metaphors and analogies, as they are relatable, familiar and concrete. Ideas must be generated from the framed problem statement. Table 5.1 offers common business problems as metaphors and offers analogies for idea generation.

Metaphors and analogies facilitate the ability to change perspective on a given subject or problem. They enable us to reframe familiar concepts into new or unfamiliar contexts, and aid with aligning innovation teams to understand how a similar problem has been solved in a different domain. Note: there is no single or right metaphor for your problem, nor is there one analogy for your solution.

5.2.2.2 Exercise: Rapid Ideation

Rapid ideation is a technique to quickly generate many ideas from a well-crafted How Might We question or well-defined problem statement. It combines problem framing with idea storming.

---

4 McClean (2016). Wales hospital uses F1 pit stop tactics for newborn resuscitation. *Financial Times*. Retrieved from ► https://www.ft.com/content/35f34152-1695-11e6-9d98-00386a18e39d.
5 Dyson (2020). About Dyson. Retrieved from ► https://www.lb.dyson.com/en-LB/community/aboutdyson.aspx.

> **How to**: Working from your How Might We question, generate many ideas that aims to answer the question. Refrain from judgement.
> - Generate many metaphors to reflect the problem statement.
> - Generate many analogies to reflect possible ideas as solutions.
> - Consider 'crazy, silly or bad' ideas and then discuss what makes them so crazy or bad.
> - Sketch or build the ideas for your team members to provide feedback on and to improve.
> - Vote on top ideas to prototype.
>
> Use the template provided in ▶ Chapter 8.

Accounting Business example: How might we (Accounting Firm X) reimagine our services to suit the diverse and urgent needs of our small business and corporate clients? By offering clients a toolbox (as analogy), our accounting service team can provide clients both the human resources they seek, and a set of tools they can access 24/7 (when they need them).

Instagram example: How might we (Instagram) enable amateur photographers to improve their digital photos and share them as best moments with friends and family, immediately? Instagram generated analogous ideas on improving the quality of photos, such as attaching a large telephoto lens to the smartphone, and by offering a digital version of a 'photo processing lab' to improve the quality and processing (aka filtered digitization) of the user-generated images. Both analogies were reimagined and developed as coded filters that could offer an improved image, in a small file size that could be shared quickly through social media channels.

Generating bad ideas is another proven approach to ideation. BadIdeas[6] is a creative thinking technique focused on divergent thinking with the aim to focus on the problem to solve, versus generating ideas and possible random solutions. The method highlights how having preconceived notions about a solution to a problem will limit our ability to discover new, novel and innovative alternatives. The BadIdeas technique is designed to break through existing beliefs and paradigms (outside zone) through iterations of ideas deemed impossible, impractical or weird.

Steps:
1. **Generate**: Think of contradictions (glass hammer; chocolate house; etc.)
2. **Analyze**: Why is it bad? (generate idea evaluation criteria)
3. **Creatively Synthesize**: How could this bad idea be good? (variants)
4. **To generate bad ideas, ask**: What is bad about this idea? Why is this a bad thing? Is there a different context where this would be good?
5. **To generate good ideas, ask**: What is good about this idea? Why is this a good thing? Is there a different context where this would be bad?

---

6 Dix et al. (2006). Why bad ideas are a good idea.

5.2.3 Framing Prototypes from Ideas

From the ideas generated from analogies and metaphors, begin to evolve them into a tangible form through prototyping. Prototyping is the process of building an experimental model or prototype of a product or output. The practice of prototyping can be attributed to early Egyptian and Roman architects who drew, designed and developed models of buildings. Today, designers and engineers continue to use prototyping as a learning and communication vehicle to explore and experiment with different designs, features, styles and materials. For organizations, engaging in this 'design iteration' practice, affords the testing of proposed problem spaces, future scenarios and innovative solutions—before investing heavily with resources and funds.

Rapid prototyping is a quick-thinking and making technique to convert ideas into concrete concepts, referred to as prototypes, mockups, visual concepts, pilots, storyboards or drafts. For innovation teams and organizations, prototyping enables thinking to be made visible, granting permission to all team members, stakeholders and customers to see and test divergent ideas. This ensures the collection of necessary feedback on the proposed concept—e.g. if it resolves the need or solves the problem. Rapid prototyping involves small-scale concepts to be iterated quickly and thoughtfully. These mockups test out both the framed problem and proposed solutions, and are expressed in rough sketches or paper-based or digital 3D models.

Prototypes are often described by their level of fidelity or detail, ranging from low to high. Low fidelity concepts introduce a visual representation on a napkin, sticky note, piece of paper or on screen. Visual prototypes reflect a rough look and feel of a product or platform, or a flow/navigation map if representing a service, process or customer journey. High-fidelity prototypes reveal functional aspects of the intended solution, how it might work, how users will interact with this, and perhaps what key content or messages will be included. A detailed description of prototype categories is provided in ▶ Chapter 6.

Prototyping is a core design competence and requires the ability to think visually. Visual thinking is a way of seeing, imagining or drawing information, forms or patterns and making the thoughts visible. Visuals make information easier to convey, process and remember, as they offer more meaning than verbal descriptions alone. Visual thinking is an important communication process as diagrams, graphic organizers and concept maps help people problem-solve and support group work. Visual thinking is not restricted to those who can draw, paint or illustrate. It's an inclusive skill for effective communicators and leaders, for those translating spreadsheets into information or synthesizing insights into strategies and business models.

Design-driven innovation prototypes are often presented through business process notations; flow charts; 3D models; strategic scenarios, storyboards; customer journey maps; service blueprints and/or business model canvases. For this section, it's recommended that students (or participants) engage in *rapid prototyping* practice that involves low fidelity representation of the ideas. Basic materials needed for this iterative thinking and doing exercise include sticky notes, different coloured paper sheets, card stock, tape, glue sticks, scissors, markers, pens and colouring pencils. Prototyping templates for simple sketching, customer journey maps and service blueprints are included in ▶ Chapter 8.

5.2.3.1 Exercise: Rapid Prototyping

How to rapidly prototype:

To engage in creative problem solving, the classroom (or boardroom) should be converted into a designer's studio or maker's space, to best prepare the students (or participants) to think visually and spatially. Working either independently or in real time with your teams in a physical and virtual studio environment, ensure the basic materials are available:

- Pencils, pens and markers
- Sheets of paper
- Sticky notes
- Scissors and tape
- Building blocks (optional).

If working remotely (digital studio), work with your preferred virtual or collaborative whiteboard platforms (e.g Miro or Mural software applications).

Work with your selected ideas or concepts as proposed solutions. Defer judgement on the individual and team's contributions. Be generative and practice divergent and visual thinking. Rapidly prototype by sketching on sticky notes or paper napkins or use building blocks.

Learn from each iteration and continue to improve upon sketches or mock-ups. Prepare for another 'design critique' aka feedback loop.

Understanding how the rapid prototype fits within an end-user or customer journey is important for context and future adoption. Use the Journey Map technique to quickly map out how your concept fits along a path. Use the template provided in ▶ Chapter 8.

5.2.3.2 Exercise: Journey Map

A journey map is a visual thinking technique that plots the target end-user or customer-led activities onto a timeline. The narrative map highlights key events, touchpoints and sentiment in relation to accomplishing a goal. It is used to map product, service or experience scenarios over stages.

How to:
- Define and describe a persona (end-user or customer) whose journey you are mapping.

- Map research findings (observations) by describing key events, touchpoints and associated sentiment (reference empathy map or Sift.Sort.Label analysis).
- Determine points of friction or pain or opportunity.
- Discuss with team on how to resolve.
- Package your selected journey map (as alpha prototype) for peer feedback.
- Use the template provided in ▶ Chapter 8.

5.2.4 Design Critique Session = Feedback Loop

Design-driven innovation combines methods and frameworks from management, anthropology and design. For centuries, designers have engaged in critique sessions as safe places and spaces for constructive criticism or feedback. Originally housed in a design studio, these sessions facilitate both instructor and peer-based evaluation of a concept. As 'critics', they offer positive feedback, pose clarifying questions and identify possible changes or different approaches. The design crit's purpose is to openly discuss and reflect on work-in-progress, and not to direct or converge on one idea, or jump to a final solution.

Setting up the feedback loop for the the rapid prototypes. Once the teams have generated several ideas and concepts from their HMW question [repeat How Might We…in case the reader isn't reading linearly], each member should vote on the best rough prototypes that could might the problem. It's recommended that teams employ the technique of *dotmocracy*, where each member of the team has two votes to select their top two prototypes. The question with the most votes is selected and proceeds to a round of peer or stakeholder feedback.

> **How to engage in a feedback loop**:
> - Prepare to post or share the selected ideas (as rough prototypes) into a Feedback Loop.
> - Prepare to offer valuable feedback to the other team's submission, in return.
> - When providing feedback follow the best practice of:
>   – stating what is done well
>   – seeking clarification on what is presented, then…
>   – proposing recommendations for improvements
> - Accept all feedback, return to your prototypes and implement the improvements to generate more iterations. Use the template provided in ▶ Chapter 8.

Accept all feedback, return to your HMW question and consider implementing the recommendations. With a well-articulated problem statement, you're now ready to generate novel and relevant ideas and solutions, well positioned as innovations.

5.2.5 Part II: Summary and Reflection

The most challenging part of an innovation development process is to articulate the problem in order to generate relevant and novel ideas as solutions. Contrary to popular myth, generating many ideas requires a rigorous and structured creative thinking process that begins with the problem statement, and engages in various divergent thinking devices, such as metaphorical and analogous thinking.

The BDM Step 3 (Frame) involves all the activities involved in framing insights into ideas and initial prototypes. This section serves to complete the stage and framing step where your insights and a well-stated problem statement directly impact agile ideation and rapid prototyping efforts. Another round of feedback loops should be completed based on your How Might We question and rough prototypes generated. The most effective creative problem-solving approaches focus on framing the right problem to solve and then tapping into the diverse minds from an innovation team to generate novel and relevant ideas and solutions, well positioned as design-driven innovations.

Students: Reflect on topics presented and answer the following:
- What is the value of reframing a problem?
- Why are problem diagnostic skills important?
- What was challenging when ideating and rapid prototyping?

Reflect on your experience with generating metaphors and analogies. Did you generate at least 10 ideas from your HMW question? Did you give yourself and your team permission to explore bad or crazy ideas? Did you ask how those bad or crazy ideas might actually be good and interesting if flipped? Did you build upon other team member ideas and arrive at novel and relevant ideas for your project?

'It was surprisingly difficult to change the way I thought about different issues - my (and most of my classmates) first inclination was just to go right to the solution, which feels like it's what I've always been taught. The process of asking, asking again, and rephrasing, and rephrasing the same question to understand it in different ways to get to the root of it was highly effective – especially because of the worksheet framework provided. I can see ways I can apply this to many problems in my current work and in the future'.—GEMBA student

Business Design Method Step 4: Solve

Supplementary Information The online version contains supplementary material available at (▶ https://doi.org/10.1007/978-3-030-86489-7_6).

© The Author(s), under exclusive license to Springer Nature Switzerland AG 2022
A. Beausoleil, *Business Design Thinking and Doing*,
https://doi.org/10.1007/978-3-030-86489-7_6

> **Learning Objectives**
> At the end of Part I of this chapter, readers will be able to:
> – Transform prototypes into a proposed solution.
> – Assess solution(s) through the Three Traits Framework.
> – Assess solution(s) adoption with the Five Factors Analysis.
>
> At the end of Part II of this chapter, readers will be able to:
> – Craft a compelling story of how the solution solves the problem.
> – Design a pilot implementation plan.
> – Identify key performance measures.

> **Key Outputs**:
> – Alpha Prototype.
> – Prototype Solution.
> – Pilot Implementation Plan.
> – Performance Measures.

6.1 Introduction

This chapter outlines the fourth step of the Business Design Method (Step 4: Solve) and the fourth stage of the innovation process (Implementation). It is divided into two parts that can be delivered as two sequential classes or as two distinct and separate modules. Part I introduces final prototyping and evaluation strategies. Part II introduces storytelling, implementation plan development and performance measurement design. Templates and examples for classroom-based projects (or case competition briefs) are provided in ▶ Chapter 8.

6.1.1 Warm Up Exercise: Paper Airplanes

> *Warm ups* prepare students to engage in the exploration of new topics or techniques. Similar to fitness or sport-based warm ups, individuals engage in a quick and gentle introduction to a topic and become more comfortable and confident with its relevance and broader application.
> **Paper Airplanes** is a team building activity and a prototyping sampling technique. Making paper aeroplanes and testing their effectiveness is a fun and educational experience. It encourages creative thinking, prototyping and testing (of effective aerodynamics, velocity, thrust, speed, drag, and gravity/weight and/or aesthetic design). Participants practice paper-based model making by folding and decorating

6.1 · Introduction

> their planes, and seeing the impact of their choices on the plane's design to fly far, fast, spiral or look cool.
> **Materials**:
> - Letter-size paper (white or preferably different colors).
> - Decorations (coloured pencils, pens, stickers, etc.).
> - Masking tape (to mark the launch line).
> - Measuring tape/stick (if possible).
> - A long hallway or open space (ideally 20 meters or longer).
> - Awards (i.e. bragging rights or chocolate bar as optional).
>
> **How to**: Give each participant two sheets of paper. The first sheet is for the rapid (or alpha) version. The second sheet is the beta version, which they will decorate with available materials (pens, colouring pencils, stickers, etc.).
> - Fold the first sheet using a variety of angles (test and iterate).
> - Experiment with different folds and decorative techniques.
> - Consider designs for speed, spirals, flight duration and/or beauty.
> - Fold the second sheet from learnings of the first version (as test). With the sheet decorated and folded, join the group with your final prototype.
> - Take turns sending your prototype plane towards a landing area.
>
> **Duration**: 5–10 minutes.
> **Discuss**: Ask participants to explain their different designs, their functional attributes and celebrate the trials, errors and attempts. Explain the value of prototyping in testing out ideas and concepts.

6.1.2 Solving the Right Problem Through Prototyping

The fourth step in the Business Design Method is entitled 'solve', as it outlines the importance of solving the right problem for the end-user, and the solvable problem for the organization. In general, 'problem solving' as a construct suggests a broader scope of activities that include defining a problem, determining its cause, identifying and proposing a solution, and then implementing that solution. The most adopted and practised problem-solving processes include:
- The structured Creative Problem Solving (CPS) method introduced in the mid-1950s by advertising agency executive and educator A. Osborn[1] and creative thinking scholar S. Parnes[2];
- The descriptive innovation development process spawned by communication scholars E. Rogers and F. Shoemaker[3] from the late 1960s, and

---

1 Osborn (1953, 1957, 1963, 1967). *Applied imagination: Principles and procedures of creative problem solving*. New York: Charles Scribner's Sons.
2 Parnes (1960). *Instructors manual for semester courses in creative problem solving*. Creative Education Foundation.
3 Rogers and Shoemaker (1971). *Communication of innovations; A cross-cultural approach*.

- The systemic approach to creative problem solving from architecture design scholars D. Koberg and J. Bagnall, published in the mid-1970s.[4]

These methods outline similar steps that involve identifying and researching the problem, generating ideas to solve the problem, and developing and implementing a plan to bring the intended solution to market. They also share similar thinking and doing modes of analysis (problem), concept development (ideas and prototypes) and synthesis (solution). Notably, the structured CPS is the most influential process and the foundational methodology for **design thinking** taught at the Hasso Platner School of Design (d.school) at Stanford University and at the University of Potsdam, and practised by design consultancies such as IDEO and Doblin, and at global corporations including IBM and GE.

In contrast, the Business Design Method's foundational framework is the innovation development process, which integrates both the structured and systemic approaches to creative problem solving. The **BDM is focussed on contextual and creative problem solving—understanding both the customer and company context**. It introduces stakeholder-centred design as a variation of human-centred design. Stakeholder-centred design is an approach to designing platforms, products and services that model both end-user and ecosystem member behaviours, are desirable, and commercially feasible and viable.

Solving, in a design-driven innovation process, focuses on the verb or action of solving (finding a solution) and not on the broader process. As an action, it aims to solve the root cause of the problem, which extends beyond the originally identified or hypothesized problem, to solve it at a greater scale, generating an **innovative** solution. Solving problems is not as simple as producing a product or service and expecting the customer to buy it. It requires a well-defined and structured, yet adaptive process—one that is stakeholder-centred (external and internal). The solving stage and step in this chapter highlights how challenges and problems can be solved following a structured process, but also offers a selection of adaptive and customizable prototyping devices.

Modern and resilient organizations have been integrating the practice of prototyping to design better products, services, strategies, processes and business models for the past 20 years. Borrowing from the product designer's toolkit, prototyping enables the generation and transformation of ideas into mock-ups, models and minimum viable products (MVP). While rapid prototyping is employed to quickly generate ideas on both problem spaces and possible solutions, final prototyping builds upon the rough mock-ups generated from rapid prototyping and further involves three sequential prototyping phases called alpha, beta and pilot. Each type represents a level of fidelity and characteristics (as phases) for testing, before final solution development.

---

4   Koberg and Bagnall (1974). *The universal traveler, A soft-systems guide to: Creativity, problem solving, and the process of reaching goals* [Revised Edition].

6.1 · Introduction

Table 6.1 Prototype categories

Type	Phase and fidelity	Descriptor
Rapid prototype	Initial ideation phase. Generates simple mock-ups or low fidelity designs, such as napkin sketches, storyboards or paper-based models	The mockup quickly expresses possible and divergent ideas. It serves to make visible and tangible key concepts in order to solicit reactions and feedback and test assumptions
Alpha prototype	The first generation of an integrated prototype or proof of concept. It represents a medium fidelity design, offering a more detailed representation of the concept, introducing look, feel and function	The alpha may be a functioning mobile application, website or cardboard model that looks and acts like a final product. The alpha prototype determines if the concept actually works with both the designers, engineers and ultimately, the intended end-users (or customers)
Beta prototype	The second generation or fully integrated prototype. It represents a high-fidelity design, is informed by end-user alpha testing and suggests the concept will satisfy customers	The beta prototype is all about manufacturing, production or development (depending on the output), it defines the materials, teams or external suppliers required to produce, build or manufacture it. As a design-driven innovation, it's expected that new processes, or new suppliers, will be involved and/or integrated into existing systems and structures
Pilot prototype	The final generation of a fully integrated and developed prototype as solution. It represents the critical validation or trial event of the innovative proof of concept. It is the highest level of fidelity and is packaged and polished for the intended market	A pilot is a trial episode in the film and television industries, an engineering validation trial (EVT) for industrial design firms, a field trial for technology companies, and a market trial for product or service brands. It offers a final review on how the new solution may be adopted, and directly informs the final details for development, manufacturing, pricing and go-to-market strategies

All prototypes require multiple iterations, and depending on the intended output (strategy, business model, service or product), each will require different tools, methods and decisions. It's important for innovation teams to consider how the prototype designs will integrate with existing operational or manufacturing systems. They must determine if the systems and structures (human and technological) must evolve or be adapted to accommodate the new 'design'. The following table (◘ Table 6.1) outlines the common categories of prototypes, associated application phases, level of fidelity and descriptions.

Prototyping is an experimental and integrative method for designing, testing and validating whether the proposed solution actually solves the intended problem. It combines art, science and business, and is highly adaptive to what you are trying to solve (e.g. a product, service, marketing, strategic, or system design problem). The goal is to make low fidelity versions of the solution (as prototypes) that allow key questions to be asked and answered at each development and increased fidelity phase, strategically offering critical feedback from end-users at every phase.

Evidence of highly successful and influential practice with rigorous prototyping include:

- American inventor Thomas Edison, who is often cited as generating over 10,000 prototypes (with his R&D team) that resulted in over 1000 commercial patents, and notable products such as the incandescent light bulb, the phonograph, motion picture cameras and many other electric powered devices.
- British design engineer James Dyson, who worked with his team generated over 5000 prototypes for his bagless vacuum.
- Danish architect and designer Arne Jacobsen and his company, which generated thousands of sketches and prototypes for furniture, textiles, wallpaper and silverware, famously offering the world simple and well-designed chairs inspired by eggs, ants and swans. The work ultimately influenced modern furniture design from the mid-twentieth century to today.

6.1.3 Evaluating Problems Through Prototypes

At this point the project teams should have generated rapid prototypes, captured feedback and will be ready to begin developing the alpha version.

The alpha prototype determines if the concept actually works for both the intended end-users (or customers) and the designers. The alpha prototype may be a detailed roadmap, blueprint, functioning mobile application or cardboard model that looks and acts like a final product.

Design-driven innovation demands that the prototyping phases reflect human-centred design principles, especially in engaging end-users throughout the process. Innovation teams should be resourceful and use whatever materials and platforms are available to prototype and test their ideas—i.e. pen and paper, marker and sticky notes, physical or digital whiteboards, flow-chart makers, building blocks. The most commonly used business design techniques include the journey or experience map, storyboards, the business model canvas and service blueprint.

The **journey or experience map** offers a rapid prototyping technique to generate a basic narrative or story of customer needs and drivers across an interactive journey with a company's product or service, suggesting a new or improved experience design.

Storyboards offer both rapid and alpha prototypes of a sequence of events from both the end-user and organizational perspectives. They're useful in conveying priorities of customer needs, the organizational resolution for those needs, how the key events will flow and how contexts, conflicts and solutions work together. In the next section (this chapter, Part II), storyboards are recommended for designing implementation and go-to-market plans.

The **service blueprint** offers an alpha prototype of a new service design, mapping the complexities of the internal processes and systems responsible for service delivery, along with critical factors impacting the customer experience. The blueprint is useful for the organization (e.g. increased efficiency), and for helping produce positive benefits for both customers and employees.

The **business model canvas** offers an alpha prototype of a business model that outlines how an organization creates value for customers, while delivering return on investment to shareholders. It's useful for companies in identifying target market segments, offering desirable services or products, and sustaining financial stability.

Design-driven innovation demands that the prototyping phases reflect human-centred design principles, especially in engaging end-users throughout the process. Innovation teams should be resourceful and use whatever materials and platforms are available to prototype and test their ideas—i.e. pen and paper, marker and sticky notes, physical or digital whiteboards, flow-chart makers, building blocks.

For the class project (or business challenge), the following techniques listed in ◘ Table 6.2 are recommended based on the problem type.

Prototyping creates value for both end-users (customers) and organizations by testing problems and solutions using low-tech materials. Prototyping is a design-driven method that enables teams and organizations to develop and test new, improved and desirable products or services or experiences—and can be integrated into most development processes and structures. Your tested alpha prototypes will lead to a final prototype, supported by a strategic and effective pilot implementation or go-to-market plan.

The storyboarding technique provided in ► Chapter 5 and the three-act story structure from this chapter are optional techniques for prototyping an implementation or market trial plan—where your solution solves both the end-users' need and the business problem, returning a profit or driving impact for the organization.

6.1.4 Evaluation Strategies for Prototypal Solutions

Prototyping is a comprehensive and agile activity for generating ideas, developing and iterating concepts as alpha prototypes. These prototypes provide enough functionality to test with your intended end-users or customers, and are critical for deep understanding and practice with human-centred design. The alpha prototype also serves as an evaluation strategy with internal stakeholders.

Table 6.2 Problem-based Alpha prototype development techniques

Problem type	Alpha prototyping technique	Application
Poor customer experience	**Journey map**: A diagram that visualizes the customer (end-user) experience with a product or service. It maps key events, needs and gaps over three phases from the customer's point of view. A template is provided in ▶ Chapter 8	• Create a map with three key interaction stages (pre, during and post) • Identify the key elements (needs and touchpoints) that occur during each of the stages (pre, during and post interaction) • Identify and map needs and observed sentiments across stages • Identify gaps and discuss surfaced issues • Generate new version from findings
Unmet customer or internal stakeholder need	**Storyboard**: A graphic organizer that displays both images and text in a sequence for the purpose of showing a story narrative. It simulates scenario planning, except focuses on the end-user (as hero), positioning the organization to offer a resolution (as proposed solution) to the hero. A template is provided in ▶ Chapter 8	• Create a series of panels like a comic book. Draw boxes for the images and lines below for the descriptive text • Identify the main character (i.e. persona), and the current context • Identify the main conflict (i.e. need, motivation, pain, etc.) and the context • Identify the resolution (i.e. proposed solution) and describe the new context • Sketch simple figures and background in the panels. Add text below each panel • Complete the storyboard and test with your team and end-users/customers
Poor service design	**Service blueprint**: A process chart that shows a service delivery process from both the end-user (customer's) and internal stakeholder's POV. It maps both the 'frontstage' and 'backstage' delivery phases to identify key issues. A template is provided in ▶ Chapter 8	• Create a blueprint based on the organization's business process chart or model • Identify and map the key phases based on *how* the organization delivers a service; show both frontstage and backstage • Identify and map *how* the end-user/customer interacts with the service in the frontstage • Identify and map the key deliverables within each phase and across both stages • Identify gaps and discuss surfaced issues • Generate new version from findings

(continued)

6.1 · Introduction

Problem type	Alpha prototyping technique	Application
Poor customer loyalty; or high employee turnover; or, outdated business model	**Business model canvas**[a]: A graphic organizer that documents and maps existing business models and aids in the development of new models. It captures nine building blocks of a company's relationship with customers, employees, suppliers and shareholders. See footnote for template	• Download a template of the Business Model Canvas • Identify key customers, partners and relationships • Identify the organization's value proposition to its customers • Identify key resources, offers and financial activities • Complete the nine blocks with descriptive text and context • Identify issues and opportunities • Discuss and test with internal stakeholders. Reference the canvas for planning

[a]Osterwalder et al. (2011). Business Model Generation: A handbook for visionaries, game changers and challengers. *African Journal of Business Management*, 5(7), 22–30

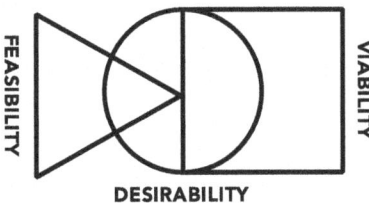

Fig. 6.1 Visual model of the three interrelated traits of designed innovations

Successful solutions are often characterized as desirable for the end-user, and feasible and viable for the organization offering them. These dimensions were first introduced as the three-lenses of innovation[5] by design consultancy IDEO in 2001, and describe the desirability lens as focussed on the customer (do they want it), the feasibility lens focussed on the organizational competencies, technologies and systems (can we do it), and the viability lens (can we profit from it). The three-lenses offer an important reframing of business trade-offs to strategic tensions, suggesting companies balance their innovation efforts to incorporate all three POVs. The lenses have evolved from perspectives to evaluative traits inherent in design-driven innovation. A visual model is presented to show the traits interrelationship (Fig. 6.1).

To evaluate which alpha prototype best displays design-driven innovation qualities, compare each prototype against the Three Traits Framework model.

---

5 Kelley (2001). *The art of innovation: Lessons in creativity from IDEO, America's leading design firm* (Vol. 10). Broadway Business.

The Three Traits Framework is an evaluation technique to assess if a prototype meets all three stakeholder needs of desirability, feasibility and viability. This framework reflects three interconnected characteristics of designed solutions that meet both external stakeholders (customers) and internal stakeholders (company) needs, abilities and motivations.

Innovation teams should reference ◘ Table 6.3 to guide their **qualitative** discussions of which alpha prototype might progress to beta development, based on the balance of desirability, feasibility and viability.

To assist the innovation project teams to **quantify** and rank their prototypes, use the simple criteria set provided in ◘ Table 6.4. The Three Traits Decision-Making Framework table is useful to compare design solutions/recommendations against

◘ **Table 6.3** Three traits framework for discussion

Trait	Description/Query	Qualities
○ Desirability	Is it needed or wanted? Does the end-user/customer need or desire the new solution?	• Does it resolve a real need? • Does it solve a real problem? • Does it serve both customer and company?
△ Feasibility	Is it do-able? Does the company have the capabilities to offer and deliver the new solution?	• Do capabilities exist to support it? • Do infrastructures exist to support it? • Is there a willingness to resource it?
□ Viability	Is it profitable and sustainable? Does the new solution create value and generate revenues and/or impact for the company?	• Can we profit from it? • Can we generate societal impact from it? • Is it a financially sustainable investment?

◘ **Table 6.4** Three traits decision-making framework (Y = 1/N = 0)

Prototype	Desirability	Feasibility	Viability	Total/Rank
Concept 1	Customer = Y/N Company = Y/N	Capabilities = Y/N Infrastructure = Y/N Willingness = Y/N	Cost/Investment = Y/N Profit/Impact = Y/N Strategic Fit = Y/N	=____ #____
Concept 2	Customer = Y/N Company = Y/N	Capabilities = Y/N Infrastructure = Y/N Willingness = Y/N	Cost/Investment = Y/N Profit/Impact = Y/N Strategic Fit = Y/N	=____ #____
Concept 3	Customer = Y/N Company = Y/N	Capabilities = Y/N Infrastructure = Y/N Willingness = Y/N	Cost/Investment = Y/N Profit/Impact = Y/N Strategic Fit = Y/N	=____ #____

6.1 · Introduction

Table 6.5 Prototypal solution adoption evaluation: five factors analysis

Factor	Descriptor	3-Traits Framework
Relative Advantage	The degree to which a new solution is perceived as being better than the current option. The value proposition is clear to potential adopters	Desirability: The new option is more effective or better than the current option
Compatibility	The degree to which a new solution fits with the values, past experiences and needs of end-users or potential customers. It must be equally or more compatible than the current option	Desirability: The new option is compatible with my beliefs and values, is useful and credible
Complexity	The degree to which a new solution is perceived as easy to understand and simple to use by potential adopters	Desirability: The new option is easy to understand and use
Trialability	The degree to which a new solution may be experimented with, or trialled, on a limited basis. The new solution can be sampled, enabling potential adopters to directly experience it	Desirability + Feasibility: The new option can be sampled, experimented with easily or can be modified to suit user needs
Observability	The degree to which the results of the new solution are positive and visible to potential end-users or customers. Seeing others adopt the new solution is correlated with increased adoption	Desirability + Viability: The new option shows clear benefits, positive impact and early adoption is obvious and visible

one another using specific criteria (as dimensions) based on specific goals and project objectives. A worksheet is provided in ▶ Chapter 8.

Deciding on which prototype best balances across all three dimensions of desirability, feasibility and viability is an important first step in strategic problem solving. However, improving the successful adoption rate for the final prototypal solution itself (focused on desirability) requires additional evaluation and analysis.

To assess the best prototype solution based on potential adoption (i.e. buy, use or consume) consider comparing the final list of prototypes against the Rogers' Five Factors Analysis.[6] This well-researched analysis framework evaluates prototype adoption through five key attributes which complements the three-traits of design-driven innovation. This five key attributes (Table 6.5) of a proposed

---

6 Rogers (1962–2003). Diffusion of innovations. *Diffusion of innovations*.

solution's probability to be adopted are: relative advantage, compatibility, complexity, trialability and, observability.

To identify the key features and characteristics for the prototype solution, refer to the Five Factors Analysis template in ▶ Chapter 8.

6.1.5 Part I: Summary and Reflection

The first part of the implementation stage or BDM Step 4 (solve) introduced the value of prototyping, and the types and categories of prototypes to facilitate a well-designed and innovative solution. Prototypes are most successful when key stakeholders (external and internal) can experience and interact with them. What you learn from those interactions will help shape and improve ideas into successful solutions.

Students: Reflect on topics presented and answer the following:
– What is the value of prototyping phases and types?
– What are the key traits to evaluate rapid and alpha prototypes?
– What are the key factors to evaluate specific innovative solutions?

Reflect on the experience with solving problems through prototyping. As with each chapter or module, take a few moments to reflect on key learnings and moments from the exercises. Capture your thoughts and questions in a notebook.

6.2 Part II: Solving Through Implementation

Part II introduces implementation plan development, storytelling and performance measures design. Story-based frameworks are introduced and serve as the most effective approach to stakeholder-buy-in of new strategies, products, services, plans and measures. Templates for the exercises are provided in ▶ Chapter 8.

6.2.1 Warm Up Exercise: Story Madlib

Warm ups prepare students to engage in the exploration of new topics or techniques. Similar to fitness or sport-based warm ups, individuals engage in a quick and gentle introduction to a topic and become more comfortable and confident with its relevance and broader application.

Story Madlib can be used as an icebreaker activity and as a creative thinking and storytelling technique. Storytelling skills are essential to one's ability to inspire and influence others. Story Madlibs create a participatory and immersive experience for

> both tellers and listeners. Stories follow a basic format also referred to as the hero's journey where a relatable hero begins their journey in a familiar world/context, then faces a series of conflicts, learns to navigate an undesirable world, and returns triumphant over the conflict and is transformed.
> **How to:** Use a simple 'madlib' story template to write a short story.
> Once upon a time, _____(insert the hero/persona), was _____(the context).
> Every day, _____(hero/persona) _____ _____(the conflict).
> Until one day, _____(hero/persona), discovered _____ _____(resolution).
> In the end, _____(hero/persona) was_____ _____(triumph).
> - Use simple words to describe the need (conflict) in context.
> - Use emotional words to describe their motivation and their triumph over the conflict, and how they transformed.
> - Generate a funny, silly or real story.
>
> **Duration**: 2 minutes.
>
> **Discuss**: Ask participants to share your story madlib with the cohort. Ask participants to explain their different designs, their functional attributes and celebrate the trials, errors and attempts. Explain the value of prototyping in testing out ideas and concepts. Use the worksheet provided in ▶ Chapter 8.

6.2.2 Storytelling

Stories connect us. They are everywhere. They help us make sense of the world and communicate our values and beliefs. A good story makes us think and feel, and speaks to us in ways that numbers, data, and slides simply can't. Storytelling follows a basic format of a beginning, middle and end. A common story framework is the hero's journey, where a relatable hero begins their journey in a familiar world/context (the beginning), faces a series of challenges and conflicts, learns to navigate the undesirable world (the middle), and arrives triumphant and is transformed (the end).

Humans are hard-wired for stories. We tell and consume them in the form of books, movies, music, television series, podcasts or theatrical performances. In business, stories are at the core of startup pitches, sales presentations and employee recognition awards. A business model tells the story of how a company will create value for customers and prosper. A marketing campaign tells a story about customers' relationship with a product or service. A product experience shapes a story about connection and understanding. Storytelling is one of the most important skills for leaders and managers, as it showcases one's ability to inspire and influence others. Effective storytellers focus on one or two salient points and bookend their story with them and weave in emotional and relevant elements that resonate.

Well-told stories create desire and offer conflict, challenges, a turning point, and a resolution—clearly, informatively and inspirationally. Storyboards (introduced in ▶ Chapter 5) are a very effective technique for breaking a story into scenes (or parts), then working on the details of one scene at a time, focussing on the most important ones. Introducing constraints (time, resources, funding, etc.) is critical to forcing creative and resourceful options, managing expectations, introducing relevant measures and emphasizing only vital information.

Another storytelling technique that reflects a simplified version of the hero's journey is the Three-Act Story structure, which frames a story into three acts: (1) beginning (character in context), (2) middle (conflict in context) and (3) end (conclusion and resolution).

Storytelling affords innovation teams to quickly envision and map how the final prototype (as proposed solution) will resolve the end-user's need and solve the business or organizational problem. Examples of organizational 'stories' that summarize the problem, prototype and solution include:

Case-story example: *Mary Kay Cosmetics*
Character in context: Mary, a young working woman in 1960s is unable to progress into a leadership position, faces discrimination and inequality.
Conflict and context: Frustrated, she leaves the company, writes a book to assist women in business. She uses all her savings, buys and experiments with skin lotion formulas, and invests in a new cosmetic line.
Resolution and conclusion: She prototypes a version of the 'at-home sales model' from Tupperware and trains a women sales team. Driven to empower women, she shares her profits with her saleswomen and creates a home-party format involving multiple customers. She develops a recognition program, making successful women visible to everyone (Pink Cadillac).

Case-story example: *Shopify*
Character in context: Two enterprising computer programmers and avid snowboarders, Tobias and Scott, join forces to develop and market a new line of snowboarding products, while working for an industrial manufacturing company.
Conflict and context: After researching and trialling several e-commerce platforms, they run into numerous challenges and decide to prototype their own. They launch the final prototype, and discover sales for snowboarding equipment were seasonal.
Resolution and conclusion: Driven to design a better e-commerce platform that was affordable and easy to set up for small, independent startups (and non-programmers), they offer subscriptions to their platform. The platform meets the needs of other startup and SME 'e-retailers', and sales grow.

Case-story example: *TD Lab*
Character in context: Senior leaders at the Canadian TD Bank Group seek to position TD as a 'bank of the future'. They need to better understand evolving customer needs, and develop innovative capacity throughout the corporation.

Conflict and context: Bank culture is risk-averse, but new product and service development requires new thinking and experimenting attitudes and processes. They need the flexibility to try new things internally, while maintaining existing financial services, systems and structures.

Resolution and conclusion: TD partners with the University of Waterloo and establishes their first 'corporate innovation co-lab' focussed on future customers—university students. The prototype and test a new 'lab' model: engage and pay students to co-design AI applications and programs, which are further tested and fully implemented thru TD.

Basic story structures (◘ Fig. 6.1) serve as the most effective frameworks to craft new strategies, products, services or business models. They are equally effective with securing stakeholder buy-in. They offer innovation teams an aligned narrative (and visual) that connects, guides and inspires senior stakeholders to buy in and support their progress forward. Story structures enable scenario or futures thinking, which involves contextualizing past and present events (insights) with a view to proposing alternative futures (solutions). The value of scenario-oriented storytelling is to envision how your innovative solution will be introduced, potentially used and ultimately adopted (◘ Fig. 6.2).

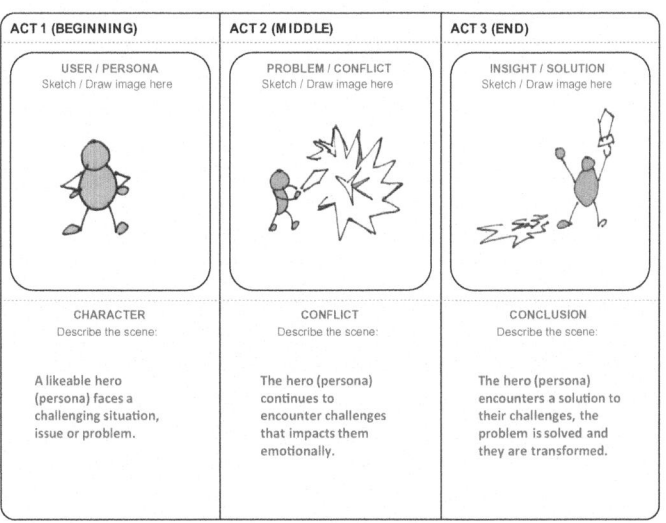

◘ Fig. 6.2 Sample three-act story structure

6.2.2.1 Exercise: Three-Act Story

> The three-act story is a technique to quickly narrate a story across three parts: the beginning, middle and end. Each part highlights a plot point that drive the overall narrative, creating a complete story structure for your final prototype.
> **How to**:
> - Identify the character (persona) and the original context (Act 1), their needs as they encounter conflict (problem) (Act 2) and where a resolution to the conflict and characters is revealed (prototype-solution) (Act 3).
> - Use the Three-Act Story structure as your guide and answer the following questions: Who, What, Why, Where, When and How
>   - Who (key character)
>   - What (goal)
>   - Why (issues/needs/insights)
>   - Where (company + context)
>   - When (timing)
>   - How (problem is solved)
> - Introduce your final prototype as part of the resolution to the hero's (aka persona) needs; show and explain how it functions.
> - Propose how your solution has resolved the hero's need and describe their transformation or positive ending.
> - Quickly iterate many versions before 'inking' your final version and sharing with internal stakeholders.
>
> *"At IMAX when we're looking at implementing new processes and workflows, I want to be able to tell those stories where I can label and identify somebody (as persona) with three words, and that everyone kind of knows who that person is and their story... like Instagram's amateur professional photographer persona". (GEMBA student)*

6.2.3 Designing a Pilot Implementation Plan

Implementation is the final stage of any project. An implementation plan is a document that outlines the key steps, activities and resources required to bring a solution to market and put it into practice. Implementation plans can benefit greatly from prototyping it as a pilot or trial, as each plan should reflect new and distinctive pathways and processes that detail how a new solution is implemented.

Innovation project managers will benefit from designing a pilot implementation plan by breaking down the process into smaller steps for a smaller targeted market test, defining the timeline, resources and minimal capital needed. As a pilot or market trial, organizations and their innovation teams can learn from the feedback and adjust their final go-to-market plan, ensuring a broader adoption of the designed solution.

A pilot implementation plan reflects the common elements of a full implementation plan, but at a reduced scale and using simplified steps. The pilot or trial (as a model) affords the team an opportunity to learn from a small target segment and adjust accordingly for the larger market rollout. Designing a pilot implementation plan reflects the application of the Occam's Razor principle which favours simple explanations over complicated ones. Occam's Razor[7] implies the need to minimize the output (i.e. prototype or plan) to essential elements only, decreasing confusion and increasing clarity and function. practised extensively by information and communication designers, an effective plan should present only the necessary information in very subtle, yet clear and effective ways.

Designing an effective implementation plan demands the application of human-centred design principles. Implementation is both a communication and navigation process. It's vital to communicate to internal stakeholders the plan's role as the strategic vision. This will lead to increased cooperation and buy-in from across functions and departments, and ultimately aid in fostering a sustainable innovation culture.

Navigation of the elements and complexities of implementation is best experienced through the design and delivery of a pilot or trial plan. Most implementation plans are comprised of the following key elements: goals, target segment, tasks, resources and responsibilities, success metrics and evaluation strategies.

The following list provides a set of actions and questions required for the design of an effective pilot implementation plan:

- **Define goals**: What do you want to accomplish from introducing this new solution?
- **Identify target**: Who will you target for this pilot? Where will you locate and engage them?
- **Schedule tasks**: Which tasks, milestones and what deadlines and project timelines are required for the pilot?
- **Allocate resources and responsibilities**: What resources (time, money, and personnel) are needed to execute the pilot? Who will do what?
- **Measure success**: How will you determine and measure success from the trial?
- **Evaluate go-to-market strategy**: How will you evaluate the progress and measures during and after the pilot? How will you collect and integrate feedback? How often?

Like a recipe, the key elements represent the core ingredients that require further instructions on how best to integrate them and serve up the final dish to the end-user or customer. Design-driven implementation requires intent, ingredients and

---

7   Domingos (1999). The role of Occam's razor in knowledge discovery. *Data Mining and Knowledge Discovery*, *3*(4), 409–425.

instructions that involve both thinking and doing. Prototyping techniques such as journey maps, storyboards and blueprints are used extensively as planning techniques and borrow from information, communication and building designers' toolkits. Design techniques permeate business processes. For example, roadmaps simulate journey maps, MS PowerPoint presentations act as storyboards, and business plans, business models and website designs are like blueprints. Although you can use journey maps, storyboards and blueprints for prototyping plans, wayfinding is proposed for designing an integrative pilot implementation plan.

6.2.3.1 Wayfinding: Designing Better Plans and Pathways

Wayfinding is an effective strategy for designing clear pathways in new and unfamiliar places and situations. Wayfinding uses systems thinking to solve spatial problems. It encompasses all of the ways in which humans orient themselves in and navigate physical or virtual spaces. Systems thinking takes a holistic approach to understanding how different parts of a system behave, operates and interrelates. Wayfinding[8] combines information systems, signals and symbols to guide people through a new environment with the aim to enhance their understanding and experience of the space and services perceived as new or unfamiliar. Originally introduced by architects, this approach is used by anthropologists, biologists, psychologists and marketers, as it effectively influences orienting behaviour.

The **value of wayfinding** for organizations is as a communication tool, as it educates and informs project stakeholders and implementation teams where to begin and how to navigate to the intended destination. Wayfinding also offers a collaborative approach to planning, and supports an innovation-readiness for new systems, processes and for customers for new features and functions of the solution. By using this technique, the implementation plan is embraced and adopted by internal stakeholders, who in turn strategically guide the end-user to the new solution.

Implementation plans (and innovation roadmapping tools) can benefit greatly by incorporating wayfinding principles and visual language systems into their design.

Consider applying the following principles to your implementation plan design:
1. Develop a comprehensive, clear and consistent visual communication system with concise messaging.
2. Show only required information that is relevant to the location and navigation path.
3. Remove excessive information, for both internal and external stakeholders (i.e. innovation teams and end-users/customers).

---

[8] Gibson (2009). *The wayfinding handbook: Information design for public places*. Princeton Architectural Press.

PILOT IMPLEMENTATION PLAN (CHART BUILDER)

An implementation plan is a document that outlines the steps required to bring a solution to market and put it into practice.

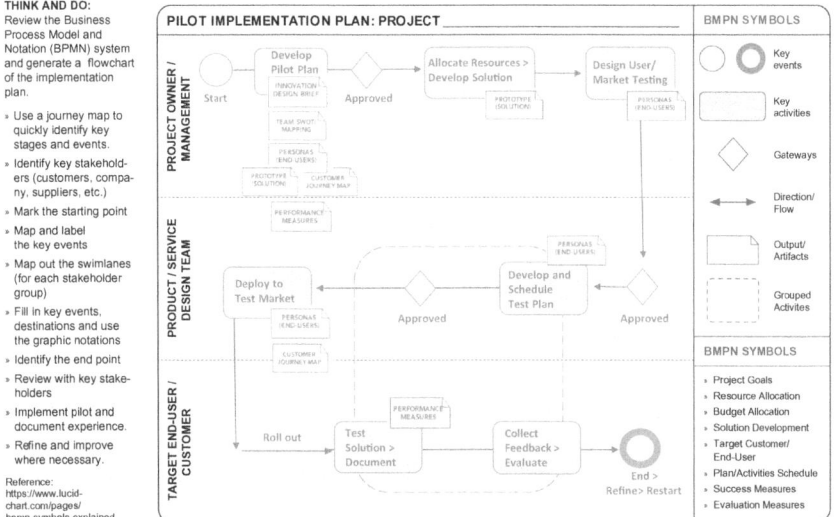

THINK AND DO:
Review the Business Process Model and Notation (BPMN) system and generate a flowchart of the implementation plan.

» Use a journey map to quickly identify key stages and events.
» Identify key stakeholders (customers, company, suppliers, etc.)
» Mark the starting point
» Map and label the key events
» Map out the swimlanes (for each stakeholder group)
» Fill in key events, destinations and use the graphic notations
» Identify the end point
» Review with key stakeholders
» Implement pilot and document experience.
» Refine and improve where necessary.

Reference:
https://www.lucidchart.com/pages/bpmn-symbols-explained

BDM STEP 4: SOLVE | PILOT IMPLEMENTATION PLAN (CHART BUILDER) WORKSHEET

◼ **Fig. 6.3** Sample BMPN chart of a pilot implementation plan

To quickly and effectively design a wayfinding system, use a standard business process notation tool. The Business Process Model Notation (BPMN) system[9] offers a universal communication system that can be customized for all types of plans and processes. BPMN is a graphic organizer that charts and models the key steps of a planned business process from end to end. It's designed to cover many types of process-based or flow-chart models and is comprised of graphical symbols and icons that represent key events (i.e. start and end), process types, directional flow, collaborations, conversations, document types and department levels.

BPMN's value is to offer a common language for bridging potential communication gaps that frequently exist between project owners, solution designers and implementers. An example of a pilot implementation plan design using BPMN is shown in ◼ Fig. 6.3. It highlights key events, activities, gates and process flow. Of note, it also shows and integrates the output (artifacts) generated from each of the Business Design Method steps.

The artefacts developed across the design-driven innovation process serve as important reference documents to facilitate a rapid, effective and aligned implementation plan across key stakeholder groups. Examples of the BDM outputs (as artifacts) are outlined in ◼ Fig. 6.4.

To increase your literacy with the Business Process Model Notation system, review and reference the complete guide to BPMN available from their website

---

9 von Rosing et al. (2015). *Business Process Model and Notation-BPMN*.

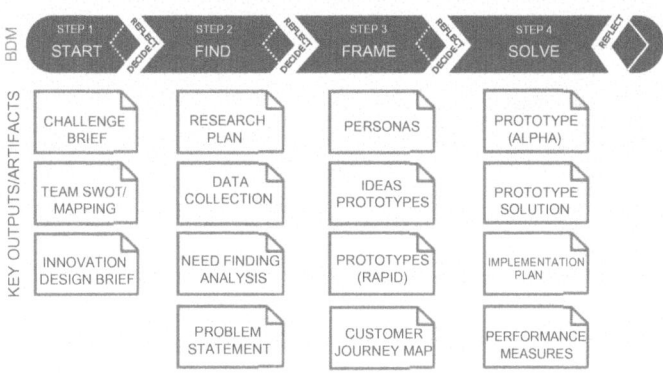

□ Fig. 6.4　List of key outputs and artefacts from each BDM step

source: ► https://www.omg.org/news/whitepapers/Business_Process_Model_and_Notation.pdf.

Story structures and the BMPN system are effective techniques that help shape the strategy and overarching vision for an implementation plan. They offer innovation teams an aligned narrative (and visual) that connects, guides and inspires them to progress forward. For time and task management, the creative approach to problem solving recommends that you make the necessary time available to meet your goal, based on available resources and priorities. Apply the most effective time-task approach (i.e. scheduler, project management application, etc.) to design and deliver an implementation plan pilot. The pilot implementation plan building template is located in ► Chapter 8.

6.2.4　Designing Performance Measures

Prototypes serve as proof of concept models that communicate and test ideas with both solution designers and end-users. Design-driven innovation demands an iterative approach to most activities, from generating problem hypotheses, to insights and proposed solutions. In addition to implementation plans, evaluation models also benefit from iterations and prototyping.

Testing ideas, solutions and plans introduces the notion of risk-reward and failure-success. The risk-reward relationship suggests the higher the risk, the greater the potential reward, while the failure-success relationship requires a mental model shift that accepts failure as a pre-condition of success.

Success metrics generally indicate an end goal or final objective, but are rarely used to define and measure progress-based achievements or milestones leading to the end goal. Design-driven innovation requires performance measures of both progress (including failure as trial and error) and success. Performance measures are evaluative indicators that represent progress towards a desired impact of a project and the degree of impact or success. The most relevant indicators for

◘ Table 6.6 KPIs vs CPMs: sample performance metrics and measures

Traditional KPIs	Contemporary Performance Measures (CPMs)
Financial Performance Index	Financial Performance Strategies
Net Profit Margin	Profitability Analysis
Revenue per Client	Customer Experience Value
Customer Retention Score	Customer Satisfaction and Retention Scale
Employee Engagement Rate	Employee Satisfaction and Retention Scale
Conversion Rate	Innovation Development Project Launches
Operational Efficiency Ratio	Quality Process Management Value

design-driven innovation projects are Contemporary Performance Measures.[10] **These modern performance measures offer a holistic approach to success, learning from both the process and the output and the trials and errors along the journey.**

Contemporary Performance Measures (or CPMs) are a set of qualitative and quantitative measures to gauge a company's non-financial and financial performance. CPMs evolved from Key Performance Indicators (KPIs), which are a set of quantitative measures or metrics used to gauge a company's overall long-term financial performance. While KPIs are cost and profit-oriented, CPMs are information and behaviour-oriented. KPIs use cost-accounting and financial frameworks such as profit-loss analysis and financial forecasting models, while CPMs use multi-dimensional and customizable frameworks such as the Balanced Scorecard[11] and the Performance Prism[12] for management decision-making. Sample measures for both KPIs and CPMs are outlined in ◘ Table 6.6.

CPMs use dashboards, while KPIs use spreadsheets to communicate performance measures. Modern organizations seeking to foster an innovative culture, knowledge-based systems and structures, and looking to design sustainable business models, are adopting CPMs and evolving their traditional KPIs. CPMs are primarily non-financial measures related to business strategy. CPMs change over time as needs change, are simple and easy to use, provide fast feedback to operators and managers, and are designed to foster improvement rather than to simply monitor performance.

Design-driven innovation positions customers (external and internal) as the principle barometer of growth, and the most accurate predictor of organizational performance. Therefore, new Innovation Performance Measures (IPMs) are required as part of an evolution from CPMs to measures that better reflect the progress, success and failure (as learnings) of the innovation development and

---

10 Franco-Santos et al. (2012). Contemporary performance measurement systems: A review of their consequences and a framework for research. *Management Accounting Research, 23*(2), 79–119.
11 Kaplan and Norton (2005). The balanced scorecard: Measures that drive performance. *Harvard Business Review, 83*(7), 172.
12 Neely et al. (2001). The performance prism in practice. *Measuring Business Excellence.*

Table 6.7 Innovation performance measures and the three-factors framework

Factor	Key questions	IPMs (examples only)
Desirable	Will customers want your solution? Do they need it? How will you measure their desire or delight—financially and non-financially (quantitatively and qualitatively)?	Financial: • New product/service sales • Customer lifetime value • Online marketing ROI
		Non-Financial: • Customer satisfaction score • Earned media mentions • Customer engagement
Feasible	Does the company have the capabilities to offer and deliver the innovative solution? How will you evaluate the company's abilities to design and deliver—financially and non-financially (quantitatively and qualitatively)?	Financial: • Operational efficiency • Human capital cost • Technology infrastructure investment
		Non-Financial: • Core competency levels • Employee retention • Employee engagement scale
Viable	Will your solution create customer value and generate revenues? How will you measure impact—financially and non-financially (quantitatively and qualitatively)?	Financial: • Revenue per client • Cost per Acquisition • Revenue share of innovations
		Non-Financial: • Net Promoter Score (NPS) • Innovation rate = number of inventions/number of new products (innovations) • Waste reduction goals

design process. The proposed IPMs reflect CPMs and integrate Customer Success Indicators (CSI). CSIs are customer centred KPIs that include customer retention, conversion rate and Net Promoter Score (NPS). CSIs orient companies to focus more on fostering a customer service culture by: gaining customer loyalty with quality products, offering excellent customer support service and retaining engaged employees. A sample list of IPMs is outlined in ◘ Table 6.7.

Innovation Performance Measures (IPMs) require a different framework for decision-making. The Three-Factors measurement framework is introduced as a contemporary performance measures (CPMs) technique to identify and design relevant measures as key indicators of an innovative solution's progress and success. The Three-Factors framework aids in identifying both non-financial and financial measures across the three critical innovation factors for a firm: desirable, feasible and viable.

What specific measures (indicators) will you define for your proposed prototype solution? Refer to the Three-Factors Measurement Framework template in ► Chapter 8 to identify the project's performance measures.

Case: **How Creative BC designed its rise to relevance**
When a new CEO joined Creative BC in 2015, the organization was meeting the minimal expectations of what a non-profit quasi-government agency offered their creative industry clients.

Creative BC (CrBC) is an independently managed society mandated by the provincial government to develop and grow the creative industry sector in British Columbia, Canada. Through programs and services, CrBC supports the province's creative industries, which include motion picture, music, publishing, interactive and digital media industries.

At the start of 2016, the agency was seen by many as a necessary evil where film, book, animation and other industries could get much-needed government funding and then get to work. The existing programs were outdated and did not reflect the industries' changing needs. The office location and physical space were not conducive to collaborative and strategic activities, which are necessary to deliver on their mandate to aggressively grow and sustain the creative industries. The entry door was blocked by a pillar, the teams were divided into small offices and across two floors accessible only from the outside. The CEO observed these issues as symbolic of a closed organization, highlighting that her own office was positioned at the very back of the building, at the end of long a dark hallway. If she was in, and you had a reason to talk to her, you would navigate the labyrinth to that back office and discover a young woman exuding a mix of warmth, candour and confidence—stemming from her years in the broadcast and telecommunications industries.

The new CEO faced the challenge of evolving Creative BC from grant funder to strategic partner to B.C.'s cultural and creative industry organizations. Following many discussions with a design-driven innovation researcher at the University of British Columbia, the CEO embraced an accelerated design planning process tasked with discovering client needs, and delivering a strategic plan, within four months. This initiative was positioned as an action research study to design and deliver a service innovation plan and document the process and impact.

Motivated to better define client-centred strategic goals and key performance measures, the CEO and researcher outlined a three-month intervention involving the business design steps of starting, finding, framing and solving. Over 80 stakeholders (internal and external) were invited to participate in the series of design sessions, with the aim to gain insight into client needs, helping Creative BC transform into a strategic partner, and provide evidence of a design-driven innovation approach.

The task: build a clearer mandate and stakeholder trust
A central question in the generative sessions (workshops) of 2016 was how Creative BC might expand beyond a role of funding mechanism to become an organization that could proactively help grow B.C.'s cultural industries. Using a design-driven innovation approach, planning sessions involved empathy interviews, prototyping concepts, scenarios and action plans as a way to quickly determine whether a concept, strategy or action should be pursued or discarded.

The initial business challenges included:

- Understanding the size, scale, impact and potential of the creative industries British Columbia's and Canada's economy (beyond basic GDP and jobs statistics).
- Improving the perception of B.C.'s creative industries' market value.
- Providing B.C.'s creative sector with a distinct identity that transcended such U.S.-based concepts as 'Hollywood North' and 'Silicon North'.
- Creating a better balance in B.C.'s cultural industries between a thirst for new ideas through entrepreneurial drive, and the promotion of existing expertise.
- Strengthening the use of industry-specific expertise and successes in B.C.—such as in film and television, and interactive media and gaming—to engage in more innovative and sustainable business practices.
- Gathering and positioning data and market intelligence on B.C.'s creative ecosystem to make informed decisions on growth opportunities, funding programs and talent retention activities.
- Pushing creative industry leaders to practise 'outside-in', customer-centric thinking and action.
- Helping industry overcome the negative effects of the high costs of working and living in B.C., home to one of the most livable but expensive cities in the world.

The methods: From the outset, the task was to produce an 'innovation', in the name of a service innovation plan for B.C.'s creative industries. The goal was to produce a flexible, cross-disciplinary and strategic approach that would be a practical and innovative response to a volatile and competitive environment. A version of the business design process (as strategic design) had been delivered to UBC students and a variety of organizations over six years. The process involved framing and reframing needs and issues, by gathering a set of observations, searching for important patterns and leading to a customer-centric identification of challenges and opportunities for Creative BC's clients and stakeholders.

The design sessions introduced a suite of techniques that explored client needs, challenge framing and problem solving. A stakeholder map was co-created with stakeholders to identify, show and discuss the relationships between Creative BC and their clients, collaborators and competitors. Business frameworks such as SWOT were combined with empathy maps to identity issues and needs relating to the industry clients and collaborators. Session participants engaged in storyboarding to prototype scenarios and new program offerings. Creative BC's internal stakeholders, including board members co-created the organization's first Balanced Scorecard with clear and actionable goals, and associated performance measures.

The impact: The business design process was not familiar to both Creative BC nor their stakeholders, and therefore was not an easy sell. The initial frustration with the non-linear process was in how different things were broken down, the complexity of the creative industry sector and how they intersected. The sessions generated important outputs, which were shared with all participants via weekly emails. Visual journey boards were installed in the CrBC offices, enabling internal stakeholders to literally see the outputs from each session and the entire progress of the strategic innovation project.

The client challenges surfaced during the session included:
- Poor communication within their own creative sector, with governments and between industry sectors.
- Lack of understanding and connection into B.C., Canada and the global creative economy.
- Lack of standardization, benchmarks and data to effectively measure their performance.
- Lack of incentives to engage and collaborate across creative industries, other jurisdictions and with other industries and sectors.
- Lack of knowledge of market needs, opportunities and emerging trends to develop new products and services.
- Volatility of Canadian currency and multi-level government priorities.

In response to those challenges, a new 'service innovation' plan highlighted four key actions:
1. Positioning B.C.'s creative industries to compete to win, chiefly through Creative BC's role as an economic development service provider and a driver of collaboration in the creative sector.
2. Creating a growth culture for B.C.'s creative industries, through experimentation and innovation.
3. Showing and telling B.C.'s creative industries stories.
4. Attracting, building and retaining the best creative talent.

The key performance measures for this initiative were mapped across the four action strategic framework and included:
- Business Strategy: Position B.C.'s creative industries to compete to win. *Measures: Government and industry funding; GDP; job creation: program applications; industry awards; etc.*
- Growth Strategy: Create a growth culture for B.C.'s creative industries. *Measures: New industry association partnerships: data collection programs; business collaboration projects; etc.*
- Communication Strategy: Show and Tell B.C.'s creative industry stories. *Measures: promotion programs; media releases; media impressions; job postings; diversity index; etc.*
- Resource Strategy: Attract, build and retain the best creative talent. *Measures: Creative industry data programs: Start-up investment programs; cross-sector training programs; etc.*
- Additionally, key business performance measures were added to include:

Stakeholder engagement: Because so many stakeholders were invited to those 2016 sessions that helped bake a new strategic plan, there's a new confidence that Creative BC is doing the right things for industry. 'To me, the biggest thing that came out of that design exercise was the building of trust, not only from within the organization itself, but from our industry stakeholders', says the chair of the Creative BC board, whose experience includes 25 years with a notable TV production company. 'The consultation process ensured that their voices were heard. And those voices helped us identify Creative BC's challenges, including getting buy-in from government'.

Trusted strategic expertise: It used to be difficult for Creative BC to get meetings with a Government of BC minister or deputy minister, but that has changed. Creative BC's CEO is now a recognized player in B.C.'s creative industries, a tireless advocate who finds herself at the table for key discussions. 'Creative BC now has, not just an active voice, but a clear and responsible voice in the creative ecosystem that incudes government and the industry associations', says an EVP of a north American film production company and recent Creative BC board member. 'This voice is not just a cheerleader, and not just a contrarian. The leadership is clear in terms of how industry should deal with government, and also very clear in terms of weighing in on what industry should be paying attention to'.

Empathic and Inclusive Leadership: One of those areas is inclusion and diversity, hot button issues that film EVP says B.C.'s creative industries tended to approach with what she calls 'conflict avoidance'. The new CEO stepped up with a 'willingness to make people uncomfortable' around those issues, coming in with such a strong voice around anything was a bit of a shock to the system, 'It definitely has to do with the fact that she's a woman, and a woman of colour. But it's also because the culture in those groups, as defined mainly by the old white man leadership—individuals I absolutely adore, by the way—were very conflict avoidant. She came in ready to shake those things up'.

Innovate the Creative Industries Impact Index: One of the key findings of the design-driven innovation workshops was a need to properly measure the impacts of B.C.'s cultural industries. Only then could you gauge their growth or how that growth might be influenced by funding. The challenge was to ensure that Creative BC wasn't using a mix of scattered data devoid of rigour and consistency. Following the diffusion of the new service innovation plan, the Creative BC executives developed a Creative Industries Economic Results Assessment framework (CIERA) to measure GDP, jobs and output in B.C. The prototype integrates public datasets from Statistics Canada and delivers economic indicators for the sector. It measures nine enabling factors as key indicators to measure the sector's 'health' and societal value contribution.

Currently, Creative BC works out of a bright new office, and thanks to a timely switch from a reliance on paper files to a sophisticated electronics database, finds itself better equipped—especially during the COVID-19 pandemic—to deliver on its core mandate of getting funding out to members of B.C.'s cultural industries. In 2019, those industries represented $5.15 billion in direct, indirect and induced gross domestic product. And while there's still some debate about exactly what Creative BC should be, it's now considered to be much more than a funding apparatus, even as it awarded more than $10.2 million in grants to 635 B.C. creators and companies in 2019–2020.

The CEO's provocative approach would never have worked, however, without some acknowledgement among those stakeholder groups that Creative BC was representing their interests. Creative BC earned that mandate through the design-driven strategic planning that helped everyone zero in on how the agency needed to change.

6.2.5 Part II: Review and Reflection

The implementation stage or **BDM Step 4: Solve**, involves the critical activities associated with final prototyping, solution development and implementation planning and evaluation. Implementation plans, similar to ideas and proposed solutions, benefit greatly from prototyping and testing. Considering these plans are designed to deliver a new and innovative solution, they should reflect an organization's adaptation to market changes and evolving economic climates. Well-designed plans contain elements and internal structures that are recombined and rearranged, reflecting the innovative or novel solution's introduction and diffusion pathway. Performance measures also require careful thought and strategic crafting. It's important to identify the right innovation performance measures (IPMs) that assess the levels of desirability, feasibility and viability with the designed solution. The most effective frameworks offer both the ability to qualify and quantify the measures and the probabilities of achieving them.

Students: Reflect on topics presented and answer the following:
- What is the value of prototyping an implementation plan?
- How might you develop influential storytelling skills?
- What are examples of key innovation performance measures?

Reflect on the experience with prototyping, storytelling, implementation plan development and evaluation.

"This course really challenged me to think creatively in designing a solution. It was interesting to see how much our group pivoted as we progressed through our research and prototyping. Also, it goes to say how I was able to build my collaborative skills."—Commerce student

Reflective Practice and Design

Supplementary Information The online version contains supplementary material available at (▶ https://doi.org/10.1007/978-3-030-86489-7_7).

© The Author(s), under exclusive license to Springer Nature Switzerland AG 2022
A. Beausoleil, *Business Design Thinking and Doing*,
https://doi.org/10.1007/978-3-030-86489-7_7

> **Learning Objectives**
> At the end of this chapter, readers will be able to:
> – Describe the importance of reflective practice.
> – Assess learning challenges and successes.
> – Reflect on the value of reflection on business design.

7.1 Introduction

This chapter introduces the practice and value of reflection. It outlines different strategies and frameworks for reflective practice in design-oriented activities and beyond. Although each chapter (as module) offers a series of reflection prompts, this chapter outlines why reflection is important for innovation participants, managers and leaders. It also offers a set of reflection techniques for individuals and teams to pause and reconsider each stage and step before proceeding to the next one.

7.1.1 Warm Up Exercise: Success Paths

> *Warm ups* prepare students to engage in the exploration of new topics or techniques. Similar to fitness or sport-based warm ups, individuals engage in a quick and gentle introduction to a topic and become more comfortable and confident with its relevance and broader application.
> **Success Paths** is a reflective thinking exercise involving one's experience with a new project and its path towards success. Reflect on your individual experience with launching a new project, and your relationship with success.
> **How to**: Think of a past experience associated with a new project:
>
> – Take a sheet of paper (or tablet), use a pen/pencil (or stylus), draw two boxes side by side. Label one box as (A) and the other box as (B).
> – In box (A) quickly draw a line that represents a success path.
> – In box (B) quickly draw a line that represents a realistic pathway towards success.
>
> **Duration**: 1 minute.
> **Discuss**: Ask students/participants to share their two success paths with their cohort. Discuss the differences and/or similarities between the two paths. Explain that typically, the first path to success is smooth, unidirectional and leans upward to the right, which is an aspirational vision of the experience. Next, explain that the second path typically reflects past experiences, with the line drawn to show circles or sharp angles, and is multi-directional before moving upward to the right. Discuss the meaning of these, the difference between perceived and realistic success pathways, and highlight that the path to success is full of uncertainty and complications.

> **Reflective Prompt**: Ask students/participants to reflect on their sketches as visual representations of their experience with success. Can they further describe their positive and negative experience with success? What issues do the pathways raise? How can we learn to better navigate and lead others through the unpaved paths of uncertainty? Use the template provided in ▶ Chapter 8.

7.2 Reflection Is the Most Impactful Strategy

Through their leaders, managers and teams, organizations require the development of skills and competencies that can be shared within and sustained. Through the practice of reflection, companies learn how to grow and what to focus on so that work continues to improve and prosperity ensues.

Reflection is a cognitive theory and practice that we all benefit from, regardless of sector, role or rank. Cognitive and social psychologists have long studied the relation between thought and action, particularly how beliefs, self-perceptions and intentions shape and direct our behaviour. Essentially, what people think, believe and feel affects how they behave. Introduce an environment or situation, and our thoughts and actions (as interactions) are further affected. Design-driven innovation creates an environment that requires a balance of thinking and doing. Thinking requires reflection, while doing is action informed from that reflection.

How we behave or act is directly correlated to our thoughts, making **reflection the most impactful and important strategy for all of us**. Through reflection and reflective practice, we develop the ability to better define problems, think critically and creatively, negotiate and navigate uncertainty and complexity, and communicate effectively and empathically.

Reflection involves self-analysis through reflective thinking. Reflective thinking is the process of self-examination of one's own knowledge, feelings, values and beliefs in order to understand and justify one's actions. Reflective thinking is focussed on why we do things the way we do, and helps us consider other approaches.

Critical reflective thinking, or critical reflection, involves analyzing a situation, proposing a justification and challenging our assumption of that justification. This process of critical analysis, synthesis and questioning has guided organizational leaders to make more informed decisions in their respective contexts.

Reflection is triggered by a series of prompts. For example, managers may ask themselves:

- Are my values aligned with my organization?
- Do we have a sustainable business model?
- Am I following my business plan? And if not, what could I be doing differently?
- Do we need to evolve our products, services or processes to better align with customer needs?
- Do I have the right skill sets to reach my goals?

- Are we actively investing in employee skills development?
- Which problem are we trying to solve? Why is it important?

Reflective practice puts value in our past experiences as a starting point for learning. With reflective thinking frameworks, we think about our experiences in purposeful ways, seek to understand and learn from them, and then take strategic action. Reflection requires deliberate or conscious thinking about things, and making decisions (doing). It's practised through **cycles** of experiences, learnings and actions, which are key to moving forward and evolving as professionals, managers and leaders. **Reflective practice is all about learning through and from experiences**. Reflection offers a systematic way for managers to assess situations, for teams to question assumptions, and for instructors to assess student progress and teaching impact.

Over the past 50 years, various frameworks have been employed by multiple sectors, and they're summarized and briefly described in ◘ Table 7.1.

Schön's reflective model[1] is often cited as the foundational model, as it introduced a '**reflection-in-action** and **reflection-on-action**' framework based on reflecting during and after an event. Reflection-in-action describes the capacity of individuals to consciously think about what they are doing while they are doing it (as it happens). Reflection-on-action describes the capacity of individuals to have hindsight or reflect our past reflections (after it happens). Schön observed that both reflection types aim to influence one's behaviour—immediately as 'in-action' or afterwards as in 'on-action'. Both are highly valued as strategies for self-improvement and personal growth.

Kolb's learning model[2] outlines four stages for reflection through educational experiences: **concrete experience, reflective observation, abstract conceptualization active experimentation**. This model is referred to as the 'experiential learning model', and is based on our own experiences, which are reviewed, analyzed and evaluated systematically across four stages. Once this process is completed, the new experiences will form the starting point for the next cycle.

Gibbs' reflective cycle model[3] proposes a systematic way for people to think about a past experience (event or activity) and is described as 'learning by doing'. He introduced six phases or stages that include: **describe** the experience **identify** the feelings and thoughts about the experience; **evaluate** the experience, both good and bad; **analyze** and make sense of the situation; **conclude** on what you learned and what you could have done differently; and, **create an action plan** for how you would deal with similar situations in the future, or general changes you might find appropriate. This model can be used by individuals or teams—either on a single event or situation, or on repeated events—and can be serve to frame

---

1   Shön (1983). *The reflective practitioner*. New York: Basic Books.
2   Kolb (1984). *Experiential learning: Experience as the source of learning and development*. Englewood Cliffs, NJ: Prentice Hall.
3   Gibbs (1988). *Learning by doing: A guide to teaching and learning methods.* London: Further Education Unit. Oxford: Oxford Polytechnic.

☐ **Table 7.1** Reflective practice frameworks (adapted for this textbook)

Framework	Author(s)	Key elements
Reflective Model	Schön (1978)	1. **Reflection-in-action**: the capacity to consciously think about what you are doing while you are doing it (as it happens) 2. **Reflection-on-action**: the capacity to have hindsight or reflect on your past reflections (after it happens)
Kolb Learning Model	Kolb (1984)	1. **Concrete experience**: the conscious and physical experience of a situation, and a description of what you see, how you feel and what you think 2. **Reflective observation**: from your description of the experience, a deeper reflection on what has happened in that situation. Ask…. what worked? what failed? why did the situation arise? And why did you behave the way you did? etc 3. **Abstract conceptualization**: based on the answers to your reflective observation questions, ask what could you have done better or differently? how can you improve? 4. **Active experimentation**: take your own reflections and thoughts and identify improvements and experiment with new strategies
Reflective Cycle Model	Gibb (1988)	1. **Describe** the experience 2. **Describe** the feelings and thoughts about the experience 3. **Evaluate** the experience, both good and bad 4. **Analyze** and make sense of the situation 5. **Conclude** what you learned and what you could have done differently 6. **Create an action plan** for how you would deal with similar situations in the future, or general changes you might find appropriate
Critical Reflection Model	Rolfe, G., Freshwater, D., & Jasper, M. (2001)	1. **Descriptive: What** …did you learn?… were you trying to achieve?…feeling did it evoke in others? 2. **Theoretical: So What**…does it tell me?…could I have done to improve it? …is my new understanding of…? 3. **Action-oriented: Now What**…do I need to do to make things better? … might be the consequences of change?

(continued)

◨ **Table 7.1** (continued)

Framework	Author(s)	Key elements
Five Rs Reflection Framework	Bain, J.D., Ballantyne, R., Mills, C., & Lester, N.C. (2002)	1. **Reporting**: what happened? who was involved? 2. **Responding**: what worked? how did you feel? 3. **Relating**: what is relevant? how does this connect with other experiences? 4. **Reasoning**: what is your explanation based upon? 5. **Reconstructing**: what conclusions can you draw upon?
ERA Cycle of Reflective Practice Model	Jasper, M. (2013)	1. **Experience**: a thing that happens to you (a situation) 2. **Reflection**: reflective processes that enable learning from the experience 3. **Action**: results from the new perspectives that are taken

project team meetings. Management coaches use this model to guide executives to think more deeply about an experience, activity or event, making them aware of their own actions. That reflection makes them more able to adjust and change their behaviour.

Rolfe et al.'s critical reflection model[4] offers a three-question framework: what, so what and now what. The questions act as prompts to examine an experience, relate the experience to wider knowledge and identify implications for your specific practice. This framework is a popular practice in health care.

Bain et al.'s 5Rs model[5] describes five elements as stages of reflective practice that include: **reporting, responding, reasoning, relating and reconstructing**. This model guides a critical reflection of a learning experience. The first stage reports on the experience. The second responds to the experience through observations and thoughts. The third stage relates the observations to past experiences and existing knowledge. The fourth stage provides reasons for significant learnings from the experience, and the fifth stage reconstructs the experience based on the significant learnings, then plans for improvements and future actions.

And finally, Jasper's ERA model[6] is a simplified version of Rolfe et al.'s model and offers novice reflection practitioners three steps: **experience, reflection** and **action**. This framework is based on building understanding from an experience, reflecting on and learning from that experience, and then having the reflected experience lead to action.

---

4 Rolfe et al. (2001). Critical reflection for nursing and the helping professions a User's Guide.
5 Bain et al. (2002) *Reflecting on practice: Student teachers' perspectives*. Kansas City: Post Pressed, Flaxton.
6 Jasper (2003). *Beginning reflective practice*. Nelson Thornes.

Regardless of which model or framework you choose, reflection demands commitment and repeated practice. For innovation design and development teams, they offer a foundational strategy to meet the following objectives:

- To identify new skills and new ways of learning.
- To identify new courses of action.
- To explore different ways of solving problems.
- To build self-awareness of our thoughts and actions.
- To demonstrate competence and confidence in one's abilities.
- To build evidence or a business case from observations.
- To help us make decisions or resolve uncertainty.
- For personal or professional development.

Designers are taught to challenge the assumptions imposed on a problem space. We ask questions, collect facts and craft insights to better define a needs-based problem. As reflective creative problem solvers, we view and define problems from unarticulated desires and cobble ideas from multiple disciplines.

In organizations, reflection is often practised by challenging the status quo, questioning assumptions or flipping orthodoxies (as ingrained assumptions). The phrase '**challenge the status quo**' suggests an exploration of the current state of affairs or how things are currently done and then, asking 'what if' and 'why not'. By questioning and exploring existing processes, systems and products, we can better understand the influential values and beliefs resulting in actions or behaviours (e.g. what if we replaced fresh produce plastic bags with cardboard boxes?).

Questioning assumptions describes the act of critically examining a belief, opinion, statement or bias. Considering that assumptions may be biased, incorrect or misguided, it's important to question and examine their validity. Questions might include 'why', 'how' and 'what is' (e.g. why do rushed grocery shoppers not use baskets?).

Flipping orthodoxies is the act of upturning or inverting tightly held organizational beliefs and paradigms to see how they can be improved. Asking 'what if', 'why and why not' and 'what next'? (e.g. why don't we reorganize our store shelves to combine fresh produce with shelf-stable foods?).

> **Business examples**: Netflix challenged the status quo of the video rental business and offered home delivery and convenient returns. Whole Foods questioned the assumption that grocery shoppers were task-oriented vs experience-seeking and sustainably motivated. Amazon flipped several orthodoxies from its online book selling business model and e-book offerings to launch convenient online ordering and delivery of everything, including fresh groceries.

While existing systems and orthodoxies are important in creating standardized and efficient practices for individuals and institutions, they can also lead to risk aversion, change avoidance and biased decision-making. And that can prevent organizations from improving and innovating. To challenge the status quo, question assumptions or flip orthodoxies, courage is required. We must be brave and grant ourselves permission to challenge, question and explore the choices, decisions and actions of ourselves and others.

So, how can individuals and teams challenge the status quo in their organizations? Consider the following principles:

- Create a culture of curiosity (at all levels).
- Encourage measures focussed on questions vs answers.
- Practice asking the right questions (hint: use 5 Whys).
- Prioritize problems and needs.
- Gather allies and collaborators.
- Lead by example.
- Defer judgement and retain your objectivity.
- Bravely persevere.

7.2.1 Teaching, Learning and Assessing Reflective Practice

Reflective practice, or reflection, is the process of exploring and examining ourselves, our teams, organizations and experiences. Reflection through introspection helps us gain deep insight into our choices and decisions, so that we can assess how to move forward.

Introspection is an individual process that demands personal 'thinking' time spent alone in self-reflection, self-examination and self-exploration. Instructors and trainers can teach students to self-reflect (or introspect) by asking them the right questions. The 'right' questions should direct the students (or participants) to:

- reflect on their personal perceptions of their abilities vis-à-vis their understanding of a specific body of knowledge or topic.
- see the importance and significance of their own learning process.
- be motivated by the process of learning.
- confidently express their thoughts, feelings and emotions.

Asking questions at the end of each chapter, module or exercise is reflective practice.

The most common technique for reflection is writing, using words to describe and probe an experience. A reflective essay or paper is most often used for a self-analysis of a reading, video, podcast or situation (as experience). The essay aims to illustrate the writer's understanding and impression of the material, their feelings about it, how it affects their point of view, and how it may affect possible decisions or actions in the future.

The narrative follows the traditional format of an introduction, body and conclusion. The popular reflection essay (paper or blog) is most aligned with the

Bains et al. (2002) 5Rs reflective model comprised of reporting, responding, reasoning, relating and reconstructing. This model guides both teacher and student along the reflective practice path (◘ Table 7.2).

Reflection activities enable productive cognitive processing time, and that's essential for students (participants and leaders) to make sense of a new experience, situation or information. Reflective practice can be adapted to diverse contexts and constraints. The following exercise (Reflection Paper) can be introduced at any stage of the innovation development process or following any lesson, module or chapter.

◘ Table 7.2 Bain's 5Rs of reflection framework

Elementa	Description	Reflective questions
Reporting	Provide a descriptive account of the situation	• What happened, what did the situation involve? • Who was involved? • What seems significant to pay attention to?
Responding	Record your response to the situation or issue	• What worked well? How do I know it worked well? • What worked least well? Why do I think that? • How did I feel, and what made me feel that way? How were others feeling, and what made them feel that way? • How did I respond emotionally/personally/behaviourally to the situation?
Relating	Describe your understanding of the situation/issue and how it relates to a context	• What body of knowledge is relevant—and in what ways? • How does this connect with other personal/professional experiences I have had, and in what ways?
Reasoning	Explore and explain the situation/issue	• What is my explanation for what happened, and on what is it based?
Reconstructing	Draw a conclusion and develop an action plan based on insightful understanding of the situation/issue	• What conclusions can I draw? How do I justify these? • With hindsight, would I do something differently next time and why? • What has this taught me about my practice? about myself? • How will I use this experience to further improve my practice in the future?

7.2.1.1 Exercise: Reflection Paper

A reflection paper is a document that outlines an analysis of an experience (or document, video, book, podcast that was heard and experienced). It aims to illustrate your understanding of the material, and how it affects your point of view and possible decisions or actions in future.

Description
- Write a description of the experience
- What are the key issues from this description that are important?

Reflection
- What was I trying to achieve?
- Why did I act as I did?
- What are the consequences of my actions?
  - For the end-user (or customer)?
  - For my team and organization?
  - For myself?
- How did I feel about this experience when it was happening?
- How did the end-user/customer feel about it?
- How do I know how the end-user/customer felt about it?

Influencing factors
- What internal factors influenced my decision-making and actions?
- What external factors influenced my decision-making and actions?
- What sources of knowledge did or should have influenced my decision-making and actions?

Alternative strategies
- Could I have dealt better with the situation?
- What other choices did I have?
- What would be the consequences of these other choices?

Learning
- How can I make sense of this experience in light of past experience and future practice?
- How do I feel about this experience, now?
- Have I taken effective action to support myself and others as a result of this experience?
- How has this experience changed my way of knowing or acting?

A template is provided in ▶ Chapter 8.

Adapted from Johns, C. (1994) Nuances of reflection. Journal of Clinical Nursing 3, 71–75.

Reflection devices can be seen everywhere from childhood diaries to online blogs. Other reflection techniques include journaling, one-minute paper, free writing and free drawing. Instructors and facilitators can act as coaches to guide students or participants through the practice of reflection.

7.2.1.2 Exercise: Journaling

Journaling is reflective writing technique that involves regular recording of events or thoughts. By capturing your thoughts through writing notes, you make them visible and gain insight into what is difficult to see. Journaling is an effective tool for problem framing and problem solving.
How to: Find a journaling medium that suits your needs (paper based or electronic). Make a habit of journaling, writing down your thoughts, ideas and questions regularly.

7.2.1.3 Exercise: One-Minute Paper

A one-minute paper is a reflection-on-action thinking technique introduced at the end of a lesson or topic, and it lasts 60-seconds (one minute). Participants are asked to reflect on the topic or lesson and generate a short paper that captures one key learning and one question about that learning.
How to: Take a blank sheet of paper (or blank computer document), introduce the key learning, reflect on it and which question and/or action it elicits, and generate a conclusion from your quick reflection. Take one minute to complete the paper.

7.2.1.4 Exercise: Free Writing

Free writing is a reflection-in-action technique in which a person writes continuously for a set period of time without regard to grammar, spelling or structure. It produces rough sentences and encourages judgement-free writing. It is helpful with writer's block, creative thinking and warming up to writing a full essay or paper.

How to: Take a blank sheet of paper (blank computer document), plunge in and start to write. If you don't know what to say, write that. Write whatever comes to your mind, whether it's on the subject or off it. Keep writing for a minimum of five minutes.

7.2.1.5 Exercise: Free Drawing

Free drawing is a reflection-in-action technique in which a person draws or sketches continuously for a set period of time without regard to aesthetic, topic or artistic judgement. It is helpful with artist's block, creative thinking and warming up to designing, crafting or communicating an idea or concept.

> **How to**: Take a blank sheet of paper (or blank computer document), plunge in and start to sketch using the language of lines. Sketch whatever comes to your mind, whether it is on the subject or off it. Take small risks with expressing yourself visually. Keep sketching for a minimum of five minutes.

Reflection is also a useful systematic reviewing process for teachers that's used to assess a specific learning experience and how the students are progressing (or not) through a lesson. Again, the 5Rs model serves as an effective reflection assessment framework and is particularly useful for designing rubrics (i.e. for the reflective essay or one-minute paper). A scoring table (◘ Table 7.3) suggests values based on levels, ranging from 1 = reporting to 5 = reconstructing. For trainers, consider applying the levels to a competency or performance measures chart.

7.2.2 Reflecting on Business Management Tools

Reflective practice harnesses the power of critical thinking for any situation, in a classroom or workplace. Reflection is all about self-improvement.

◘ **Table 7.3** Reflective practice rubric example (applying Bain's 5Rs model)

Levels	Description	Performance criteria
Reporting (Level 1)	Narrative describes the experience or event with no evidence of reflection	The student describes an experience as a series of observations with no judgement or insight
Responding (Level 2)	Narrative outlines learnings without explicit links to supporting evidence	The student makes an observation or judgement without making any further inferences or detailing the reasons for the judgement
Relating (Level 3)	Narrative provides analysis from both personal assessment and external evidence of lessons learned	The student identifies key observations of the experience that has personal meaning, and connects it with prior or current experience
Reasoning (Level 4)	Narrative explicitly refers to prior experiences and describes how they informed behaviour	The student integrates the key observations and judgements into an associative relationship, involving transformation or conceptualization
Reconstructing (Level 5)	Narrative integrates previous experience with current events and insights to inform future action	The student extracts and internalizes the personal significance of the experience, and describes ways to extend learning from the reflection

Reflective thinking involves a structured way of thinking back on school or workplace experience, and related actions. Reflective practice is designed to help students (and employees) to think more deeply about an experience, how it made you feel, and what you can learn from it. Reflective thinking is an important and practical tool for informed and confident decision-making that leads to trusting your own decisions and becoming a better team member (or employee).

Traditional management tools such as SWOT, Porter's Five Forces, PESTLE analysis and Blue Ocean Strategy (BOS) frameworks aim to provide insight into external factors (and some internal capabilities) which can support a competitive advantage for a product and/or market strategy. These devices remain useful in helping organizations understand the forces and factors affecting their profitability and potential prosperity. They remain important tools to inform decisions relating to macro-level strategies involving industry sector, verticals and competitors. They provide a high-level view of their industry competitors and internal capacity, but are not designed to gain insight into a manager's or leader's motivations, beliefs or values.

Few management frameworks integrate reflection into their designs. Of note, management theorist Peter Drucker proposed a human-centred approach to management focussed on innovative and market-driven leadership. He offered tools such as management by objectives (MBO) and SMART processes.

Design-driven innovation demands reflection and introspection. The purpose of introspection is to gain self-awareness of your motivations, actions, emotions and points of view. It facilitates curiosity into your personality and how it impacts others and indicates your mindset orientation. Through repeated practice, it builds your reflective thinking muscle or reflection skills, which are necessary for developing a learning and design mindset.

In psychology, introspection is described as 'self-reflection', a process of observing one's mental and emotional states, mental processes and belief or spiritual systems. It centres on conscious thoughts, behaviours and feelings.

Business designers or 'redesigners' practice both reflection and introspection. Where introspection is observing or examining one's own mental state and processes from within, reflection encompasses introspection along with observing or examining others, sensing their choices and processes from outside oneself. Introspection and reflection share common attributes of questioning, observing and listening. These traits are shared by innovators and creative problem solvers.

> **Case Example: Reflections on Intuit's Design-Driven Transformation**
> Intuit is a California-based financial software company founded in 1983. Intuit's products include tax preparation, financial and small business accounting programs (TurboTax, Mint.com and QuickBooks). In 2007, Intuit faced a dissatisfying Net Promoter Score, highlighting poor customer recommendations for their products. Triggered by this data, Scott Cook, one of the company's co-founders, reflected on how Intuit should respond. Inspired by Apple's design-driven success, he and the CEO explored how Intuit could infuse more design into their products, mar-

> keting programs and internal processes. They sought external perspectives (i.e. experts from the consumer packaged goods company Procter & Gamble, and a professor from Stanford) and experimented with a series of workshops involving over 300 managers.
>
> Overall, the typical 'talking head-style' of the talks were not impactful. Yet, one aspect of the workshops that stuck was the 'hands-on' experience. The participant group was introduced to a business design challenge, created prototypes, received feedback and iterated/refined ideas, then importantly reflected on their learning experience. An internal assessment followed, identifying designers from across the organizations and promoting one senior designer to lead a new initiative by identifying and engaging nine other managers, who could be trained as design-driven innovation coaches (referred to as 'innovation catalysts').
>
> Over two years, the process branded as 'Design for Delight (D4D)', was refined and improved. The number of trained coaches grew from 10 to hundreds. D4D focuses on identifying customer needs (as pain points) through field research, and engaging internal teams in techniques such as 'painstorming' and 'solution jamming', which generated prototypes and innovative solutions. The impact from the D4D process and related reflection and feedback techniques and programs, has been very positive for Intuit, in terms of improved Net Promoter Scores, sales revenue and market share growth over the past 10 years.
>
> *Interpreted and adapted from Martin, R. L. (2011). The innovation catalysts. Harvard Business Review, 89(6), 82–87.*

Organizations benefit greatly by reflecting on their own innovation design and development processes. Reflection or reflective practice enables:

- innovation managers and designers to learn from their experiences.
- innovation processes to be improved, along with the proficiency of individual participants and teams.
- more conscious and insightful led decision-making.
- critical analysis of past processes.
- critical analysis of future developments and business designs.
- improved performance measures.
- integrating the practice of reflection to better navigate uncertainty adapt to economic and market changes.

By executing on each reflection cycle, innovation leaders, managers and designers will continue to learn from their experiences with the design process. They learn from the specific solution being designed, and from the interaction between solution and target consumer.

Reflective practice triggers your ability to think about possible situations and their outcomes—including considering whether the right problem was solved or if the solution was the right action. Reflection ultimately drives the organization towards designing a more sustainable innovation practice.

Reflection Prompt:
1. When do you self-reflect? What triggers it?
2. What is the benefit of reflective practice?
3. What value does reflection offer your innovation team and/or within your organization?

7.2.3 Reflecting on the Business Design Learning Journey

Each chapter in this textbook begins with a warm up exercise, which involves a reflective discussion, and concludes with a series of topic-based reflective questions. Using chapters as distinct learning units or modules provides instructors and trainers with a suite of reflective thinking techniques.

In addition, asking students (or participants) to capture their reflections in a notebook or journal will help them to both record and consolidate their learning journey. These regular entries (prompted by the end-of-chapter reflection questions) will help surface the learner's progress, challenges, recurring themes of thoughts, and influence future actions or behaviours. We gain a lot from thinking back over past experiences, including incorporating other points of view or perspectives, also referred to as feedback from others.

The feedback loops (aka design crits) introduced in Chapters 4, 5 and 6, build on the idea that other peoples' different perspectives help us gain knowledge and information that is difficult to obtain if we worked alone. The innovation teams will also benefit from completing an anonymous 360-degree team feedback form.

The **360-degree reflection and feedback** is a useful technique to reflect on your contribution and your team's contributions (what was done well, not well, etc.) to a project. It's a great way to learn about yourself, and to offer and receive feedback from everyone whose views are helpful and relevant. Be mindful of potential unconscious biases and rate your colleagues' performance honestly. Unconscious bias is a prejudice or judgement of a person, thing, or group as compared to another, that's considered unfair or unfounded.

7.2.3.1 Exercise: 360 Reflection and Evaluation

Business design (as design-driven innovation) is a team sport. This technique guides you to reflect on your own performance and provide feedback on your team members' performance during the course/unit (or project). Reflection and feedback are an important part of contributing to a meaningful collective experience.
How to: Create a 360 Reflection and Evaluation form (as a table or Excel worksheet). Rate yourself and each of your team members based on the following state-

ments. Your responses will remain confidential, and will contribute to your and your teammates' overall reflection of the learning experience.

- Communicated well and consistently (1–5).
- Set clear strategy for achieving goals (1–5).
- Adapted and aligned with changes (1–5).
- Considered the impact of decisions (1–5).
- Accepted feedback from others (1–5).
- Took initiative to resolve issues (1–5).
- Motivated others to reach their goals (1–5).

A reflective thinking technique that is both insightful and enjoyable for students (and workplace participants) is the personal learning journey map. This map guides the student (or participant) to reflect on personal learning experience with the BDM steps, activities and exercises. Students (or participants) individually generate key observations, insights and express key emotions associated with stages and are encouraged to reflect on the challenges and pleasures of their journey.

7.2.3.2 Exercise: Personal Learning Journey Map

The personal learning journey map is a reflective thinking (reflection-on-action) technique to capture, document and analyze your learning experience from a project, program or course unit.

Think and Do:
Identify and select the specific learning journey (e.g. innovation project).
Reflect on the journey stages (pre, during, end and post)
Name: _____
Experience (Project/Unit/Program): _____
Description: describe the experience

Think:
Reflect on key issues from this experience across stages
Reflect on the key activities and events within and across stages
Reflect on the varying emotional states associated with activities and stages
Do:
Identify and describe the key reflections
Identify, plot and describe the key activities or events
Identify, plot and generate a line and with dots across the sentiment emojis
Describe key insights and future actions from this reflection across each stage.
Use the template provided in ▶ Chapter 8.

Today's volatile, uncertain, complex and ambiguous (VUCA) world requires a new kind of leadership, one that chooses to carve out time to reflect on what's happened so far, to review past mistakes in order to understand why things didn't work out, and to evaluate whether changes should be made to the current course of action. This book offers the Business Design Method (BDM) as your orienteering kit—intended to prepare and guide you and your teams through the VUCA world we're currently living and working in.

Reflective practice researchers have shown that leaders who take the time to reflect on events stand out in their ability to test assumptions, think critically and creativity. They develop a mastery with making connections between seemingly unrelated events, which is a critical skill for success in this uncertain world. Throughout this textbook, it's recommended that students (or participants) take time to reflect on their individual and team-based learning experiences, behaviours and decisions. By practising self-reflection, you build self-awareness and thoughtfulness, increasing the ability to develop empathy for others, especially your customers and colleagues.

Congratulations on reaching the end of your project. Continue to reflect on your next innovation journey.

> *"This program made me think about how many times, either myself or us as an organization had looked at something through a business lens – identify the problem, slap the solution on it and move forward…now, I sit back, and think about that, and wonder."*—Multinational executive learner

Templates
and Worksheets

Supplementary Information The online version contains supplementary material available at (▶ https://doi.org/10.1007/978-3-030-86489-7_8).

© The Author(s), under exclusive license to Springer Nature Switzerland AG 2022
A. Beausoleil, *Business Design Thinking and Doing*,
https://doi.org/10.1007/978-3-030-86489-7_8

8.1 Introduction

This chapter provides a suite of techniques and design templates, referenced across Chapters 1 through 7, to aid instructors, students or participants in innovative thinking and doing. Design templates are pre-made designs and documents that can be customized to suit the context (i.e. project or challenge), subject or topic. The techniques for each chapter are listed in ◘ Table 8.1. The templates can be used both as instructional aids and as worksheets, which are documents that guide the work or tasks to be completed.

Business design thinking and doing makes the process of innovation involving problems and solutions tangible, visible and actionable. The following methods, templates and worksheets facilitate your learning and practice of design-driven innovation—approaching problems , concrete, clear and easily intelligible to a wide variety of stakeholders.

◘ Table 8.1 Chapter-based templates/worksheets list

Chapter	List of templates/worksheets
▶ Chapter 1	• Warm Up: Word Association • Case Mapping
▶ Chapter 2	• Warm Up: Design an Object • Personal Thinking Map
▶ Chapter 3 BDM Step 1: Start	• Warm Up: Story of Me • Challenge Brief (2 pages) • Warm Up: Pass the Message • Personal SWOT • Team SWOT • Innovation Design Brief (2 pages) • Stakeholder Map (Internal and External) • Five Whys Analysis
▶ Chapter 4 BDM Step 2: Find	• Warm Up: Trading Card • Lean Research Plan (2 pages) • PDP Framework • POEMS Framework • Empathy Interview Script • Warm Up: Items Sorting • Sift.Sort.Label (3 pages) • Insight Statements • Problem Statement • Feedback Sheet: Problem Statement

(continued)

8.1 · Introduction

Table 8.1 (Continued)

Chapter	List of templates/worksheets
▶ Chapter 5 BDM Step 3: Frame	• Warm Up: Alternative Uses • Empathy Map • Persona • How Might We Question • Feedback Sheet: HMW Question • Warm Up: Analogy Maker • Rapid Ideation • Rapid Prototyping • Journey Map • Feedback Sheet: Rapid Prototypes
▶ Chapter 6 BDM Step 4: Solve	• Warm Up: Paper Airplane • Storyboards (3 pages) • Service Blueprint • Three Traits Framework • Five Factors Analysis • Warm Up: Story Madlib • Three-Act Story Builder • Pilot Implementation Plan Builder • Three Factors Measurement Framework
▶ Chapter 7	• Warm Up: Success Paths • Reflection Paper • Personal Learning Journey Map

8.2 ▶ Chapter 1: Templates and Worksheets

Warm Up: Word Association Template (◘ Fig. 8.1).
Case Mapping Template (◘ Fig. 8.2).

WARM UP: WORD ASSOCIATION

Warm ups prepare students to engage in the exploration of new topics or techniques. Similar to fitness or sport-based warm ups, individuals engage in a gentle introduction with reference to a topic and become more comfortable and confident with its relevance and broader application.

WORD ASSOCIATION is a common word game involving an exchange of words or phrases that are related. The game introduces a word and prompts the participants to generate words that come to their mind, or reflect on a deeper meaning of the word presented.

HOW TO: Take a sheet of paper/pen or tablet/stylus and create a mind map with the word 'innovation' at the centre.

- » Think of words or images that you associate with this word.
- » Quickly list at least three words that come to mind.
- » Prepare to share with cohort.

DURATION: 1 minute

DISCUSS: What patterns do you detect? What common or shared meaning has surfaced? Discuss how one word can present many different and diverse perspectives and meanings.

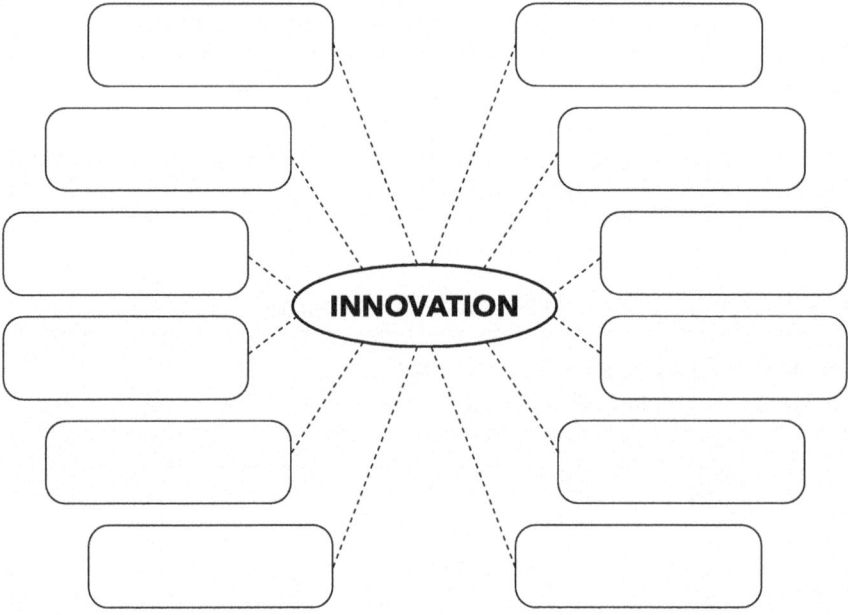

WARM UP: WORD ASSOCIATION WORKSHEET

Fig. 8.1 Word association template/worksheet

8.2 · Chapter 1: Templates and Worksheets

CASE MAPPING

Case mapping is a technique to visually reconstruct and analyze relevant information from a case study. It guides individuals and teams to think analytically and visually, aiding in the exploration and surfacing of key problems, issues, decisions and actions within a case.

THINK AND DO:

- Identify a business case or article to analyze.
- Refer to the questions in each stage to guide your analysis.
- Use the template to list items or use sticky-notes and whiteboard to place answers to the questions in each column.
- Summarize your analysis and discuss with group.

BUSINESS CASE

INITIATION	INVESTIGATION	INTEGRATION	IMPLEMENTATION
» What problem was the company trying to solve? » For whom? » What triggered the start of the innovation project?	» What did their customers actually need? » Why did it matter to the customers and company stakeholders? » What insights did they develop?	» Did they reframe their original problem? » How did they engage end-users and stakeholders? » Did they generate and test prototypes? » How did they propose to solve the problem?	» How did they design and deliver the solution? » How did they measure its impact? » Did they solve the problem? » What did they learn from the experience?

ANALYSIS AND REFLECTION

CASE MAPPING WORKSHEET

Fig. 8.2 Case mapping template/worksheet

8.3 ▶ Chapter 2: **Templates and Worksheets**

Warm Up: Design an Object Template (◘ Fig. 8.3).
Personal Thinking Map Template (◘ Fig. 8.4).

WARM UP: DESIGN AN OBJECT

Warm ups prepare students to engage in the exploration of new topics or techniques. Similar to fitness or sport-based warm ups, individuals engage in a gentle introduction with reference to a topic and become more comfortable and confident with its relevance and broader application.

DESIGN AN OBJECT is a design thinking exercise practiced at IBM which involves two prompts that elicit two different yet meaningful outcomes. One focuses on the functional needs associated with an object, the other focuses on the emotional needs of the object's end user.

HOW TO: Take a sheet of paper/pen or tablet/stylus and draw a line in the centre to create two panels or sections.

» In the top of the left panel, write "Design a vase"
» Generate sketches or words that come to mind.
» In the top of the right panel, write "Design a way for people to enjoy flowers"
» Generate sketches or words that come to mind.

DURATION: 3 minutes (1.5 min per panel)

DISCUSS: What is observed when reframing a question? Did you sense empathy for end-users? What needs did you surface? Discuss the differences between functional and emotional needs.

DESIGN A VASE	DESIGN A WAY FOR PEOPLE TO ENJOY FLOWERS

WARM UP: DESIGN AN OBJECT WORKSHEET

◘ Fig. 8.3 Design and object template/worksheet

8.3 · Chapter 2: Templates and Worksheets

PERSONAL THINKING MAP

A personal thinking map is a visual thinking technique to reflect and then express your thinking process in simple steps or stages, making your decision-making process visible.

THINK AND DO:

- Reflect on the Business Design Method steps
- Identify a past situation involving adopting a new idea, object or technology (i.e. a simple everyday example)
- Use the worksheet (or paper/tablet) to sketch out the steps involved in your thinking and actions
- Annotate your mapping with key decisions or actions
- Reflect on how it compares with the BDM steps

PAST SITUATION (DESCRIBE):

BDM — STEP 1 START — STEP 2 FIND — STEP 3 FRAME — STEP 4 SOLVE

KEY ISSUES AND OPPORTUNITIES

PERSONAL THINKING MAP WORKSHEET

Fig. 8.4 Personal thinking map template/worksheet

8.4 ► Chapter 3: BDM Step 1: START Templates and Worksheets

Story of Me Template (◘ Fig. 8.5).
Warm Up: Pass the Message Template (◘ Fig. 8.6).
Challenge Brief/Project-Based Course Outline Template (page 1 of 2) (◘ Fig. 8.7).
Challenge Brief/Project-Based Course Outline Template (page 2 of 2) (◘ Fig. 8.8).
Personal SWOT Template (◘ Fig. 8.9).
Team SWOT Template (◘ Fig. 8.10).
Innovation Design Brief Template (page 1 of 2) (◘ Fig. 8.11).
Innovation Design Brief Template (page 2 of 2) (◘ Fig. 8.12).
Stakeholder Map (Internal) Template (◘ Fig. 8.13).
Stakeholder Map (External) Template (◘ Fig. 8.14).
Five Whys Analysis Template (◘ Fig. 8.15).

8.4 · Chapter 3: BDM Step 1: START Templates and Worksheets

WARM UP: STORY OF ME

Warm ups prepare students to engage in the exploration of new topics or techniques. Similar to fitness or sport-based warm ups, individuals engage in a gentle introduction with reference to a topic and become more comfortable and confident with its relevance and broader application.

STORY OF ME can be used as an icebreaker activity and as a visual and associative thinking technique on a topic you're familiar with (yourself). It also engages participants in reflective practice: where you are now; how you got here; and where you might be going. It encourages futures thinking and is used as a team forming exercise.

HOW TO: Take a sheet of paper/pen OR a tablet/stylus and divide the sheet into three equal sections (draw lines): label "Past" on the left; "Now" in the centre and "Future". Write your name at the top and then:
- » Describe/sketch your NOW (you are here)
- » Describe/sketch your PAST
- » Describe/sketch your FUTURE
- » Use few words or images (keep it simple)

DURATION: 2 minutes

DISCUSS: Share your personal map with your cohort.

NAME: _____

PAST
EXPERIENCE
REPUTATION

NOW
PROJECT

FUTURE
AMBITION
LEGACY

BDM STEP 1: START | WARM UP: STORY OF ME WORKSHEET

Fig. 8.5 Story of me template/worksheet

WARM UP: PASS THE MESSAGE

Warm ups prepare students to engage in the exploration of new topics or techniques. Similar to fitness or sport-based warm ups, individuals engage in a gentle introduction with reference to a topic and become more comfortable and confident with its relevance and broader application.

PASS THE MESSAGE can be used as an icebreaker activity and as a group communications exercise. It engages participants to translate information using words and illustrations. It encourages analytical and creative thinking, and is used as a team forming exercise.

HOW TO: Divide the cohort into groups of four or five people. Give each group one sheet of paper and a pencil.
  » The first person in each group writes a sentence/message at the top of the paper and folds the paper to cover the sentence. (Any sentence at all).
  » This person passes the paper to their colleague on the left, who unfolds the paper, reads the sentence, folds it back, and in the next section illustrates their interpretation of it.
  » Keeping the original statement hidden under the fold, the paper is then passed to the next person, who looks at the drawing, folds it back, and writes the sentence of what they think it is.
  » The paper continues to be passed along like this until each person has had a turn.
  » Return the folded paper to the first person who unfolds it and shares with group.

DURATION: 5 minutes

DISCUSS: This fun exercise illustrates how quickly a message can be altered even when passed from person to person in a relatively short period of time. It highlights that people interpret information differently and that the intent of the original message can be completely lost. Ask: How does this relate to team projects? (i.e. clear communication, multiple perspectives, alignment, etc.)

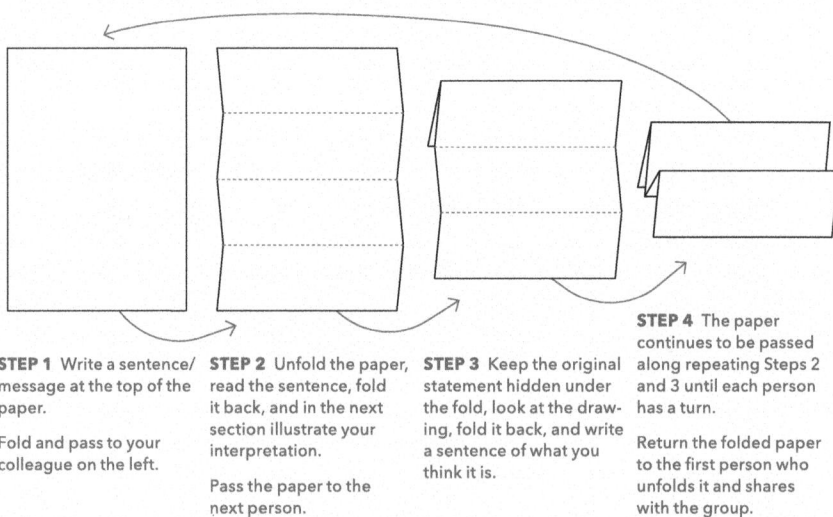

STEP 1 Write a sentence/message at the top of the paper.

Fold and pass to your colleague on the left.

STEP 2 Unfold the paper, read the sentence, fold it back, and in the next section illustrate your interpretation.

Pass the paper to the next person.

STEP 3 Keep the original statement hidden under the fold, look at the drawing, fold it back, and write a sentence of what you think it is.

STEP 4 The paper continues to be passed along repeating Steps 2 and 3 until each person has a turn.

Return the folded paper to the first person who unfolds it and shares with the group.

BDM STEP 1: START | WARM UP: PASS THE MESSAGE WORKSHEET

◘ **Fig. 8.6** Pass the message template/worksheet

8.4 · Chapter 3: BDM Step 1: START Templates and Worksheets

CHALLENGE BRIEF (PROJECT-BASED LEARNING UNIT OUTLINE)

A challenge brief outlines a real-world problem or a complex research question that is willfully vague and intentionally broad.

AIM Describe the goal of the project.

LEARNING OBJECTIVES Describe a list of learning objectives and outputs.

METHODS Identify methods and related techniques that will be applied to the projects.

CONTEXT Describe the context of this challenge, both at a systems level (economic, industry sector) and organizational (market segment) level.

SYSTEMS LEVEL	ORGANIZATIONAL LEVEL

BDM STEP 1: START | CHALLENGE BRIEF (PROJECT-BASED LEARNING UNIT OUTLINE) WORKSHEET

Fig. 8.7 Challenge brief template/worksheet (page 1 of 2)

CHALLENGE BRIEF
(PROJECT-BASED LEARNING UNIT OUTLINE), continued

ASSESSMENT

MEASURES Describe how the different learning objectives will be measured (i.e. assignments)

SCHEDULE Outline the schedule (i.e. item / weighting / due)

SUPPLEMENTARY MATERIAL List the supporting readings, worksheets or templates that will be provided to students.

BDM STEP 1: START | CHALLENGE BRIEF (PROJECT-BASED LEARNING UNIT OUTLINE) WORKSHEET

Fig. 8.8 Challenge brief template/worksheet (page 2 of 2)

PERSONAL SWOT

The Personal SWOT is a version of the original organizational analysis framework (Strengths, Weaknesses, Opportunities, Threats) applied to individuals. It's designed to generate personal reflection and self-awareness.

Complete each quadrant and reflect further upon your answers. Prepare to share the highlights of your personal SWOT with your project team for the team SWOT.

STRENGTHS

THINK: What are my strengths?
» What do I do well?
» What unique resources can I draw on?
» What do others see as my strengths?

WEAKNESSES

THINK: What are my weaknesses?
» What could I improve?
» Where do I have fewer resources than others?
» What are others likely to see as weaknesses?

ME

DO: List your thoughts and highlight the most relevant in each quadrant

OPPORTUNITIES

THINK: What opportunities can I chase?
» What opportunities are open to me?
» What trends could I take advantage of?
» How can I turn my strengths into opportunities?

THREATS

THINK: What threats do I face?
» What threats could harm me?
» What is my competition doing?
» What threats do my weaknesses expose me to?

BDM STEP 1: START | PERSONAL SWOT WORKSHEET

Fig. 8.9 Personal SWOT template/worksheet

TEAM SWOT

The team SWOT is a version of the original organizational analysis framework (Strengths, Weaknesses, Opportunities, Threats) applied to project teams or groups. It facilitates a dialogue and enables curiosity and empathy for others. Take turns sharing highlights from your personal SWOT, and add key attributes to build one aggregated team SWOT profile.

Complete each quadrant and reflect on your answers.

STRENGTHS	**WEAKNESSES**
THINK: What are our strengths? » What do we do well? » What unique resources can we draw on? » What do others see as our strengths?	**THINK:** What are our weaknesses? » What could we improve? » Where do we have fewer resources than others? » What are others likely to see as weaknesses?

WE

DO: Discuss, then select the most relevant attributes in each quadrant

THINK: What opportunities can we chase? » What opportunities are open to us? » What trends can we take advantage of? » How can we turn our strengths into opportunities?	**THINK:** What threats do we face? » What threats could harm/impact us? » What is our competition doing? » What threats do our weaknesses expose us to?
OPPORTUNITIES	**THREATS**

BDM STEP 1: START | TEAM SWOT WORKSHEET

Fig. 8.10 Team SWOT template/worksheet

INNOVATION DESIGN BRIEF

The Innovation Design Brief is a framework that outlines a design project based on an assumed business problem. It's developed by a person or team in consultation with a client or company. It frames, aligns and guides project teams to investigate a problem hypothesis, along with perceived company and customer motivations, and it directly informs the lean research plan. Note: It reflects assumptions, biases and facts.

PROBLEM HYPOTHESIS

What business problem(s) are you *trying* to solve? (aka problem hypothesis)

What customer problem(s) are you *trying* to address? (aka needs)

	KEY INTERNAL STAKEHOLDERS	KEY EXTERNAL STAKEHOLDERS
STAKEHOLDER MAP Who is invested in this problem? Who is impacted by this problem? Identify both internal and external stakeholders. Use the stakeholder map template to guide you.	Collaborate with (Top 2): Consult with (Top 2): Keep informed (Top 2):	Collaborate with (Top 2): Consult with (Top 2): Keep informed (Top 2):
STAKEHOLDER MOTIVATIONS Why does solving this problem matter to the company (hint: internal stakeholders)? What is their motivation (aka why?) Why does solving this problem matter to the customer or end-user (hint: external stakeholders)? What is their motivation (aka why?)		

BDM STEP 1: START | INNOVATION DESIGN BRIEF WORKSHEET

Fig. 8.11 Innovation design brief template/worksheet (page 1 of 2)

INNOVATION DESIGN BRIEF, continued

TARGET END-USER
Who is our intended customer/end-user for this problem? (hint: external stakeholder)

SCHEDULE AND TIMELINE

Who will participate in the innovation project?	What are the required tasks and roles?	What is the project timeline?

BUDGET (N/A) for class project.

REFERENCES What are all the sources and links associated with this brief? Follow appropriate citation protocols from your desk research.

BDM STEP 1: START | INNOVATION DESIGN BRIEF WORKSHEET

Fig. 8.12 Innovation design brief template/worksheet (page 2 of 2)

8.4 · Chapter 3: BDM Step 1: START Templates and Worksheets

STAKEHOLDER MAP (INTERNAL)

The stakeholder map is a framework to identify key stakeholders, their roles and relationships, associated with the innovation project. Use this map to identify project participants (internal stakeholders) and research populations (external stakeholders) for the project.

THINK AND DO: Once you have generated a list (i.e. simple spreadsheet) of possible stakeholders, apply a criterial set to further prioritize participant stakeholders for the project: e.g.

- » What is their interest level relating to this project? (low/med/high)
- » What is their influence level relating to this project? (low/med/high)

INTERNAL STAKEHOLDERS List your internal stakeholders (project lead, team, champions, etc.)

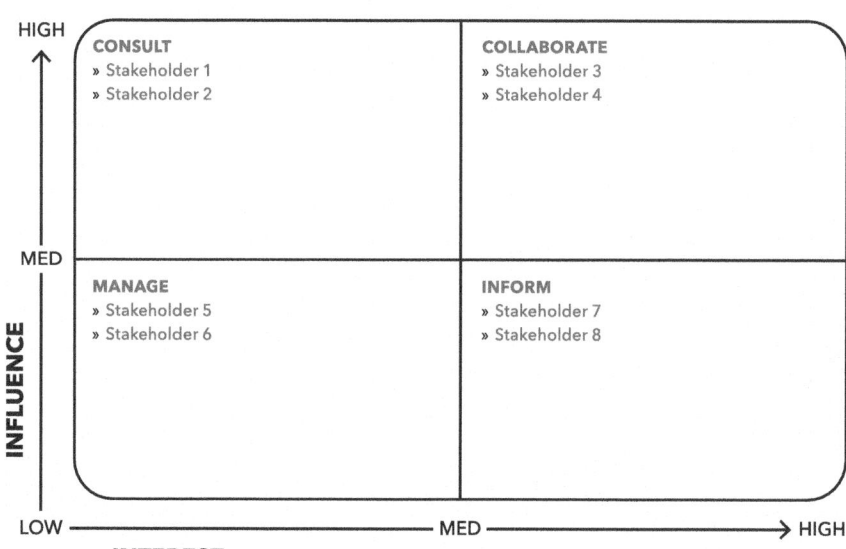

NOTES Reflect on list of key stakeholders, discuss and refine with team. Summarize list and add to the innovation design brief.

BDM STEP 1: START | STAKEHOLDER MAP (INTERNAL) WORKSHEET

Fig. 8.13 Stakeholder map (internal) template/worksheet

STAKEHOLDER MAP (EXTERNAL), continued

The stakeholder map is a framework to identify key stakeholders, their roles and relationships, associated with the innovation project. Use this map to identify project participants (internal stakeholders) and research populations (external stakeholders) for the project.

THINK AND DO: Once you have generated a list (i.e. simple spreadsheet) of possible stakeholders, apply a criterial set to further prioritize participant stakeholders for the project: e.g.

» What is their interest level relating to this project? (low/med/high)
» What is their influence level relating to this project? (low/med/high)

EXTERNAL STAKEHOLDERS List your external stakeholders (e.g. customers, suppliers, partners, etc.)

_____
_____
_____

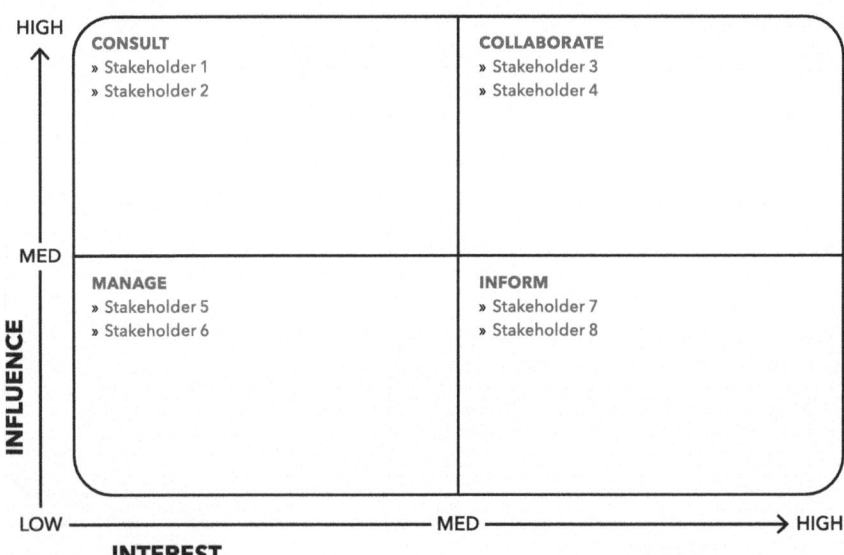

NOTES Reflect on list of key stakeholders, discuss and refine with team. Summarize list and add to the innovation design brief.

BDM STEP 1: START | STAKEHOLDER MAP (EXTERNAL) WORKSHEET

Fig. 8.14 Stakeholder map (external) template/worksheet

8.4 · Chapter 3: BDM Step 1: START Templates and Worksheets

FIVE WHYS ANALYSIS

The Five Whys (5 Whys) is a basic root cause analysis technique. It's helpful when defining a problem or determining its root cause, easy to learn and use.

THINK AND DO: Start with looking at any problem and asking "why"? and "what caused this problem"? The first "why" generally prompts a second, third, fourth and fifth "why" until the root cause becomes apparent.

THE PROBLEM HYPOTHESIS IS _____

_____

WHY DOES THIS PROBLEM EXIST? WHAT CAUSED THE PROBLEM?

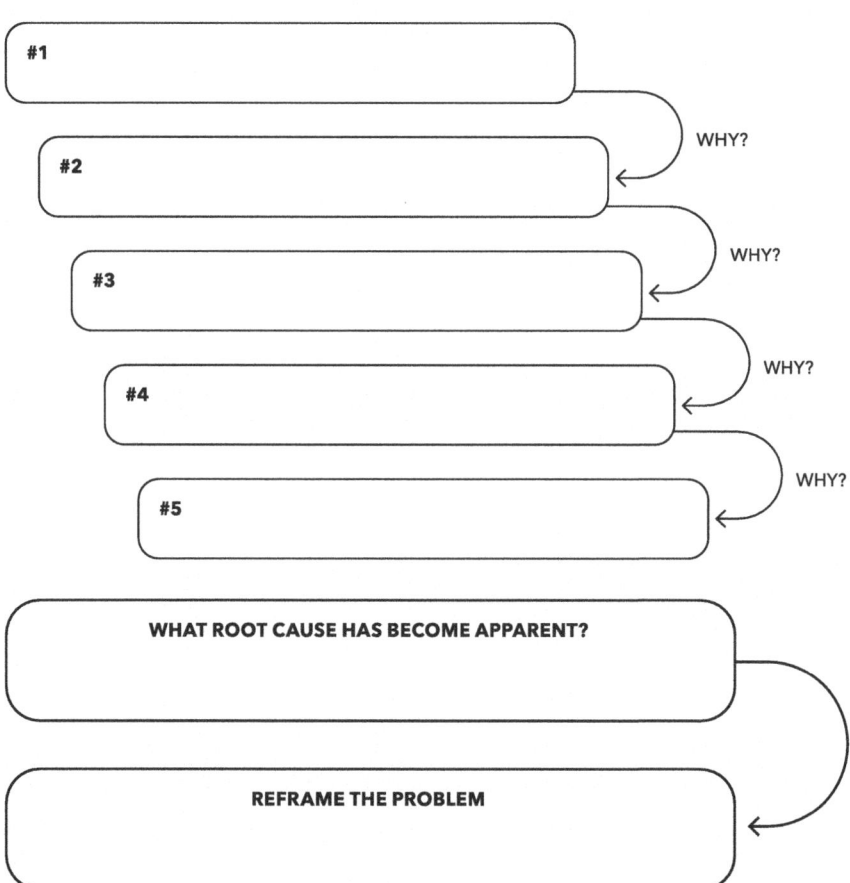

BDM STEP 1: START | FIVE WHYS ANALYSIS WORKSHEET

Fig. 8.15 Five whys analysis template/worksheet

8.5 ▶ Chapter 4: BDM Step 2: FIND Templates and Worksheets

Trading Card Template (◘ Fig. 8.16).
Lean Field Research Plan Template (page 1 of 2) (◘ Fig. 8.17).
Lean Field Research Plan Template (page 2 of 2) (◘ Fig. 8.18).
PDP Framework Template (◘ Fig. 8.19).
POEMS Framework Template (◘ Fig. 8.20).
Empathy Interview Script Template(◘ Fig. 8.21).
Warm Up: Items Sorting Template (◘ Fig. 8.22).
Sift.Sort.Label Template (page 1 of 3) (◘ Fig. 8.23).
Sift.Sort.Label Template (page 2 of 3) (◘ Fig. 8.24).
Sift.Sort.Label Template (page 3 of 3) (◘ Fig. 8.25).
Insight Statements Template (◘ Fig. 8.26).
Problem Statement Template (◘ Fig. 8.27).
Feedback Sheet: Problem Statement Template (◘ Fig. 8.28).

WARM UP: TRADING CARD

Warm ups prepare students to engage in the exploration of new topics or techniques. Similar to fitness or sport-based warm ups, individuals engage in a gentle introduction with reference to a topic and become more comfortable and confident with its relevance and broader application.

TRADING CARD can be used as an icebreaker activity for a class, meeting or workshop, and as an interviewing and visual thinking technique. It provides a quick and structured way to ask basic questions of an interviewee and record observations. Designed for teams of two, it aims to build rapport between individuals, and facilitates active listening and visual thinking skills.

HOW TO: Take a sheet of plain paper or use a new page in your tablet. With a pen or stylus, divide the sheet into two sections. In one section draw a large box and label it 'image'. In the other section write down the following words and add a line: Name, From, Current Position (Job Title), and Superpower.

After the sheet or page is complete (as your template), turn to a colleague or peer and ask the following questions. Fill in the lines with their responses to: "What is your name; Where are you from; What is a current position or job title; and, What is your special talent (aka superpower)?" From this information, quickly sketch an image of your peer in the box. (Stick figures are great)

Ask your peer to interview you. Note: one person asks the questions, listens, writes the answers in the lines and creates a quick sketch of the person. Take turns being the interviewer and interviewee.

DURATION: 3 minutes

DISCUSS: Introduce your colleague to the cohort by sharing the trading card you created for them.

BDM STEP 2: FIND | WARM UP: TRADING CARD WORKSHEET

Fig. 8.16 Trading card template/worksheet

LEAN FIELD RESEARCH PLAN

A lean field research plan is a simplified document that outlines the target study population (end-users or customers), the context and locations to lead qualitative data collection.

THINK: How will the team investigate the problem hypothesis? Who will the team observe or interview? Where and when will then team members lead the field research? Who will be leading which task?

THINK AND DO:

RESEARCH METHODS, OBJECTIVES AND OUTPUTS

Which methods will be employed?	What objectives do you want to achieve?	What outputs will be generated?

FIELD RESEARCH

Where and when will you observe and interview your target customer/end-user?	What additional locations or proxies should be considered?

BDM STEP 2: FIND | LEAN RESEARCH PLAN WORKSHEET

Fig. 8.17 Lean field research plan template/worksheet (page 1 of 2)

LEAN FIELD RESEARCH PLAN, continued

RESEARCH TEAM SCHEDULE Who will participate in which research method? With time constraints, provide details of team members and associated research tasks, activities (feasible and realistic).

TEAM MEMBERS Who?	ASSOCIATED RESEARCH TASKS/ACTIVITIES What? When?

RESEARCH LOCATION(S) List field research study locations (address, time, duration).

ADDRESS	TIME	DURATION

DISCUSS with team members and complete your research plan

BDM STEP 2: FIND | LEAN RESEARCH PLAN WORKSHEET

■ **Fig. 8.18** Lean research plan template/worksheet (page 2 of 2)

OBSERVATIONAL RESEARCH: PDP FRAMEWORK

The PDP framework organizes notetaking for observational research and facilitates alignment with team generated datasets. It guides the identification of a contextual experience of people arriving (pre-experience), during (experience) and leaving (post-experience). It observes both broad and specific behaviour and interactions within an environment.

THINK AND DO: **BE FACTUAL:** describe only what actually happened.
 BE RELEVANT: include details of direct quotes and information about the context of the observed experience.

PROJECT TITLE	ACTIVITY AND LOCATION	DATE
PRE » How do people arrive? » How do people behave as they arrive? » What are they doing or carrying? » What might it suggest?	**DURING** » How do they move through the space (i.e. store)? » What is their visible emotional state? » What do they do while interacting with _____ ?	**POST** » How do people behave as they leave? » What are they doing? Why? » What else do you observe?
NOTES Review field notes and circle or highlight key words or phrases or events that elicited both common and outlier behaviour. Summarize and share with your project team for data sorting and analysis.		**CONFIDENTIALITY** Follow human ethics and privacy protocols, and secure informed verbal consent from individuals you directly engage. Obtain verbal consent. Protect the identity of the study participant with a numeric code or a random name.

■ **Fig. 8.19** PDP framework template/worksheet

POEMS FRAMEWORK

The P.O.E.M.S. framework organizes notetaking for observational research relating to a specific activity and facilitates alignment with team generated datasets. It guides the observation of people, objects, environments, messages and services of an activity.

THINK AND DO: **BE FACTUAL:** describe only what actually happened.
BE RELEVANT: include details of direct quotes and information about the context of the observed experience.

PROJECT TITLE		ACTIVITY AND LOCATION		DATE
PEOPLE Who do you see? How do you describe them demographically? What are their roles based on behavior?	**OBJECTS** What objects are people holding, carrying, or interacting with? (e.g. bags, books, furniture, etc.)	**ENVIRONMENT** What elements in the place/space do you see? e.g. lighting, furniture, etc.	**MESSAGES** What can you read? What can you hear?	**SERVICES** What services and systems are enabling the activity?

SUMMARY/NOTES Review field notes and circle or highlight key words or phrases or events that elicited both common and outlier behaviour. Summarize and share with your project team for data sorting and analysis.

CONFIDENTIALITY Follow human ethics and privacy protocols, and secure informed verbal consent from individuals you directly engage. Obtain verbal consent. Protect the identity of the study participant with a numeric code or a random name.

BDM STEP 2: FIND | POEMS FRAMEWORK WORKSHEET

Fig. 8.20 POEMS framework template/worksheet

EMPATHY INTERVIEW SCRIPT

The Empathy Interview script is a tool to guide researchers on scripting an open-ended interview with end-users or customers. It enables a casual dialogue with end-users, eliciting user-generated quotes relating to the experience under study.

THINK AND DO: As a project/research team, ensure all members follow the same script, to ensure consistent data collection. Have a notebook and or voice recording device available. Seek verbal consent.

BUILD RAPPORT
Hello, I'm _____ *(introduce yourself)*. I'm working on a research project focused on _____ (e.g. grocery shopping experience) and was hoping you had a few minutes to talk about your best and worst experiences.

If no, approach another target end user or customer.

If yes, ask "Before we begin, may I have your verbal consent to take notes or capture this interview with a digital recording assistant? Rest assured that your comments will remain anonymous. Please answer only what is comfortable. Thank you."

ACTIVELY LISTEN Allow them to answer and capture their story using a notebook or digital recording application.	**OBSERVE** Facial behaviour or body language for emotional cues such as excitement or frustration.

ASK,
Can you share one of your best experiences with _____?
Don't lead the interviewee.
Listen, take notes – prompt for further 'stories' by adding: *why? can you elaborate? when?* etc.

FOLLOW UP BY ASKING,
Can you share one of your worst experiences with _____?
Don't lead the interviewee.
Listen, take notes – prompt for further 'stories' by adding: *why? how so? when?* etc.

WRAP-UP "Thank you for taking the time to share your story today."

REVIEW Code your notes with key themes and meet with your project team to begin data sorting and analysis. Highlight key words or phrases that elicited emotional responses.

CONFIDENTIALITY Follow human ethics and privacy protocols, and secure informed verbal consent from individuals you directly engage. Obtain verbal consent. Ptrotect the identity of the study participant with a numeric code or a random name.

BDM STEP 2: FIND | EMPATHY INTERVIEW SCRIPT WORKSHEET

Fig. 8.21 Empathy interview script template/worksheet

8.5 · Chapter 4: BDM Step 2: FIND Templates and Worksheets

WARM UP: ITEMS SORTING

Warm ups prepare students to engage in the exploration of new topics or techniques. Similar to fitness or sport-based warm ups, individuals engage in a gentle introduction with reference to a topic and become more comfortable and confident with its relevance and broader application.

ITEMS SORTING is an analytical thinking technique that can be applied to all domains, sectors and topics. It engages participants to observe, sift, sort and group items into categories. It encourages divergent and convergent thinking and is used to introduce unstructured data analysis.

HOW TO: Provide students with a copy of the Items Sort Exercise template from Chapter 8:

» Observe the following objects (e.g. grocery items)
» Sort the objects into common and contextual categories.
» Categorize objects with common similarities (e.g. shape); label.
» Categorize objects with contextual similarities (e.g. use); label.
» Generate 1–3 groups/labels

DURATION: 2 minutes.

DISCUSS: Share your categories with your cohort. Data sorting involves the ability to see similarities and differences between data points (as words or objects). It involves visual thinking, pattern recognition and the ability to create categories and groupings that reflect common or contextual themes.

THINK AND DO: Sort the objects on the left, then label.

milk, cheese, fries, pineapple, chips, pear, carrot, donut, yogurt, banana, pizza, strawberry

CATEGORIZE Objects with common similarities (e.g. shape)

LABEL:	LABEL:	LABEL:

CATEGORIZE Objects with contextual similarities (e.g. use)

LABEL:	LABEL:	LABEL:

▫ **Fig. 8.22** Items sorting template/worksheet

SIFT.SORT.LABEL.

Sift.Sort.Label is a qualitative data sorting technique. Project teams sift through their observational and interview data, sort the data into clusters or categories, then label each cluster with an overarching theme.

THINK AND DO:

SIFT Sift out or discard the least useful data. Create a list or generate one sticky-note per important data point. Sift through facts and interpretations, and check for bias.

BDM STEP 2: FIND | SIFT.SORT.LABEL. WORKSHEET

Fig. 8.23 Sift.Sort.Label template/worksheet (page 1 of 3)

8.5 · Chapter 4: BDM Step 2: FIND Templates and Worksheets

SIFT.SORT.LABEL., continued

THINK AND DO:

SORT Sort the key data points according to theme, pattern or meaning and group.

BDM STEP 2: FIND | SIFT.SORT.LABEL. WORKSHEET

◘ **Fig. 8.24** Sift.Sort.Label template/worksheet (page 2 of 3)

SIFT.SORT.LABEL., continued

THINK AND DO:

Fig. 8.25 Sift.Sort.Label template/worksheet (page 3 of 3)

8.5 · Chapter 4: BDM Step 2: FIND Templates and Worksheets

INSIGHT STATEMENTS

Insight statements is an analysis-synthesis technique to summarize observations and findings from research activities.

THINK: Use the following three sentences as prompts to draw out insights from your research data (observations and interviews).

DO:

WE OBSERVED AND/OR HEARD (OBSERVATIONS/NEEDS) Use this space to write what was observed and/or heard.

WE LEARNED (FINDINGS/THEMES) Use this space to write what was learned.

WE INFER (NEEDS-BASED PROBLEM = INSIGHT) Use this space to write what was inferred.

INTERATION #1

INTERATION #2

INTERATION #3

THINK The third and concluding statement reflects your data analysis and synthesis of key themes. The third statement is your insight statement that reframes the original problem hypothesis.

BDM STEP 2: FIND | INSIGHT STATEMENTS WORKSHEET

◘ **Fig. 8.26** Insight statements template/worksheet

PROBLEM STATEMENT

A problem statement is a communication tool that clearly defines the problem your project ultimately addresses, who it involves, and why it matters.

THINK AND DO: Work from the concluding insight statement and infuse your target end-user or customer segment.

INSIGHT (AKA WE INFER) STATEMENT

_____

_____

_____

_____

_____

PROBLEM STATEMENT

The problem we _____ are trying to solve for
                          «company»

_____ end-user/customer (who), is their need
            «who»

_____, so/because
                          «what»

_____
                      «why it matters»

_____.

NOTES Brainstorm before finalizing your problem statement.

EXAMPLES

» The problem Instagram (company) is trying to solve for smart phone users (who) is to improve the quality and size of their photos and size (what) so they can share them as best moments in real time (why).
» The problem Grocer X (company) is trying to solve for the busy young family shoppers (who) is to how to balance routine with discovery of new items (what), so they can stay on budget and introduce new meal options to their families (why).
» The problem Manufacturer X (company) is trying to solve for engineering teams (who) to innovatively problem solve within a rigid process (what), so they can feel more creative and confident (why).

BDM STEP 2: FIND | PROBLEM STATEMENT WORKSHEET

Fig. 8.27 Problem statement template/worksheet

FEEDBACK SHEET AND PROBLEM STATEMENTS

A feedback loop is a simple technique to test a concept, idea or statement with peers, stakeholders or end users/customers, for the purpose of improving the concept or statement.

HOW TO:

- » Prepare to post or share the selected problem statement into a Feedback Loop.
- » Prepare to offer valuable feedback to the other team's submission, in return.
- » **THINK:** When providing feedback follow the best practice of:
    - » state what is done well
    - » seek clarification on what is presented, then…
    - » propose recommendations for improvements.

FEEDBACK Collect and record feedback from your team members.	
What did you do well?	Proposed recommendations:

DO: Accept all feedback, return to your problem statement and implement the suggestions and improvements.

REVISED PROBLEM STATEMENT

The problem we _____ are trying to solve for
                        «company»

_____ end-user/customer (who), is their need
            «who»

_____, so/because
                        «what»

_____
                    «why it matters»

_____.

BDM STEP 2: FIND | FEEDBACK SHEET AND PROBLEM STATEMENTS WORKSHEET

Fig. 8.28 Problem statement feedback sheet template/worksheet

8.6 ► Chapter 5: BDM Step 3: FRAME Templates

Warm Up: Alternative Uses Template (◘ Fig. 8.29).
Empathy Map Template (◘ Fig. 8.30).
Persona Template (◘ Fig. 8.31).
How Might We Question Template (◘ Fig. 8.32).
Feedback Sheet: HMW Question Template (◘ Fig. 8.33).
Warm Up: Analogy Maker Template (◘ Fig. 8.34).
Rapid Ideation Template (◘ Fig. 8.35).
Rapid Prototyping Template (◘ Fig. 8.36).
Journey Map Template (◘ Fig. 8.37).
Feedback Sheet: Rapid Prototypes Template (◘ Fig. 8.38).

8.6 · Chapter 5: BDM Step 3: FRAME Templates

WARM UP: ALTERNATIVE USES

Warm ups prepare students to engage in the exploration of new topics or techniques. Similar to fitness or sport-based warm ups, individuals engage in a gentle introduction with reference to a topic and become more comfortable and confident with its relevance and broader application.

ALTERNATIVE USES are great as an icebreaker activity or as a purposeful creative thinking technique. They engage participants to think divergently and generate options for alternative uses of simple objects such as a pencil, hammer or paper clip. In business, this technique is used to surface 'functional fixedness' or unconscious bias toward existing processes, systems or products. Repeated practice of this technique helps develop the ability to reframe orthodoxies, explore different perspectives and think more creatively.

HOW TO: Take a sheet of paper/pen OR a tablet/stylus and prepare to respond to a visual prompt. The prompt is a simple drawing of a pencil:

» Ask participants to consider alternative uses for this object
» Ask participants to generate as many alternative ideas as possible

DURATION: 2 minutes

DISCUSS: Ask participants to share their most 'alternative' use ideas. Reflect on divergent thinking and its application to organizations.

THINK AND DO: Consider alternative uses for this object, then generate as many alternative ideas as possible.

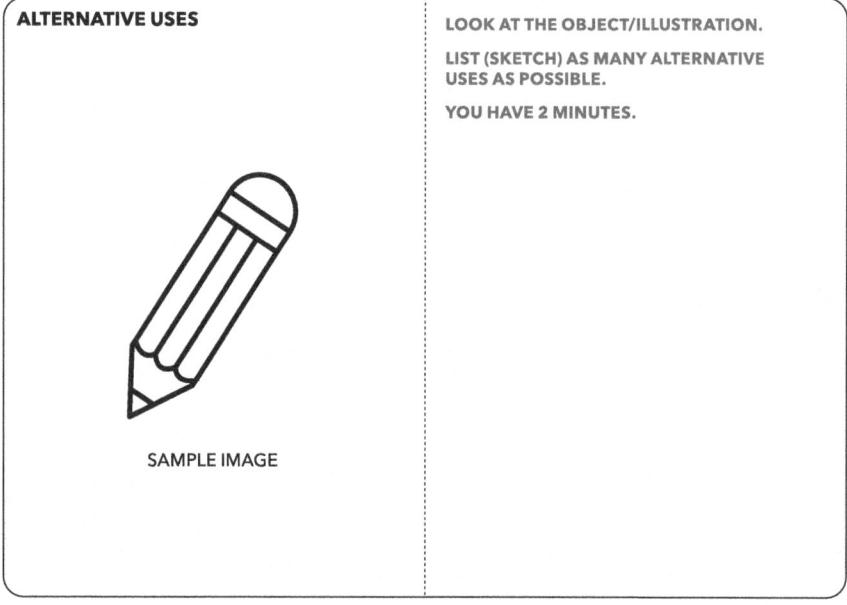

BDM STEP 3: FRAME | WARM UP: ALTERNATIVE USES WORKSHEET

Fig. 8.29 Alternative uses template/worksheet

EMPATHY MAP

An empathy map is a persona prototyping technique that sorts observational and interview data across four quadrants of what the end-user says, does, thinks and feels. It's a useful technique to build empathy for end-users or customers by understanding their needs, desires and motivations.

THINK AND DO: Map end user or customer research data onto the four quadrants. The left quadrants highlight facts (i.e. quotes and actions) and the right quadrants highlight interpretations. The map directly informs the development of personas.

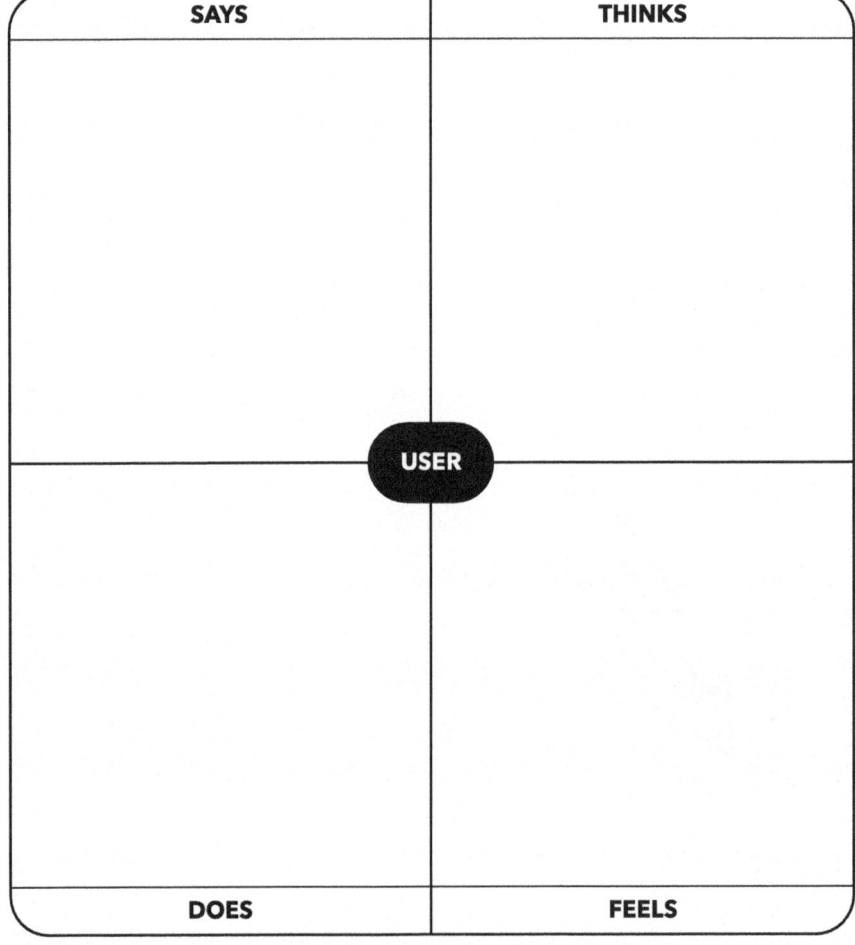

BDM STEP 3: FRAME | EMPATHY MAP WORKSHEET

◘ **Fig. 8.30** Empathy map template/worksheet

PERSONA

Persona is a technique to generate archetypal models of end-users, customers or stakeholders from research activities.

THINK AND DO: Reference your dataset (data analysis from the Sift.Sort.Label and empathy map techniques) to build your persona(s).

PROFILE IMAGE/SKETCH	
	PROFILE NAME _____
	PROFILE TYPE _____
	DEMOGRAPHICS
	Occupation _____
	Age _____
	Location _____

PERSONAL GOALS AND MOTIVATIONS What are their goals, drivers or motivations?

BEHAVIOURAL PROFILE (traits and habits, lifestyle choices)

NEEDS AND WANTS (pains and gains relative to project)

DO: Each team member generates one persona. As a project team, share personas, discuss, combine and select two or three personas for the next step.

BDM STEP 3: FRAME | PERSONA WORKSHEET

Fig. 8.31 Persona template/worksheet

HOW MIGHT WE QUESTION

The How Might We question is a divergent thinking technique that launches idea generation. The three words are placed at the start of the problem statement, reframing the statement into a question.

THINK: Reframe your problem statement into a problem-solving question. Insert your persona(s) into the formula.

DO: Fill in the blanks. Iterate, and generate many versions.

How Might We _____ _____
        «company»   «active verb»

_____ to _____
  «persona»   «problem statement»

_____

_____?

How Might We _____ _____
        «company»   «active verb»

_____ to _____
  «persona»   «problem statement»

_____

_____?

How Might We _____ _____
        «company»   «active verb»

_____ to _____
  «persona»   «problem statement»

_____

_____?

EXAMPLES
- » How might we (Instagram) enable (verb) smart phone users (persona) to improve the quality and size of their photos, so they can share them as best moments in real time (problem statement)?
- » How might we (Grocer X) inspire (verb) busy young family shoppers (persona) to balance routine with discovery of new items, so they can stay on budget and introduce new meal options to their families (problem statement)?
- » How might we (Manufacturer X) support (verb) engineering teams (persona) to innovatively problem solve within a rigid process, so they can feel more creative and confident (problem statement)?

BDM STEP 3: FRAME | HOW MIGHT WE QUESTION WORKSHEET

Fig. 8.32 How Might We template/worksheet

FEEDBACK SHEET AND HOW MIGHT WE QUESTIONS

A feedback loop is a simple technique to test a concept, idea or statement with peers, stakeholders or end users/customers, for the purpose of improving the concept or statement.

THINK AND DO:

» Prepare to post or share the selected HMW question into a Feedback Loop.
» Prepare to offer valuable feedback to the other team's submission, in return.
» When providing feedback follow the best practice of:
  » state what is done well
  » seek clarification on what is presented, then…
  » propose recommendations for improvements.

FEEDBACK Collect and record feedback from your team members.

What did you do well?	Proposed recommendations:

DO: Accept all feedback, return to your HMW question and implement the improvements to generate more iterations of the HMW question.

REVISED HMW QUESTION

How Might We _____ _____
                    «company»   «active verb»

_____ to _____
       «persona»   «problem statement»

_____

_____?

BDM STEP 3: FRAME | FEEDBACK SHEET: HMW QUESTION WORKSHEET

Fig. 8.33 How Might We feedback sheet template/worksheet

WARM UP: ANALOGY MAKER

Warm ups prepare students to engage in the exploration of new topics or techniques. Similar to fitness or sport-based warm ups, individuals engage in a gentle introduction with reference to a topic and become more comfortable and confident with its relevance and broader application.

ANALOGY MAKER can be used as an icebreaker activity and creative thinking technique. Analogies are word puzzles that are used to compare and connect two seemingly unrelated concepts. The activity introduces one problem statement as a prompt. Participants are asked to generate at least two metaphors and analogies in order to practice idea generation.

HOW TO: Take a sheet of paper/pen OR a tablet/stylus and generate a few metaphors and analogies that answer the presented statement.
- » Example: Finding my car keys was once like finding a needle in a hay-stack (metaphor); Now, finding my car keys is like having a magnet, simple to locate and quick to detect.
- » Prompt: Cooking a meal was once like _____ (metaphor); now, cooking is _____ (analogy).
- » Generate at least two different metaphors and associated analogies.

Don't overthink. Keep it simple

DURATION: 2 minutes

DISCUSS: Ask a few participants to share their analogies.

THINK AND DO:
Generate a few metaphors and analogies that answer the presented statement.

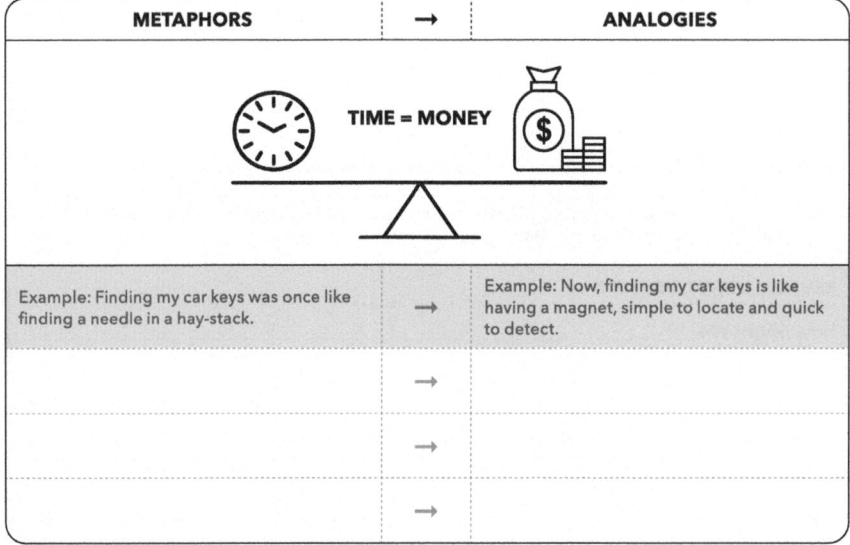

BDM STEP 3: FRAME | WARM UP: ANALOGY MAKER WORKSHEET

◼ **Fig. 8.34** Analogy maker template/worksheet

RAPID IDEATION

Rapid ideation is a technique to quickly generate many ideas from a well-crafted How Might We question or well-defined problem statement.

THINK AND DO: Working from your How Might We question, generate many ideas that aim to answer the question. Refrain from judgement on team member ideas.

- » Generate many metaphors to reflect the problem statement.
- » Generate many analogies to reflect possible ideas as solutions.
- » Consider 'crazy, silly or bad' ideas and then discuss what makes each so crazy or bad.
- » Sketch or build the ideas for your team members to comment, provide feedback and improve.
- » Vote on the top two or three ideas to further prototype.

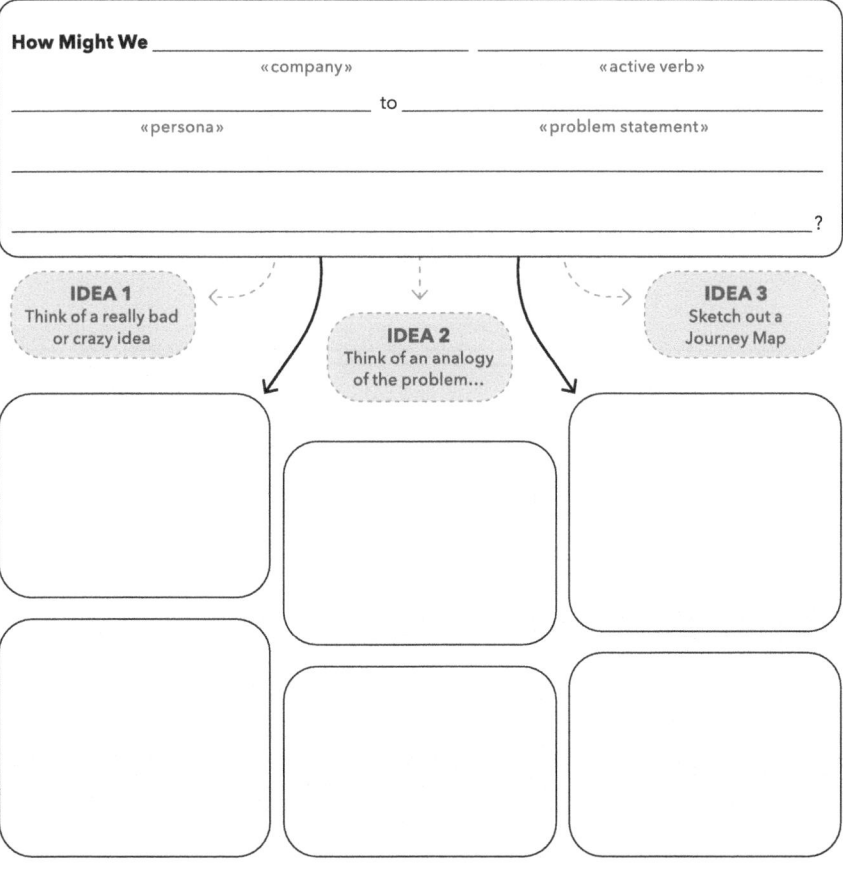

◘ **Fig. 8.35** Rapid ideation template/worksheet

RAPID PROTOTYPING

Rapid prototyping is a technique used to quickly generate tangible or physical concepts from ideas. It's iterative and uses available materials to quickly prototype and test 'visible' concepts with end users or customers.

THINK AND DO: Working individually or in teams, select the best ideas to prototype. Gather basic materials (pencils, markers, sticky-notes, paper, scissors, tape or building blocks).

THINK: Choose ideas and concepts (as proposed solutions) to visualize or make concrete.

DO: Rapidly prototype by sketching on sticky-notes or paper napkins, or use building blocks.

THINK AND DO: Learn from each iteration and continue to improve upon sketches or mock-ups. Prepare for another 'design critique' (feedback loop).

FEEDBACK Collect and record feedback from your team members.	
What did you/we do well?	Proposed recommendations:

BDM STEP 3: FRAME | RAPID PROTOTYPING WORKSHEET

■ **Fig. 8.36** Rapid prototyping template/worksheet

8.6 · Chapter 5: BDM Step 3: FRAME Templates

JOURNEY MAP

A journey map is a visual thinking and rapid prototyping technique that plots the end-user or customer relationship with a product or experience over a time period. It offers a basic narrative of key events or touchpoints and sentiment when interacting with a proposed solution (as prototype). It's used to map product, service or experience scenarios over stages.

THINK AND DO: Working individually or in teams, select the best ideas to prototype. Gather basic materials (pencils, markers, sticky-notes, paper, scissors, tape or building blocks).

PERSONA PROFILE: _____

JOURNEY PHASES
(pre-interaction, during interaction, post-interaction)

INTERACTION	PRE	DURING	POST
KEY EVENTS AND TOUCHPOINTS			
ASSOCIATED SENTIMENT WITH NEW SOLUTION :D :| :C			
KEY ISSUES OR OPPORTUNITIES			

FEEDBACK Package your selected journey map (as a rapid prototype) for peer feedback.

What did you/we do well?   Proposed recommendations:

BDM STEP 3: FRAME | JOURNEY MAP WORKSHEET

Fig. 8.37 Journey map template/worksheet

FEEDBACK SHEET AND RAPID PROTOTYPES

A feedback loop is a simple technique to test a concept, idea or prototype with peers, stakeholders or end users/customers, for the purpose of improving the concept or prototype.

HOW TO:

- » Prepare to post or share the selected prototypes into a Feedback Loop.
- » Prepare to offer valuable feedback to the other team's submission, in return.
- » **THINK:** When providing feedback follow the best practice of:
    - » state what is done well
    - » seek clarification on what is presented, then…
    - » propose recommendations for improvements.

FEEDBACK Collect and record feedback from your team members.

What did you do well?	Proposed recommendations:

DO: Accept all feedback, return to your ideas, discuss and implement the improvements to the next iterations of prototypes discussed in Chapter 6.

DISCUSSION NOTES

BDM STEP 3: FRAME | FEEDBACK SHEET: RAPID PROTOTYPES WORKSHEET

Fig. 8.38 Rapid prototypes feedback sheet template/worksheet

8.7 ▶ Chapter 6: **BDM Step 4: SOLVE Templates**

Warm Up: Paper Airplanes Template (◘ Fig. 8.39).
Storyboarding Template (page 1 of 3) (◘ Fig. 8.40).
Storyboarding Template (page 2 of 3) (◘ Fig. 8.41).
Storyboarding Template (page 3 of 3) (◘ Fig. 8.42).
Service Blueprint Template (◘ Fig. 8.43).
Three Traits Framework Template (◘ Fig. 8.44).
Five Factors Analysis Template (◘ Fig. 8.45).
Warm Up: Story Madlib Template (◘ Fig. 8.46).
Three-Act Story Template (◘ Fig. 8.47).
Pilot Implementation Plan (Chart Builder) Template (◘ Fig. 8.48).
Three-Factors Measurement Framework Template (◘ Fig. 8.49).

WARM UP: PAPER AIRPLANES

Warm ups prepare students to engage in the exploration of new topics or techniques. Similar to fitness or sport-based warm ups, individuals engage in a gentle introduction with reference to a topic and become more comfortable and confident with its relevance and broader application.

PAPER AIRPLANES can be used as an icebreaker, a team building activity and as a prototyping technique. Making paper airplanes and testing their effectiveness is a fun and educational experience. It encourages creative thinking, prototyping and testing (of effective aerodynamics, velocity, thrust, speed, drag, and gravity/weight and/or aesthetic design). Participants practice paper-based model making by folding and decorating their planes, and seeing the impact of their choices on the plane's design to fly far, fast, spiral, or look cool.

MATERIALS:
- » Letter-size paper (white or preferably different colors)
- » Decorations (coloured pencils, pens, stickers, etc.)
- » Masking tape (to mark the launch line)
- » Measuring tape/stick (if possible)
- » A long hallway or open space (ideally 20 metres or longer)
- » Awards (i.e. bragging rights or chocolate bar as optional)

HOW TO: Take two sheets of paper. The first sheet is your rapid and alpha version. Your second sheet is your beta version, which you will decorate with available materials (pens, colouring pencils, stickers, etc).
- » Fold the first sheet using a variety of angles (test and iterate)
- » Experiment with different folds and decorative techniques
- » Consider designs for speed, spirals, flight duration, and/or beauty.
- » Fold the second sheet from learnings of the first version (as test), decorate and fold, join the group with your final prototype
- » Take turns sending your prototype plane towards a landing area.

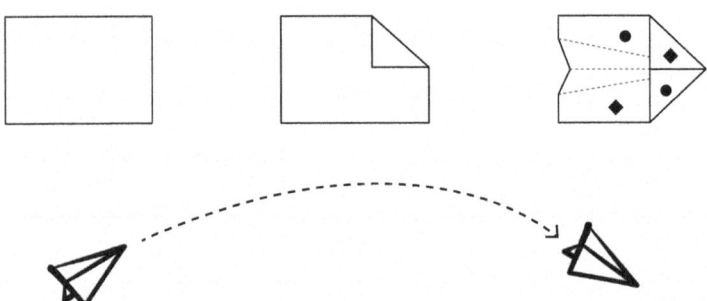

DURATION: 5-10 minutes.

DISCUSS: Participants explain their different designs, their functional attributes and celebrate the trials, errors and attempts. Explain the value of prototyping in testing out ideas and concepts.

BDM STEP 4: SOLVE | WARM UP: PAPER AIRPLANES WORKSHEET

◧ Fig. 8.39   Paper aeroplanes template/worksheet

8.7 · Chapter 6: BDM Step 4: SOLVE Templates

STORYBOARDING (AS PROTOTYPING)

Storyboarding is a visual thinking technique to communicate the flow of a story, strategy, scenario, presentation or customer journey. A storyboard a sequence of boxes or panels intended for rough drawings and notes that represent key story elements. When combined, the panels form a prototype of the story flow, aiding teams and stakeholders to visibly see the narrative.

THINK AND DO: Select a template that best suits your project needs (A) Comic book (B) Hero's Journey or (C) Moonshot.

(A) COMIC BOOK Create rough drawings and notes that represent key story elements.

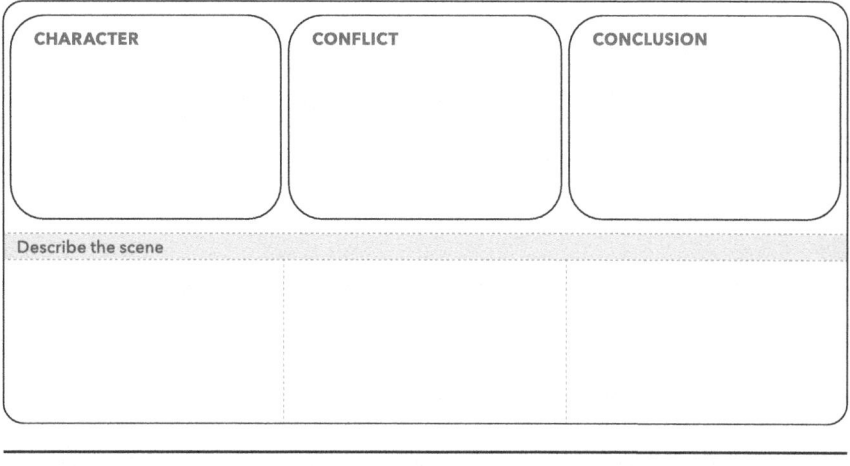

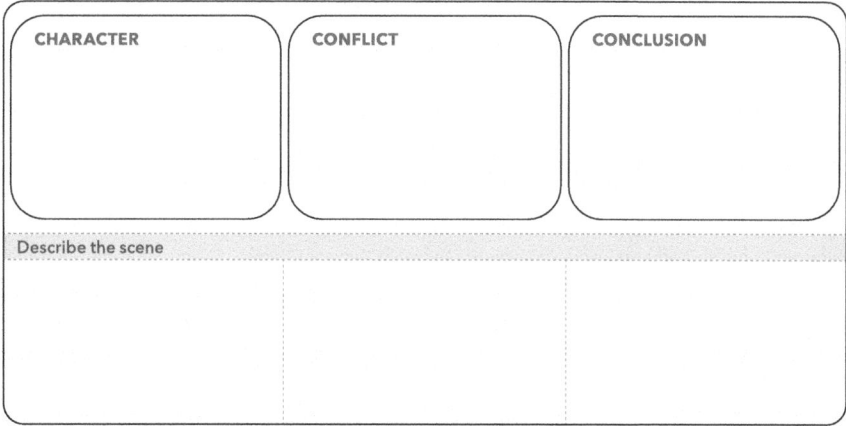

BDM STEP 4: SOLVE | STORYBOARDING (COMIC BOOK) WORKSHEET

Fig. 8.40 Storyboarding template/worksheet (page 1 of 3)

STORYBOARDING (AS PROTOTYPING), continued

Storyboarding is a visual thinking technique to communicate the flow of a story, strategy, scenario, presentation or customer journey. A storyboard a sequence of boxes or panels intended for rough drawings and notes that represent key story elements. When combined, the panels form a prototype of the story flow, aiding teams and stakeholders to visibly see the narrative.

THINK AND DO: Select a template that best suits your project needs (A) Comic book (B) Hero's Journey or (C) Moonshot.

(B) HERO'S JOURNEY Create rough drawings and notes that represent key story elements.

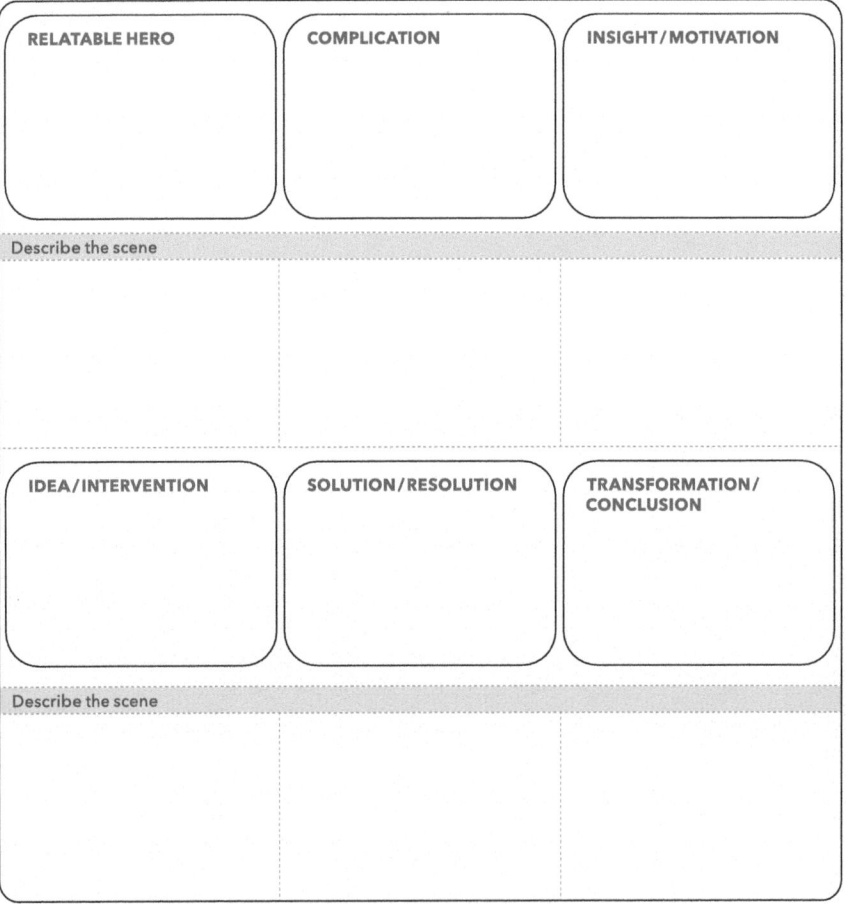

BDM STEP 4: SOLVE | STORYBOARDING (HERO'S JOURNEY) WORKSHEET

Fig. 8.41 Storyboarding template/worksheet (page 2 of 3)

8.7 · Chapter 6: BDM Step 4: SOLVE Templates

STORYBOARDING (AS PROTOTYPING), continued

Storyboarding is a visual thinking technique to communicate the flow of a story, strategy, scenario, presentation or customer journey. A storyboard a sequence of boxes or panels intended for rough drawings and notes that represent key story elements. When combined, the panels form a prototype of the story flow, aiding teams and stakeholders to visibly see the narrative.

THINK AND DO: Select a template that best suits your project needs (A) Comic book (B) Hero's Journey or (C) Moonshot.

(C) MOONSHOT Create rough drawings and notes that represent key story elements.

BDM STEP 4: SOLVE | STORYBOARDING (MOONSHOT) WORKSHEET

◘ **Fig. 8.42** Storyboarding template/worksheet (page 3 of 3)

SERVICE BLUEPRINT (AS PROTOTYPE)

A service blueprint is a visual thinking technique to map key interactions between a company's service offering and associated customer touchpoints, and internal processes. The blueprint is a useful framework to prototype new service designs, as well as to diagnose service delivery performance.

THINK AND DO:

- Identify a customer-persona and their service journey
- Map out their customer experience and key actions.
- Map out the customer's touchpoints with the company's internal processes
- Identify both customer and company 'swim lanes' and map out relationships, responsibilities and actions.
- Discuss key pain points, inefficiencies and opportunities
- Iterate and generate improved blueprint and seek feedback.

CUSTOMER PERSONA Who?	SERVICE JOURNEY What?			
Draw arrows indicate the connections between interactions.				
CUSTOMER ACTIONS Line of interaction				
ONSTAGE ACTIONS Line of visibility				
BACKSTAGE ACTIONS Line of internal interaction				
SUPPORT PROCESSES				
FEEDBACK Collect and record feedback from your team members.	What did you do well?		Proposed recommendations:	

BDM STEP 4: SOLVE | SERVICE BLUEPRINT WORKSHEET

▪ **Fig. 8.43** Service blueprint template/worksheet

THREE TRAITS FRAMEWORK

The Three Traits Framework is an evaluation technique to assess the prototype (or proposed solution) meets all three critical stakeholder needs (external and internal/ customer and company).

THINK AND DO:

1. Desirability: Is it needed or wanted?
2. Feasibility: Is it do-able?
3. Viability: Is it profitable and sustainable?

PROTOTYPE TITLE.		CONCEPT 1		CONCEPT 2		CONCEPT 3	
DESIRABILITY Is it needed or wanted?	CUSTOMER =	Yes	No	Yes	No	Yes	No
	COMPANY =	Yes	No	Yes	No	Yes	No
FEASIBILITY Can the company develop and deliver it?	CAPABILITIES =	Yes	No	Yes	No	Yes	No
	INFRASTRUCTURE =	Yes	No	Yes	No	Yes	No
	WILLINGNESS =	Yes	No	Yes	No	Yes	No
VISIBILITY Will it create value and generate revenues and/or impact?	COST/INVESTMENT =	Yes	No	Yes	No	Yes	No
	PROFIT/IMPACT =	Yes	No	Yes	No	Yes	No
	STRATEGIC FIT =	Yes	No	Yes	No	Yes	No
RANK How does it rank?		# _____		# _____		# _____	

BDM STEP 4: SOLVE | THREE TRAITS FRAMEWORK WORKSHEET

Fig. 8.44 Three traits framework template/worksheet

FIVE FACTORS ANALYSIS

The Five Factors Analysis is an evaluative framework to assess if the prototype (as proposed solution) meets the five critical factors for end-user or customer adoption.

THINK AND DO: Review the five factors and descriptive qualifiers. Generate a list of characteristics that reflect each factor from your prototype (as proposed solution).

FIVE FACTORS ANALYSIS

The Five Factors Analysis is an evaluative framework to assess if the prototype (as proposed solution) meets the five critical factors for end-user or customer adoption.

FACTOR	QUALIFIER	CHARACTERISTICS
RELATIVE ADVANTAGE	Is the proposed solution perceived as being better than current option?	e.g. offers 2x speed
COMPATIBILITY	Does the proposed solution fit the values and needs of end-users or potential customers?	e.g. brand extension
COMPLEXITY	Is the proposed solution easy to understand and simple to use?	e.g. ease of use
TRIALABILITY	Can the proposed solution be sampled or trialed? Has it been tested?	e.g. market trial
OBSERVABILITY	Has the proposed solution received positive feedback? Have others adopted it?	e.g. expert review

BDM STEP 4: SOLVE | FIVE FACTORS ANALYSIS WORKSHEET

Fig. 8.45 Five factors analysis template/worksheet

WARM UP: STORY MADLIB

Warm ups prepare students to engage in the exploration of new topics or techniques. Similar to fitness or sport-based warm ups, individuals engage in a gentle introduction with reference to a topic and become more comfortable and confident with its relevance and broader application.

STORY MADLIB can be used as an icebreaker activity and creative thinking and storytelling technique. Storytelling skills are essential to one's ability to inspire and influence others. Story madlibs create a participatory and immersive experience for both tellers and listeners. Stories follow a basic format also referred to as the hero's journey where a relatable hero begins their journey in a familiar world/context, then faces a series of conflicts, learns to navigate an undesirable world, and returns triumphant over the conflict and is transformed.

HOW TO: Use a simple 'madlib' story template to write a short story: Once upon a time, [insert the hero/persona], was [the context]. Every day, he/she/they [the conflict]. Until one day, [hero/persona], discovered [resolution]. In the end, [hero/persona] was [triumph].

» Use simple words to describe the need (conflict) in context
» Use emotional words to describe their motivation and their triumph over the conflict, and how they transformed.
» Generate a funny, silly or real story

DURATION: 2 minutes

DISCUSS: Share your story madlib with the cohort.

Once upon a time, _____ «insert the hero/persona» **was** _____ «the context»

_____ .

Every day, he/she/they _____ «the conflict»

_____ .

Until one day, _____ «hero/persona» **discovered** _____ «resolution»

_____ .

In the end, _____ «hero/persona» **was** _____ «triumph»

_____ .

EXAMPLE: Once upon a time, **Jack** (hero) was **considering how to increase sales at his bike shop** (the context). Every day, **Jack** (hero/persona) **had problems with getting enough bikes from manufacturers to meet the demands of his customers**. Until one day, **Jack** (hero/persona), discovered **that joining forces with other bike shops for larger orders increased his ability to secure supply from manufacturers** (resolution). In the end, **Jack** (hero/persona) was **able to increase his annual bike sales by 20%** (the triumph).

BDM STEP 4: SOLVE | WARM UP: STORY MADLIB WORKSHEET

Fig. 8.46 Story Madlib template/worksheet

THREE-ACT STORY BUILDER

The three-act story is a technique to quickly narrate a story across three parts: the beginning, middle and end. Each part highlights a plot point that drives the overall narrative, creating a complete story structure for your final prototype.

THINK AND DO:
Reflect on your persona and prototype. Generate stories (or scenarios) that reflect how your persona interacts with the prototype and is transformed.

» Notes: Introduce your final prototype as part of the resolution to the hero's (aka persona) needs; show and explain how it functions

» Propose how your solution has resolved the hero's need and describe their transformation or positive ending.

» Quickly iterate many versions before 'inking' your final version and sharing with internal stakeholders.

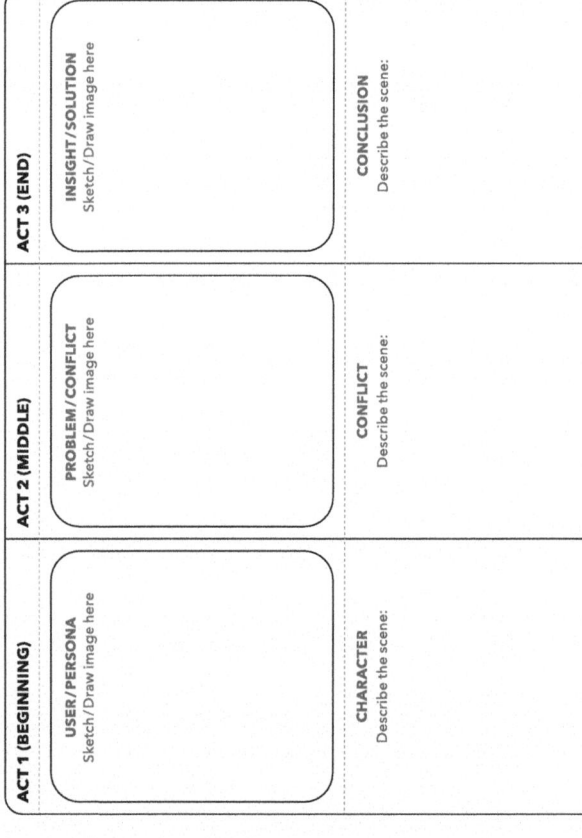

Fig. 8.47 Three-act template/worksheet

8.7 · Chapter 6: BDM Step 4: SOLVE Templates

PILOT IMPLEMENTATION PLAN (CHART BUILDER)

An implementation plan is a document that outlines the steps required to bring a solution to market and put it into practice.

THINK AND DO:

Review the Business Process Model and Notation (BPMN) system and generate a flowchart of the implementation plan.

- Use a journey map to quickly identify key stages and events.
- Identify key stakeholders (customers, company, suppliers, etc.)
- Mark the starting point
- Map and label the key events
- Map out the swimlanes (for each stakeholder group)
- Fill in key events, destinations and use the graphic notations
- Identify the end point
- Review with key stakeholders
- Implement pilot and document experience.
- Refine and improve where necessary.

Reference:
https://www.lucid-chart.com/pages/bpmn-symbols-explained

PILOT IMPLEMENTATION PLAN: PROJECT _____

PROJECT OWNER / MANAGEMENT

PRODUCT/SERVICE DESIGN TEAM

TARGET END-USER / CUSTOMER

BMPN SYMBOLS

- ○ Key events
- ▭ Key activities
- ◇ Gateways
- ↕ Direction/Flow
- 📄 Output/Artifacts
- ⬚ Grouped Activites

BMPN SYMBOLS

- Project Goals
- Resource Allocation
- Budget Allocation
- Solution Development
- Target Customer/End-User
- Plan/Activities Schedule
- Success Measures
- Evaluation Measures

BDM STEP 4: SOLVE | PILOT IMPLEMENTATION PLAN (CHART BUILDER) WORKSHEET

Fig. 8.48 Pilot implementation plan template/worksheet

THREE FACTORS MEASUREMENT FRAMEWORK

The 3-Factors framework is a technique to identify and design distinct and relevant measures as key indicators of an innovative solution's progress and success.

THINK AND DO: Use the template below to identify both non-financial and financial measures across the three critical innovation factors (for the company): desirable, feasible and viable.

THREE FACTORS MEASUREMENT FRAMEWORK

FACTOR	KEY QUESTIONS	IPMs
DESIRABLE	How will you measure the customer's desire for and delight with the innovative solution? (quantitatively and qualitatively)	FINANCIAL:
		NON-FINANCIAL:
FEASIBLE	Does the company have the capabilities to offer and deliver the innovative solution? How will you evaluate the company's abilities to design and deliver—financially and non-financially (quantitatively and qualitatively)?	FINANCIAL:
		NON-FINANCIAL:
VIABLE	Will your solution create customer value and generate revenues (and/or impact)? How will you measure success—financially and non-financially (quantitatively and qualitatively)?	FINANCIAL:
		NON-FINANCIAL:

BDM STEP 4: SOLVE | THREE FACTORS MEASUREMENT FRAMEWORK WORKSHEET

Fig. 8.49 Three-factors measurement framework template/worksheet

8.8 ▸ Chapter 7: **Reflection Templates**

Warm Up: Success Paths Template (◘ Fig. 8.50).
Reflection Paper Template (page 1 of 2) (◘ Fig. 8.51).
Reflection Paper Template (page 2 of 2) (◘ Fig. 8.52).
Personal Learning Journey Map Template (◘ Fig. 8.53).

WARM UP: SUCCESS PATHS

Warm ups prepare students to engage in the exploration of new topics or techniques. Similar to fitness or sport-based warm ups, individuals engage in a gentle introduction with reference to a topic and become more comfortable and confident with its relevance and broader application.

SUCCESS PATHS is a reflective thinking exercise involving one's experience with a new project and its path toward success. Reflect on your individual experience with launching a new project and your relationship with success.

HOW TO: Think of a past experience associated with a new project:
- » Take a sheet of paper (or tablet), use a pen/pencil (or stylus), draw two boxes side by side.
- » Label one box as (A) and the other box as (B)
- » In box (A) quickly draw a line that represents a success path
- » In box (B) quickly draw a line that represents a realistic pathway toward success

DURATION: 1 minute

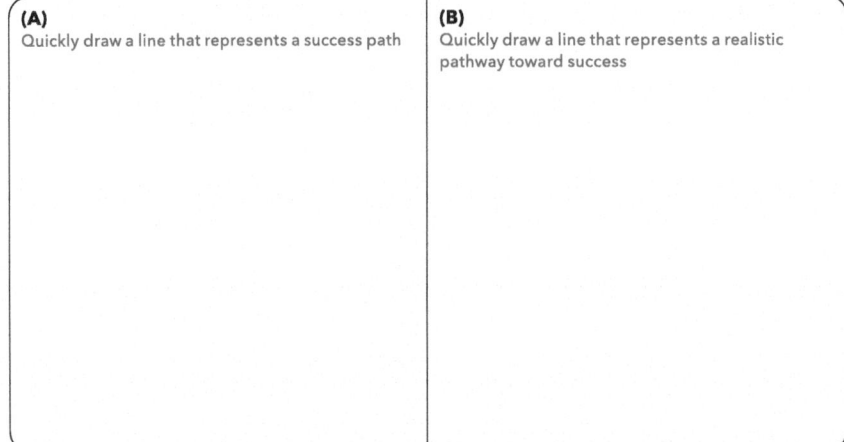

DISCUSS: Ask students/participants to share their two success paths with their cohort. Discuss the differences and/or similarities between the two paths. Explain that typically the first path to success is smooth, unidirectional and leans upward to the right, which is an aspirational vision of the experience. Next, explain the second path typically reflects past experiences, with the line drawn to show circles or sharp angles, and is multidirectional before leaning upward to the right. Discuss the meaning of these, the difference between perceived and realistic success pathways, highlighting the path is full of uncertainty and complications before arriving to its destination.

REFLECTIVE PROMPT: Ask students/participants to reflect on their sketches as visual representations of their experience with success. Can they further describe their positive and negative experience with success? What issues do the pathways raise? How can we learn to better navigate and lead others through the unpaved paths of uncertainty?

REFLECTIVE PRACTICE | SUCCESS PATHS WORKSHEET

Fig. 8.50   Success paths template/worksheet

8.8 · Chapter 7: Reflection Templates

REFLECTION PAPER

A reflection paper is a document that outlines an analysis of an experience (or document, video, book, podcast that was heard and experienced). It aims to illustrate your understanding of the material, and how it affects your point of view and possible decisions or actions in future.

DESCRIPTION
- » Write a description of the experience
- » What are the key issues from this description?

REFLECTION
- » What was I trying to achieve?
- » Why did I act as I did?
- » What are the consequences of my actions?
    - » For the end user (or customer)?
    - » For my team and organization?
    - » For myself?
- » How did I feel about this experience when it was happening?
- » How did the end-user/customer feel about it?
- » How do I know how the end-user/customer felt about it?

INFLUENCING FACTORS
- » What internal factors influenced my decision-making and actions?
- » What external factors influenced my decision-making and actions?
- » What sources of knowledge did or should have influenced my decision-making and actions?

Adapted from Johns, C. (1994). Nuances of reflection. Journal of Clinical Nursing 3 71-75

REFLECTIVE PRACTICE | REFLECTION PAPER WORKSHEET

Fig. 8.51 Reflection paper template/worksheet (page 1 of 2)

REFLECTION PAPER, continued

ALTERNATIVE STRATEGIES
» Could I have dealt better with the situation?
» What other choices did I have?
» What would be the consequences of these other choices?

LEARNING
» How can I make sense of this experience in light of past experience and future practice?
» How do I feel about this experience, now?
» Have I taken effective action to support myself and others as a result of this experience?
» How has this experience changed my way of knowing or acting?

Adapted from Johns, C. (1994). Nuances of reflection. Journal of Clinical Nursing 3 71-75

REFLECTIVE PRACTICE | REFLECTION PAPER WORKSHEET

Fig. 8.52 Reflection paper template/worksheet (page 2 of 2)

8.8 · Chapter 7: Reflection Templates

PERSONAL LEARNING JOURNEY MAP

The personal learning journey map is a reflective thinking (reflection-on-action) technique to capture, document and analyze your learning experience from a project, program or course unit.

THINK AND DO:
Identify and select the specific learning journey (e.g. innovation project).
Reflect on the journey stages (pre, during, end and post)

THINK:
- Reflect on key issues from this experience across stages
- Reflect on the key activities and events within and across stages
- Reflect on the varying emotional states associated with activities and stages

DO:
- Identify and describe the key reflections
- Identify, plot and describe the key activities or events
- Identify, plot and generate a line and with dots across the sentiment emojis
- Describe key insights and future actions from this reflection across each stage.

NAME _____   PROJECT / UNIT / PROGRAM _____

PROGRAM STAGES	BEFORE	DURING	END	POST
KEY REFLECTIONS				
:D	Simply sketch or plot key moments, behaviours and associated sentiment.			
:I				
:(				
PERSONAL INSIGHTS (Exercises, Activities, etc.)				

REFLECTIVE PRACTICE | PERSONAL LEARNING JOURNEY MAP WORKSHEET

Fig. 8.53 Personal learning journey map template/worksheet

Supplementary Information

© The Editor(s) (if applicable) and The Author(s), under exclusive license to Springer Nature Switzerland AG 2022
A. Beausoleil, *Business Design Thinking and Doing*,
https://doi.org/10.1007/978-3-030-86489-7

Appendix

This section offers a selection of pre-filled templates as samples. They aim to assist with design-driven innovation projects or workplace initiatives, and practice with the Business Design Method steps, strategies and techniques.

Challenge Brief Sample for Project-Based Course (page 1 of 2) (◘ Fig. A.1).

Challenge Brief Sample for Project-Based Course (page 2 of 2) (◘ Fig. A.2).

Innovation Design Brief Sample for Project-Based Course (page 1 of 2) (◘ Fig. A.3).

Innovation Design Brief for Project-Based Course (page 2 of 2) (◘ Fig. A.4).

Stakeholder Map (Internal) Sample for Project-Based Course (page 1 of 2) (◘ Fig. A.5).

Stakeholder Map (External) Sample for Project-Based Course (page 2 of 2) (◘ Fig. A.6).

Lean Research Plan Sample for Project-Based Course (page 1 of 2) (◘ Fig. A.7).

Lean Research Plan Sample for Project-Based Course (page 2 of 2) (◘ Fig. A.8).

Persona Sample for Project-Based Course (◘ Fig. A.9).

Appendix

CHALLENGE BRIEF (PROJECT-BASED LEARNING UNIT OUTLINE)

A challenge brief outlines a real-world problem or a complex research question that is willfully vague and intentionally broad.

AIM Describe the goal of the project.

This course presents learners with a simulated business challenge: "How might we (Grocer X) put customers at the center of our processes, systems, decisions." Through the course, learners are introduced to the tools and techniques of Business Design and simultaneously apply them to reframe the business challenge and craft a novel and relevant solution.

LEARNING OBJECTIVES Describe a list of learning objectives and outputs.

- Active practice of Business Design Method (4-step process), using management frameworks, ethnographic methods and design techniques to find, frame and solve problems
- In consulting teams, design and conduct empathic research in-field and online to gain insight;
- Experience sustained curiosity, empathy and creativity to reframe problems and offer customer-centred solutions to the industry class sponsor; and,
- Articulate and offer a novel and relevant solution to the industry sponsor.

METHODS Identify methods and related techniques that will be applied to the projects.

- 4-stage Innovation Process and Business Design method
- Innovation Team Forming
- Innovation Design Brief
- Stakeholder Maps
- Lean Ethnography (Observational Research, Empathy Interviews, Netnography)

- Data Sorting Techniques: Sort Sift Label, Affinity Maps, Empathy Maps, Personas,
- Insight Statement, HMW question
- Rapid Prototyping
- Bad Ideas Methodology
- 3 Lenses of Innovation
- Storytelling

CONTEXT Describe the context of this challenge, both at a systems level (economic, industry sector) and organizational (market segment) level.

SYSTEMS LEVEL	ORGANIZATIONAL LEVEL
The pandemic has challenged the grocery sector, resulting in inventory shortages, drop in footfalls and low employee morale. Competition is intense -organizations such as Empire Companies Limited are expanding aggressively. This simulated project seeks to help Loblaws Companies Limited solve a variety of challenges they face by engaging BD students as consultants.	Students are free to pick any challenge faced by LCL based on desk research. One example might be: Last quarter, Loblaws underperformed in key metrics. While a drop in footfalls was expected due to Covid-19 restrictions, Loblaws saw an unexpected drop in basket size and ticket size. Loblaws Companies Limited seeks to improve grocery shopper experience to remedy this.

BDM STEP 1: START | CHALLENGE BRIEF (PROJECT-BASED LEARNING UNIT OUTLINE) WORKSHEET

Fig. A.1 Challenge Brief example for curricular use (page 1 of 2)

CHALLENGE BRIEF
(PROJECT-BASED LEARNING UNIT OUTLINE), continued

ASSESSMENT

MEASURES Describe how the different learning objectives will be measured (i.e. assignments)	SCHEDULE Outline the schedule (i.e. item/weighting/due)	
Reflection 1 (Individual)	15%	Class 2
Business Design Brief (Team)	20%	Class 5
Data Collection Worksheet (Individual)	5%	Class 8
Business Design Proposal (Team)	30%	Class 12
Reflection 2 (Individual)	15%	Class 12
Participation (Individual + Team 360)	10% + 5%	Ongoing + Class 12

SUPPLEMENTARY MATERIAL List the supporting readings, worksheets or templates that will be provided to students.

- Business Design Pocketguides
- Embedding Design into Business https://rogerlmartin.com/docs/default-source/Articles/business-design/embeddingdesign (Links to an external site.)
- Innovative Thinking and Mindsets: https://www.businessmagazinegainesville.com/innovative-thinking-fixed-vs-growth-mindsets/ (Links to an external site.)
- Cyber Ethnography (aka netnography): https://en.wikipedia.org/wiki/Cyber-ethnography
- Ethnography and Design-led innovation: https://www.youtube.com/watch?v=nV0jY5Vgyml
- Design Research Plan: https://www.lullabot.com/articles/8-tools-for-a-leaner-design-research-process
- Strategy By Design: https://www.fastcompany.com/52795/strategy-design
- Forbes (2016) https://www.forbes.com/sites/billeehoward/2016/04/04/storytelling-the-new-strategic-imperative-of-business/#151d3be64d79 (Links to an external site.)
- Metaphors in Business Innovation: https://www.fastcompany.com/3065920/why-imagery-and-metaphor-are-essential-for-business-communications (Links to an external site.)
- Book Review (2012) https://graysreadinggroup.wordpress.com/2012/12/18/the-reflective-practitioner-by-donald-schon/ (Links to an external site.)
- Power of Self-Reflection: http://www.reflectiveleadership.com/

BDM STEP 1: START | CHALLENGE BRIEF (PROJECT-BASED LEARNING UNIT OUTLINE) WORKSHEET

Fig. A.2 Challenge Brief example for curricular use (page 2 of 2)

Appendix

INNOVATION DESIGN BRIEF

The Innovation Design Brief is a framework that outlines a design project based on an assumed business problem. It's developed by a person or team in consultation with a client or company. It frames, aligns and guides project teams to investigate a problem hypothesis, along with perceived company and customer motivations, and it directly informs the lean research plan. Note: It reflects assumptions, biases and facts.

PROBLEM HYPOTHESIS

The **business problem** we are trying to solve, is that Grocer X quarter-on-quarter sales are flat, accompanied by an expected drop in footfalls due to covid-19, and an unexpected drop in basket size.

The **customer problem** we are trying to solve, is that urban shoppers look frustrated while shopping at Grocer X. They are circling the same aisles repeatedly, trying to find front-line workers to help them.

	KEY INTERNAL STAKEHOLDERS	KEY EXTERNAL STAKEHOLDERS
STAKEHOLDER MAP Who is invested in this problem? Who is impacted by this problem? Identify both internal and external stakeholders. Use the stakeholder map template to guide you.	Collaborate with (Top 2): • Director – Business & Consumer Insights • Store managers Consult with (Top 2): • VP, Visual Merchandising and National Operations • VP, Store Planning and Design Keep informed (Top 2): • Back office staff • In-store marketing team	Collaborate with (Top 2): • University students not living at home • New Canadians living downtown Toronto Consult with (Top 2): • Social Media influencers • Media Agencies Keep informed (Top 2): • Brand Partners • Grocery consumer researchers
STAKEHOLDER MOTIVATIONS Why does solving this problem matter to the company (hint: internal stakeholders)? What is their motivation (aka why?) Why does solving this problem matter to the customer or end-user (hint: external stakeholders)? What is their motivation (aka why?)	In the past few years, Grocer X has invested heavily in improving their store experiences – in 2019, the company had more than 400 employees focused on digitally-driven projects and installed electronic shelf labels and expanded self-checkouts, to improve customer experience. Despite this investment, their quarter-on-quarter sales are flat and they have underperformed in key metrics. Shoppers seem to be spending lesser time in store and buying fewer items per transaction, resulting in a drop in average basket size and ticket value. Grocer X must identify and resolve the underlying issue to justify their investment.	"According to Kevin Chapman, a clinical psychologist who specializes in anxiety-related disorders, grocery store anxiety is common. Like other forms of anxiety, it stems from the inability to control the experience." – Huffpost, 16-03-2020. Grocery shopping can be a stressful experience, and the pandemic fatigue and safety concerns add to the anxiety of shoppers. Students, seniors, and young couples can be spotted looking quizzically at shelves, circling the same aisle multiple times, and chasing front-line workers to get their attention. This store is not living up to their "Live Life Well," slogan.

BDM STEP 1: START | INNOVATION DESIGN BRIEF WORKSHEET

Fig. A.3 Innovation Design Brief example for curricular use (page 1 of 2)

TARGET END-USER
Who is our intended customer/end-user for this problem? (hint: external stakeholder)

Anxious and frustrated urban shoppers at Loblaws at Carlton Street in Toronto. These could be students, seniors or young couples, who quizzically look at shelves, circle the same aisle multiple times, and chase front-line workers to get their attention.

SCHEDULE AND TIMELINE

Who will participate in the innovation project?	What are the required tasks and roles?	What is the project timeline?
Peter	Field Research	Week 7
	Data Sorting	Week 9
Marie	Field Research	Week 6
	Data Sorting	Week 9
Xi	Field Research	Week 6
	Final PPT / Storytelling	Week 11
Priya	Field Research	Week 6
	Final PPT / Storytelling	Week 11

BUDGET (N/A) for class project.

REFERENCES What are all the sources and links associated with this brief? Follow appropriate citation protocols from your desk research.

- Forbes.com. (2020). "Council Post: How Products Engage Digital Natives With Smart Packaging." https:// 2 www.forbes.com/sites/forbestechcouncil/2020/01/29/how-products-engage-digital-natives-with-smart-packaging/
- Heller, Laura. "43% Of Millennials Use a Mobile App to Grocery Shop." FierceRetail, 28 Apr. 2016, 4 www.fierceretail.com/operations/43-millennials-use-a-mobile-app-to-grocery-shop.
- "Millennials Infographic." Goldman Sachs, January 2020 www.goldmansachs.com/insights/archive/millennials/.
- Orbital Shift. "Top 5 Challenges Facing the Grocery Industry in 2018." Staff Scheduling & Time Clock Apps, 1 www.orbitalshift.com/blog/top-5-challenges-facing-the-grocery-industry-in-2018
- Stec, Bob, and Bob StecBob Stec. "Join The Robin Report Email List." The Robin Report, 21 June 2017, 6 www.therobinreport.com/why-the-consumer-is-so-frustrated-with-retail-today/
- "The Future of Grocery: How Millennials Are Changing Grocery Shopping Habits." CompuCom, 26 July 2019, 5 www.compucom.com/blog/future-grocery-how-millennials-are-changing
- Farmboy Canada. (2020, 07 30). *EMPIRE CONTINUES FARM BOY EXPANSION, ANNOUNCES THREE NEW ONTARIO LOCATIONS*. Retrieved from Farmboy Canada: https://www.farmboy.ca/empire-continues-farm-boy-expansion-announces-three-new-ontario-locations/

Fig. A.4 Innovation Design Brief example for curricular use (page 2 of 2)

Appendix

STAKEHOLDER MAP (INTERNAL)

The stakeholder map is a framework to identify key stakeholders, their roles and relationships, associated with the innovation project. Use this map to identify project participants (internal stakeholders) and research populations (external stakeholders) for the project.

....

THINK AND DO: Once you have generated a list (i.e. simple spreadsheet) of possible stakeholders, apply a criterial set to further prioritize participant stakeholders for the project: e.g.

» What is their interest level relating to this project? (low/med/high)
» What is their influence level relating to this project? (low/med/high)

INTERNAL STAKEHOLDERS List your internal stakeholders (project lead, team, champions, etc.)

GROCER X: Loyalty and Consumer Insights; Store Planning and Design; store managers and grocery staff; finance,

Inventory control, demand planning, online marketing, procurement, visual merchandising, product lead

Legal, Finance, Brand Marketing and Strategy

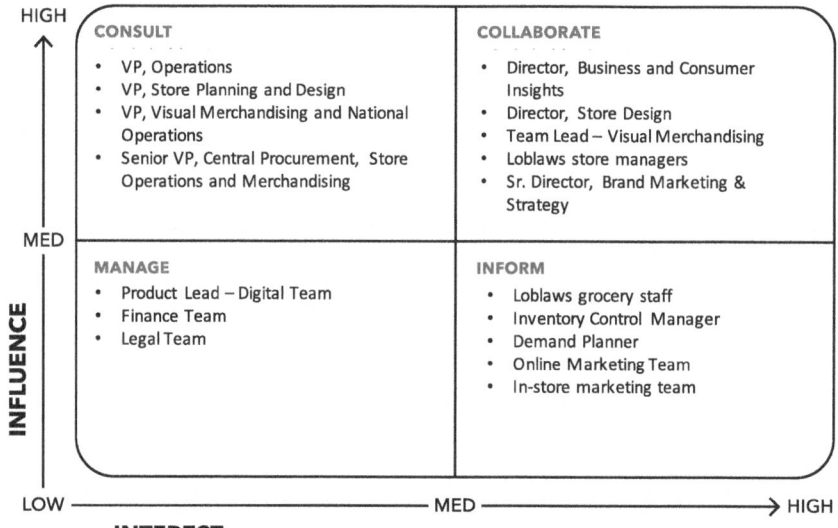

NOTES Reflect on list of key stakeholders, discuss and refine with team. Summarize list and add to the innovation design brief.
Consult: VP, Visual Merchandising and National Operations; VP, Store Planning and Design
Collaborate: Director, Business and Consumer Insights; Loblaws store managers
Inform: Loblaws grocery staff, in-store marketing team

BDM STEP 1: START | STAKEHOLDER MAP (INTERNAL) WORKSHEET

Fig. A.5 Stakeholder Map (Internal) example for curricular use (page 1 of 2)

STAKEHOLDER MAP (EXTERNAL), continued

The stakeholder map is a framework to identify key stakeholders, their roles and relationships, associated with the innovation project. Use this map to identify project participants (internal stakeholders) and research populations (external stakeholders) for the project.

THINK AND DO: Once you have generated a list (i.e. simple spreadsheet) of possible stakeholders, apply a criterial set to further prioritize participant stakeholders for the project: e.g.

» What is their interest level relating to this project? (low/med/high)
» What is their influence level relating to this project? (low/med/high)

EXTERNAL STAKEHOLDERS List your external stakeholders (e.g. customers, suppliers, partners, etc.)

GROCER X: Government agencies, Brand partners, Urban shoppers, Students, New Canadians,

Media agencies, Food banks, Vendors / Suppliers, Social Media Influencers, Educational

and research partners, psychologists, grocery consumer behavior researchers

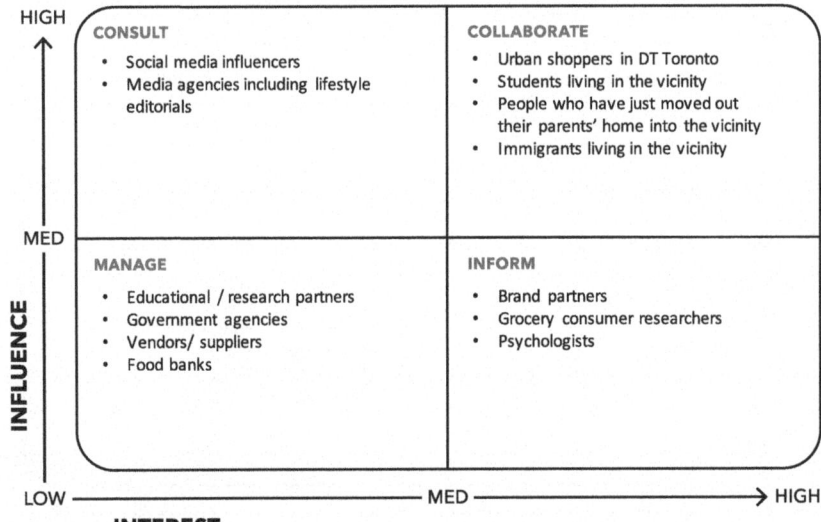

CONSULT
- Social media influencers
- Media agencies including lifestyle editorials

COLLABORATE
- Urban shoppers in DT Toronto
- Students living in the vicinity
- People who have just moved out their parents' home into the vicinity
- Immigrants living in the vicinity

MANAGE
- Educational / research partners
- Government agencies
- Vendors/ suppliers
- Food banks

INFORM
- Brand partners
- Grocery consumer researchers
- Psychologists

NOTES Reflect on list of key stakeholders, discuss and refine with team. Summarize list and add to the innovation design brief.
Consult: Social Media Influencers, Media agencies
Collaborate: Students, Immigrants
Inform: Brand Partners, Grocery consumer researchers

BDM STEP 1: START | STAKEHOLDER MAP (EXTERNAL) WORKSHEET

Fig. A.6 Stakeholder Map (External) example for curricular use (page 2 of 2)

Appendix

LEAN FIELD RESEARCH PLAN

A lean field research plan is a simplified document that outlines the target study population (end-users or customers), the context and locations to lead qualitative data collection.

THINK: How will the team investigate the problem hypothesis? Who will the team observe or interview? Where and when will then team members lead the field research? Who will be leading which task?

THINK AND DO:

RESEARCH METHODS, OBJECTIVES AND OUTPUTS

Which methods will be employed?	What objectives do you want to achieve?	What outputs will be generated?
Interviews w/ first year Rotman students	Dive into their mealplanning process	Data> consumer stories
Interviews w/ meal kit consumers	Motivations and experience with meal-kits	Data> stories of eager cooks
Interviews w/ young live-in couples	Cooking/grocery shopping process and experiences	Data> how couples manage cooking/shopping
Interviews w/ new immigrants	Grocery shopping experiences	Data> consumer stories
Observational Research and Netnography	Grocery shopping behavior / habits	Data> behavioural choices/actions

FIELD RESEARCH

Where and when will you observe and interview your target customer/end-user?	What additional locations or proxies should be considered?
First year Rotman students → Graduate house (student residence), Cafe in Rotman building, study area at Rotman	Locations where these consumers hang out offline: Madison pub on campus, Library, Metro grocery store on campus, Uoft Gym, Speciality grocery store (e.g. Indian grocery store, asian grocery store, etc.), IKEA
Meal kit consumers → Friends and family	
Young live-in couples → Rotman alum in network	Locations where these consumers hang out online: Facebook groups of GoodFood, Chefs Plate, etc, Facebook gruops of Instant pot and followers of celebrity homechefs, reddit forums for immigrants living in downtown Toronto, etc.
Immigrants → International center at UofT, friends and family	
Urban Shoppers → At Loblaws at Carlton Street, Toronto	

BDM STEP 2: FIND | LEAN RESEARCH PLAN WORKSHEET

Fig. A.7 Lean Research Plan example for curricular use (page 1 of 2)

LEAN FIELD RESEARCH PLAN, continued

RESEARCH TEAM SCHEDULE Who will participate in which research method? With time constraints, provide details of team members and associated research tasks, activities (feasible and realistic).

TEAM MEMBERS Who?	ASSOCIATED RESEARCH TASKS/ACTIVITIES What? When?
Peter	5 Empathy interviews with Rotman Students and alum (young live-in couples), Week 3
Marie	5 Empathy interviews with meal kit consumers and immigrants, Week 3
Xi	Observation and 3 interviews of Urban Shoppers at Loblaws, Carlton Street, Week 3
Priya	Netnography, Observational research at proxy locations, 2 interivews, Week 3

RESEARCH LOCATION(S) List field research study locations (address, time, duration).

ADDRESS	TIME	DURATION
Loblaws, 60 Carlton Street, Toronto, M5B1J2 (weekday)	10 am	30 mins
Loblaws, 60 Carlton Street, Toronto, M5B1J2 (weekday)	6 pm	30 mins
Loblaws, 60 Carlton Street, Toronto, M5B1J2 (weekend)	10 am	30 mins
Loblaws, 60 Carlton Street, Toronto, M5B1J2 (weekend)	1 pm	30 mins
Rotman Exchange Café, 105 St. George Street, Toronto, M5S2E8	4 pm	30 mins
Centre for International Experience, UofT - 214 College Street Room 150, Main Floor Toronto, ON M5T 2Z9	11 am and 6 pm	30 mins 30 mins

DISCUSS with team members and complete your research plan

Ask: Shall we consider other grocery stores that suit our end-user/customer?

Do we investigate our end-users at other grocery stores?

Do you have other questions?

Fig. A.8 Lean Research Plan example for curricular use (page 2 of 2)

Appendix

PERSONA

Persona is a technique to generate archetypal models of end-users, customers or stakeholders from research activities.

THINK AND DO: Reference your dataset (data analysis from the Sift.Sort.Label and empathy map techniques) to build your persona(s).

PROFILE IMAGE/ SKETCH	
	**PROFILE NAME** Neha Patel (not real name) **PROFILE TYPE** Urban Shopper **DEMOGRAPHICS** Occupation: Unemployed Age: 28 years old Location: Front Street, Toronto

PERSONAL GOALS AND MOTIVATIONS What are their goals, drivers or motivations?

- Seeks to get a management job in the CPG industry as soon as possible
- Wants to build her network.
- Aims to save up and buy a house in 2 years.
- Wants to make friends and get to know neighbours
- Wants to get a driver's license.

BEHAVIOURAL PROFILE (traits and habits, lifestyle choices)

She recently moved to Toronto with her spouse on a PR. She is newly married and still getting used to living with a partner (who secured a job as a consultant) in Canada. She loves eating out. She is used to living in a joint family and seeks to make new friends. She feels excited to be in a new country, but also lonely.

NEEDS AND WANTS (pains and gains relative to project)

- Has never had to cook, so the responsibility of managing meals for herself and spouse feels overwhelming
- Wants to learn how to cook, grocery shop and living and eating in Canada.
- Curious about MealKids such as GoodFood and Chef's Plate.

DO: Each team member generates one persona. As a project team, share personas, discuss, combine and select two or three personas for the next step.

BDM STEP 3: FRAME | PERSONA WORKSHEET

Fig. A.9 Persona (Customer) example for curricular use

Glossary

This section introduces the terms relevant to design-driven innovation and how those terms apply contextually in this book.

Abductive method: A qualitative research method of seeking the simplest and most likely conclusion from incomplete observations or limited datasets.

Adoptability: The propensity or tendency to adopt new ideas or to use new technologies.

Adaptability: The propensity or tendency to acknowledge and adjust to changing conditions and/or environments.

Business design: The act of designing or redesigning an organization; a way of thinking and working that applies human-centred design to improving or transforming business activities.

Business Design Method: An approach that integrates management frameworks, anthropological methods and design principles to solve organizational challenges; a structured methodology for design-driven innovation activities.

Business design practices:
- **Business Model Design** applies scenario, organization and product design principles to devise an organization's financial sustainability.
- **Strategic Design** applies scenario design principles to increase an organization's competitive position.
- **Organization design** applies architectural design principles to the infrastructure, roles, business processes and policies within organizations.
- **Process Design or Business Process Management (BPM)** applies system design principles to model, analyze, measure, improve and automate business processes
- **Service Design** applies organization and process design principles to plan and organize people, infrastructure, communication and material components of a service.
- **Design Research** applies ethnographic and qualitative research principles to a new product, service, process or system design offering.
- **Behavioural Design** applies strategic, service and experience design principles to influence behaviour for business and/or societal intentions.
- **Experience Design (XD)** applies integrated design principles from product, process, service and system design to a holistic offering.
- **Customer Experience Design (CX)** applies communication and experience design principles to branded offerings.
- **User Experience Design (UX)** applies user interface design principles to the usability and desirability of the interaction with a product.
- **Product Design** applies the process of imagining, creating, and iterating products that solve users' problems or address specific needs in a given market.

Business Process Model Notation: A graphic organizer that charts and models the steps of a planned business process from end to end.

Case map: A diagram that visually illustrates the relationships between key concepts, inputs and outputs of a case study.

Case mapping: A technique to visually represent and analyze relevant information from a case study.

Challenge brief: A document that outlines a real-world problem or a complex research question that is willfully vague or broad, to trigger or start an innovation project.

Competencies: Individual capabilities, aptitudes and skills that an organization has decided are desirable for an employee to possess.

Contemporary performance measures: A set of qualitative and quantitative measures to gauge a company's non-financial and financial performance.

Core competencies: Skills or areas of expertise possessed by an organization that makes it particularly good at doing some things, and which make an important contribution to its success by giving it competitive advantage over other organizations.

Convergent thinking: A way of thinking that filters or reduces choices, options or ideas.

Critical thinking: A mode of thinking that involves analysis, logical and objective reasoning about a subject, problem or solution.

Deductive method: A quantitative research approach that is objective and based on numeric quantification and generalization of results. Used to test and validate a pre-specified concept or hypothesis.

Design: The thoughtful planning or drawing of a concept (product, service, process, company or policy) before it is built, developed or manufactured.

Design crit (critique): A participatory technique to facilitate the evaluation of a concept of idea with peers, instructors and project stakeholders.

Design-driven innovation: The design, development, management and implementation of an innovation that meets the needs of the target end-user or customer; a designed solution that offers value and meaning for consumers.

Design-driven innovation development model: A four-stage process that involves all the activities relating to the initiation, investigation, integration and implementation of a customer-centred innovation.

Glossary

Designer: A professional practitioner who analyzes and synthesizes ideas into tangible outputs; one who works with abstract concepts (i.e. needs, problems, ideas) and makes them concrete through divergent and convergent thinking and abductive reasoning.

Design thinker: One who applies the designer's methods and toolkit to a business challenge and generates ideas and prototypes to be further tested.

Design thinking: A creative problem-solving approach that embeds empathy into traditional design practices. It's a non-linear, iterative and experiential process for non-designers to learn how to integrate end-users into existing product, platform or service development systems.

Design research: Involves qualitative research methods critical to creating needs-centred products, services, and systems. It's used in business and public and international development sectors for improved product, services and livelihoods and better governance.

Dotmocracy: A nominal voting technique using dots or dot stickers. The item with the most dots is selected.

Divergent thinking: A way of thinking that generates many choices, options or ideas.

Empathy: A person's ability to recognize, understand and appreciate the emotions of another person or fictional character within a specific context.

Empathy interview: A design research approach to finding out as much as possible about a person's experience, situation, need or problem as a 'user' of a space, a process, product or environment. It's used to understand the choices people make and why they make them.

Empathy map: A collaborative tool for teams to use to gain a deeper insight into their users/customers. An empathy map can represent a group of users, such as a customer segment, and inform persona or character development.

Feedback loop: A simple technique to test a concept, idea or statement with peers, stakeholders or end-users/customers, for the purpose of improving the concept or statement.

Five factors analysis: An evaluative framework to assess whether the prototype (as proposed solution) meets the five critical factors for end-user or customer adoption.

Five whys analysis: A basic root cause analysis technique to better define a problem or opportunity.

Graphic organizer: A visual thinking tool that organizes thoughts and guides understanding of complex and relational information through graphical aids, such as boxes and images

How might we: A divergent thinking technique that launches idea generation. The three words are placed at the start of the problem statement, reframing the statement into a question.

Human-centred design: An approach to designing platforms, products and services that model end-user behaviour, and are intuitive, desirable and commercially viable.

Implementation plan: A document that outlines the key steps, activities and resources required to bring a solution to market and put it into practice.

Innovation: Something perceived as new, the introduction of new ways, and the development of something new that is perceived as valuable. It's both a process and the result of its process (i.e. product or service).

Innovation design brief: A guiding document that outlines the key elements of an innovation project. It launches a design project, aligns teams, and serves as a statement of intent between a company's senior stakeholders and the innovation project team/manager.

Innovation performance measures: A set of qualitative and quantitative measures or metrics used to gauge a company's overall innovation design and development performance.

Innovation process: A communication process that involves all of the activities, decisions and outputs from investigating and defining a problem, through to solving a problem, developing a solution and proposing it to the intended market.

Innovation process design: A focus on the investigation and definition of the ways/paths that guide and support innovation processes inside and outside organizations.

Innovation readiness: The willingness to be open to new experiences, accept failure as a pre-condition for success, the adoption of new ideas and adaptation to changing situations.

Innovation types:
- **Product/Service Innovation**: Improves and makes changes on what a company does.
- **Process Innovation**: Improves and makes changes on how a company does it.
- **Position Innovation**: Improves and makes changes on where and who consumes it.
- **Paradigm Innovation**: Makes changes on why it matters and what value it creates.

Glossary

Innovative competencies: Specific qualities in an individual that an organization has decided are desirable for an employee to possess, within the realm of innovation development.

Innovativeness: The willingness to experiment with new approaches of inquiry, the commitment to master new knowledge, and the ability to exhibit innovative behaviour over time.

Innovator: A person or company who adopts new ideas, thinks creatively and critically, and who copes with uncertainty; a person or company that successfully introduces a new idea to market.

Insight: An interpretation of a theme (from patterns) generated from research activities, that reflects the what, how and why of something that exists.

Insight statements: An analysis-synthesis technique to summarize observations and findings from research activities.

Lean: A business methodology that promotes an agile and rapid flow of information and value to the customer through cycles of prototyping and evaluation.

Lean Ethnography: An agile method for design researchers to observe and engage human-subjects in their natural habitats, over a short period of time.

Lean Research: An agile framework for conducting end-user or customer research and analysis in the field, online and through other qualitative methods, over a short period of time.

Need: Something that is necessary; a critical tension with a present state.

Need finding: A systematic process of discovering end-user or customer needs involving observational research and empathy interview methods.

Needs analysis: A structured and systematic process of identifying needs that employ scripted tools such as surveys and questionnaires to direct the research subject to provide answers to pre-articulated problems and issues.

Reframing: The framing or phrasing of a word, concept or expression differently. Cognitive reframing identifies, challenges and then changes the way a situation, experience, idea, and/or emotion is perceived.

PDP framework: An information organizer to categorize notes from observational research when studying an entire experience or event—pre, during and post.

Performance measures: Evaluative indicators that represent progress towards a desired impact of a project, and the degree of impact or success.

Personas: A technique to generate archetypal models of end-users, customers or stakeholders from research activities.

Personal learning journey map: A reflective thinking (reflection-on-action) technique to capture, document and analyze your learning experience from a project, program or course unit.

Personal SWOT: A reflective thinking technique using the organizational analysis framework of strengths, weaknesses, opportunities and threats, applied to individuals.

Personal thinking map: A visual thinking technique to reflect and then express your thinking process in simple steps or stages, making your cognitive decision-making process visible.

POEMS framework: An information organizer to categorize notes from observational research, when studying people, objects, environment, messages and services within a specific context.

Project-based learning: A student-centred instructional method focussed on learning by doing by working through and solving a real-world challenge, problem or project.

Problem: An issue; the difference between an existing state or situation, and a desired state or situation.

Problem diagnosis: The process of determining the right problem to solve, based on critical, reflective and empathic thinking of the situation.

Problem finding: A process that involves observing people or organizations struggling with an issue; identifying patterns in how they describe an issue; and how they respond to an issue.

Problem framing: A process that involves defining an issue, problem or context that influences how it's perceived and evaluated. It aids in explaining or making sense of an issue, context or problem, and is influenced by personal narratives and conceptual metaphors.

Problem statement: A communication technique that clearly defines the problem your project ultimately addresses, who it involves, and why it matters.

Prototype: A tangible concept, mock-up or early sample model of an idea, product or output.

Prototyping: An experimental and integrative method for designing, testing and validating whether the proposed idea or solution actually solves the defined need, issue or problem.

Qualitative research: A method of inquiry that involves a naturalistic and interpretive investigation of a subject area or phenomenon. It's used to surface meaning, unarticulated needs and motivations.
- **Primary research** involves direct engagement with the intended user/customer whenever possible. Methods include observation, interviews, focus groups, online chat rooms, questionnaires/surveys, etc.
- **Secondary research** involves reviewing and analyzing information from primary research activities. Methods include print or digital media reports, whitepapers, and industry reports from libraries and other professional/rigorous sources.
- **Tertiary research** involves citing or summarizing overviews and completed the analysis of primary and secondary research sources. Sources include industry reports, mass media published articles, Wikipedia, etc.

Rapid ideation: A creative thinking technique for the quick generation of many ideas.

Rapid prototyping: A creative thinking technique for the quick generation of tangible or physical concepts from ideas, for testing 'visible' concepts with end-users or customers.

Reflective thinking: A process of reflecting on past experiences, creating connections between experiences, analyzing and making judgements, leading to learning.

Reflection: The act of reflective thinking that involves self-analysis and self-examination of one's own knowledge, feelings, values and beliefs in order to understand and justify one's actions.

Reflection paper: A document that outlines an analysis and synthesis of an experience (or document, video, book, podcast that was heard and experienced) for the purpose of future decision-making and action.

Service blueprint: A visual thinking technique used to map key interactions between a company's service offering, associated customer touchpoints and internal processes.

Sift.Sort.Label: A qualitative data sorting technique to sift through observational data, sort the data into clusters or categories, then label each cluster with an overarching theme.

Stakeholder-centred design: An approach to designing platforms, products and services that model both end-user and ecosystem member behaviours, are desirable and commercially feasible and viable.

Stakeholder map: A framework used to identify key stakeholders (internal and external), their roles and relationships associated with the innovation project.

Storyboarding: A visual thinking technique to communicate the flow of a story, strategy, scenario, presentation or customer journey, using a sequence of panels intended for rough drawings and notes of key story elements.

Strategic design: An approach that involves strategic thinking and reflective action through the use of creative and critical thinking techniques, resulting in situated innovation. It combines human-centred and system-centred design.

Strategic Design Method: A process that integrates design (human-centered research, problem finding, design and creative thinking) and strategy (systems thinking, problem solving, practical reasoning and planning) techniques.

Strategic thinking: A process that involves articulating a goal and how the goal will be achieved through actions and resources.

Sustainable Innovation: An approach to innovation development that is designed to be maintained, sustained and supported over many cycles or years.

Systems thinking: A process that takes a holistic approach to understanding how different parts of a system behave, operate and interrelate.

Team SWOT: A reflective thinking technique using the organizational analysis framework of strengths, weaknesses, opportunities and threats, applied to a project team or work groups.

Textbook procedures:
- **Method**: A way of approaching something; a process by which a task is completed.
- **Model**: A simplified representation of a method, system or event, for others to see.
- **Strategy**: A way-forward action plan for a company, competition, product or policy.
- **Framework**: A proposed set of rules and logics used in decision-making.
- **Technique**: A tool focussed on a specific objective.
- **Worksheet**: An instructional sheet outlining tasks to be accomplished.
- **Exercise**: A designed or planned event with a specific goal or objective.

Thick data: Short for 'thick description data', thick data is a description of human motivations, drivers, needs and behaviours stated by the research subject and/or interpreted by the researcher.

Three-act story: A visual thinking technique to quickly narrate a story across three parts:the beginning, middle and end.

Three-factors framework: A critical thinking technique used to identify and design distinct and relevant measures as key indicators of an innovative solution's progress and success.

Three-traits framework: A framework designed to assess whether a prototype (or proposed solution) meets all three critical stakeholder needs (external and internal/ customer and company).

Visual thinking: A process that involves visual processing and organizing of information; an expression or display of the synthesis from visual processing.

Warm Up: An icebreaker or introductory technique to prepare students to engage in the exploration of new topics or methods.

Wayfinding: Combines information systems, signals and symbols to guide people through a new environment with the aim of enhancing their understanding and experience of the space and services perceived as new or unfamiliar.

Index

A

Abductive method 52
Adaptability 31, 37, 55
Adoptability 53

B

Behavioural design 18, 32, 53
Big data 5, 18, 53, 54
Brief(s) 7, 25, 40, 41, 45–47, 59, 60, 90
Business design (BD) 16–24, 39, 94, 112, 130, 131
Business design methods (BDM) 24–27, 31, 32, 34, 35, 37, 38, 41, 42, 64, 92, 107, 133
Business design methods (BDM) steps 16, 23–26, 30, 31, 34–36, 39, 40, 47, 50, 51, 64, 69, 70, 74–76, 80, 88, 90, 91, 100, 107, 108, 115, 132, 136, 137, 142, 154, 168, 179, 198
Business design practices 16–18, 25, 41, 70, 198
Business model canvas 85, 94, 95, 97
Business model design 18–21, 23, 92
Business process management 18
Business Process Model Notation (BPMN) 107

C

Case map 8, 9
Case mapping 8–10, 136, 137, 139
Challenge brief 25, 30, 39, 40, 42, 45–47, 136, 142, 145, 146, 199, 200
Communication 3, 5, 6, 23, 31, 39, 40, 42, 45, 47, 69, 75, 85, 91, 105–107, 113
Competencies 33–35, 37–39, 97, 119, 128
Contemporary performance measures (CPMs) 109, 110
Convergent thinking 36–38, 65
Core competencies 85, 110
Course outline 142
Creative problem solving (CPS) 34, 35, 46, 78, 86, 88, 91, 92, 123, 129
Creative thinking 39, 41, 74, 81, 82, 84, 88, 90, 91, 100, 127
Critical thinking 32, 34, 35, 40, 128
Customer experience design (CXD) 18, 19, 23

D

Data 7, 35, 36, 47, 52–60, 62–64, 66, 67, 72, 76, 77, 80, 101, 112–114, 129
Data analysis 25, 42, 50, 53, 64–69, 71, 72, 80
Data sorting 63, 65, 66, 72
Data synthesis 68
Deductive method 52
Design 7, 8, 10, 16–18, 20–24, 26, 31–34, 36–38, 40, 45, 53, 57–59, 70, 76, 78, 79, 87, 90–94, 98, 102, 106–109, 111, 136
Design critique 70, 79, 86, 87
Design-driven innovation 5, 7–10, 12, 16, 17, 19, 21–24, 26, 31–34, 37, 38, 41, 42, 46, 47, 51, 52, 57, 60, 70, 79, 80, 82, 85, 87, 88, 92–95, 97, 99, 107–109, 111, 114, 119, 129–131, 136, 198
Design-driven innovation development model 2, 7, 12
Designer 17, 20, 22, 26, 40, 45, 47, 55, 59, 70, 71, 76, 79, 83, 85–87, 92–94, 105–108, 123, 129, 130
Design research 46, 53, 57–60, 64, 71
Design thinking 4, 16, 20, 21, 24, 26, 34, 92, 136
Dotmocracy 71, 78, 79, 87

E

Empathy 16, 18, 32, 34, 35, 43, 53, 58, 77, 133
Empathy interview 50, 53, 55, 58, 62–66, 72, 111, 154, 160
Empathy map 77, 87, 112, 137, 168, 170
Employee experience design (EXD) 18, 19
End-user(s) 8, 12, 13, 16, 18–23, 36, 41, 46, 47, 51–54, 57–62, 64, 66, 69, 70, 72, 76–78, 80, 86, 91–99, 102, 105, 106, 108, 126
Evaluation 34–36, 41, 42, 70, 75, 79, 84, 87, 90, 95, 99, 100, 105, 108, 110, 115, 120, 121, 131, 133
Evaluation frameworks 97–99
Exercises 2, 4, 16, 19, 26, 30, 31, 39, 43, 44, 50, 58, 62, 65, 68, 69, 74, 77, 78, 80, 81, 83, 86, 90, 100, 104, 114, 118, 124, 126, 127, 131, 132
Experience map 94

F

Feedback loop 70, 71, 79, 86–88, 131
Five factors analysis 99, 137, 179, 186
Five whys analysis 136, 142, 153

G

Graphic organizer 85, 96, 97, 107

H

How Might We (HMW) 78–80, 83, 84, 87, 88, 137, 168, 172, 173
Human-centred design (HCD) 17–19, 23, 26, 32, 36, 64, 92, 94, 95, 105, 129

I

Ideation 8, 78, 80, 81, 84, 88, 93
Implementation 2, 6–8, 18, 19, 24, 32, 80, 90, 95, 100, 103–106, 115
Implementation plan 25, 90, 100, 104–108, 115, 137, 179, 189
Initiation 2, 6–8, 24, 30, 31, 35, 46
Innovation 2–6, 8–12, 19–22, 24, 31, 32, 34, 38, 44, 47, 75, 82, 97, 98, 104, 118, 130
Innovation design brief 25, 30, 35, 39, 41, 42, 44–47, 50, 51, 56, 58, 64, 70, 71, 136, 142, 149, 150, 198, 201, 202
Innovation development process 4, 6, 19, 24, 25, 75, 88, 91, 92, 125
Innovation performance measures (IPMs) 109, 110, 115
Innovation process 3–5, 7, 13, 33, 35, 38, 50, 51, 74, 90, 130
Innovation process design 8, 22, 23, 30, 59
Innovation readiness 5, 6, 33, 106
Innovation stages 6, 8, 10, 12, 16, 24, 26, 30, 34, 39, 47, 50, 51, 54, 74, 75, 80, 90, 125
Innovation teams 3, 7, 34, 42, 45, 47, 58, 64, 65, 70, 71, 76, 78, 83, 85, 88, 93–95, 98, 102–104, 106, 108, 131
Innovation types 22, 30, 34, 35, 38, 39
Innovative competencies 30, 32, 34, 38
Innovativeness 33, 34
Innovator 11, 33, 38, 129
Insight 3, 7, 8, 18, 24, 25, 31, 35, 36, 41–43, 46, 47, 50, 52–60, 64, 65, 67–72, 74–78, 80, 81, 85, 88, 103, 104, 108, 111, 123–125, 127–129, 132
Insight statements 68, 69, 136, 154, 165

Integration 2, 3, 7, 8, 11, 17, 18, 20, 21, 24, 32, 41, 45, 53, 55, 57, 74, 76, 92, 93, 95, 105, 107, 110, 114, 128, 129
Investigation 2, 7, 8, 13, 24, 35, 39–41, 45, 46, 50, 51, 56, 58–60, 64, 65, 68, 71, 80

J

Journey map 25, 85–87, 96, 106, 137, 168, 177

L

Lean ethnography 59
Lean research 45, 47, 50, 51, 60, 64, 136, 157, 198, 205, 206

M

Mindsets 5, 20, 21, 30–34, 37–39, 44, 77, 81, 129

N

Need finding 50–56, 58, 59, 64, 66, 71
Needs 3, 5–8, 10–12, 17–25, 31–33, 35, 36, 38, 40, 41, 44, 46, 47, 51–53, 55–60, 64–72, 74–77, 80, 82, 84, 85, 94–96, 98, 99, 101, 102, 104, 105, 109–114, 119, 121, 123, 124, 127, 130
- emotional needs 16, 57, 65, 66, 68, 69
- functional needs 16, 57, 65, 68, 69
Needs analysis 25, 55, 56

O

Observational research 50, 53, 55, 58, 60–62, 64, 65, 72
Organization design 10–12, 17, 19, 97, 109, 130

P

Paradigm innovation 22, 23
PDP framework 136, 154, 158
Performance measures 25, 90, 100, 108–113, 115, 128, 130
Personal learning journey map 132, 137, 191, 195
Personal SWOT 43, 136, 142, 147
Personal thinking map 26, 136, 140, 141
Personas 74, 76–78, 80

Index

POEMS framework 61, 62, 66, 136, 154, 159
Position innovation 22, 80, 87, 88, 109, 111
Primary research 52–54
Problem(s) 3, 5–9, 12, 18, 21, 23–25, 31–37, 39, 41, 42, 44–47, 51, 53, 55–57, 60, 62, 64–66, 69–72, 74–76, 78, 80–83, 85, 87, 88, 91, 92, 94–96, 100, 104, 106, 119, 123, 124, 130, 136
Problem diagnosis 5
Problem finding 33
Problem framing 8, 80, 83
Problem solving 5, 20, 32, 35, 36, 41, 70, 79, 91, 99, 108, 112, 127
Problem statement 25, 42, 66, 69, 71, 72, 74–76, 78–81, 83, 84, 87, 88, 136, 154, 166, 167
Process innovation 3–5, 7, 13, 33, 35, 38, 50, 51, 74, 90, 130
Product/service innovation 3, 5, 10, 13, 22
Product design 18, 21–23, 92
Project-based learning (PBL) 30, 39–42, 45
Prototype/prototyping 3, 7, 8, 18, 19, 22–25, 33, 35, 36, 41, 54, 56, 70, 71, 74, 77, 80, 81, 83–88, 90–95, 97–106, 108, 110–112, 114, 115, 130

Q

Qualitative research 42, 50–55, 58, 60, 64

R

Rapid ideation 83, 137, 168, 175
Rapid prototyping 25, 85–88, 92–94, 137, 168, 176, 178
Reflection paper 42, 125, 126, 137, 191, 193, 194
Reflection prompts 5, 6, 10, 21, 118, 131
Reflective thinking 118–120, 129, 131, 132
Reframing 7, 16, 18, 24, 35, 41, 68, 70, 75, 76, 78, 80, 83, 88, 97, 112
Rubric 128

S

Secondary research 52, 53
Service blueprint 85, 86, 94–96, 137, 179, 184
Service design 18–21, 23, 34, 95
Sift.Sort.Label 87, 136, 154, 162–164
Stages 2, 6–8, 10, 13, 24, 26, 30, 31, 36, 37, 58, 64, 71, 74, 80, 82, 86, 88, 92, 96, 100, 104, 115, 118, 120, 122, 132

Stakeholder 3, 7, 8, 13, 18, 21, 23, 25, 35, 36, 40–42, 45, 47, 64, 71, 72, 79, 85, 87, 92, 95, 96, 98, 100, 103–107, 111–113, 115, 136
Stakeholder-centred design (SCD) 18, 23, 92
Stakeholder map 46, 112, 136, 142, 151, 152, 198, 203, 204
Steps 16, 24, 26, 30, 35, 37, 58–60, 64, 66, 70, 71, 74, 75, 82, 84, 91, 92, 99, 104, 105, 107, 111, 118, 122, 132
Storyboarding 85, 93–96, 102, 106, 112, 137, 179, 181–183
Storytelling 90, 100–103, 115
Strategic design 18–20, 23, 94
Strategic thinking 32, 34, 35
Sustainable innovation 7, 12, 24, 26, 70, 105, 130
Systems thinking 18, 20, 106

T

Team forming 30, 39, 44
Team SWOT 42–44, 47, 136, 142, 148
Tertiary research 53
Textbook procedures
- exercise(s) 131
- framework(s) 121
- method(s) 40
- technique(s) 34, 82, 131
- worksheet(s) 40
Thick data 50, 53, 54, 58, 64, 65, 72
Three-act story 95, 102–104, 137, 179
Three-factors framework 110
Three-traits framework 97–99, 137, 179, 185

U

User experience design 34

V

Visual thinking 26, 51, 65, 85, 86

W

Warm up(s) 2, 16, 30, 39, 50, 65, 74, 81, 90, 100, 118, 131, 136, 137, 140, 142, 154, 168, 179, 191
Wayfinding 106, 107

The manufacturer's authorised representative in the EU is Springer Nature Customer Service Centre GmbH, Europaplatz 3, 69115 Heidelberg, Germany. If you have any concerns regarding our products, please contact ProductSafety@springernature.com

Printed and bound by CPI Group (UK) Ltd, Croydon, CR0 4YY

25/02/2026

02060499-0009